A Guide to the Scotland Ac

A Guide to the Scotland Act 1998

Alan Page LLB, PhD
Professor of Law
University of Dundee

Colin Reid MA, LLB
Professor of Law
University of Dundee

Andrea Ross LLB, LLM
Lecturer
University of Dundee

Butterworths
Edinburgh
1999

United Kingdom	Butterworths a Division of Reed Elsevier (UK) Ltd, 4 Hill Street, EDINBURGH EH2 3JZ and Halsbury House, 35 Chancery Lane, LONDON WC2A 1EL
Australia	Butterworths, a Division of Reed International Books Australia Pty Ltd, CHATSWOOD, New South Wales
Canada	Butterworths Canada Ltd, MARKHAM, Ontario
Hong Kong	Butterworths Asia (Hong Kong), HONG KONG
India	Butterworths India, NEW DELHI
Ireland	Butterworth (Ireland) Ltd, DUBLIN
Malaysia	Malayan Law Journal Sdn Bhd, KUALA LUMPUR
New Zealand	Butterworths of New Zealand Ltd, WELLINGTON
Singapore	Butterworths Asia, SINGAPORE
South Africa	Butterworths Publishers (Pty) Ltd, DURBAN
USA	Lexis Law Publishing, CHARLOTTESVILLE, Virginia

A CIP Catalogue record for this book is available from the British Library.

ISBN 0 406 98806 4

Typeset by Phoenix Photosetting, Chatham, Kent
Printed and bound in Scotland by
Thomson Litho, East Kilbride

Visit us on our website: http://www.butterworthsscotland.com

Preface

Our aim in writing this book has been to offer an explanation of the main provisions of the Scotland Act 1998. We have not aimed to present a comprehensive account of this long and complex piece of legislation, nor have we sought to provide a detailed analysis of its many provisions or of their interaction with existing laws and practice. Our hope is that by explaining the main effects of the Act we have produced a book that will be useful to lawyers and others who are keen to understand the fundamental legal basis of the new constitutional relationship between Scotland and the United Kingdom. There is a great deal more that could be said about this hugely significant piece of legislation.

In many instances though, going much beyond the sort of explanation offered here would involve a great deal of speculation. At this stage, before the first elections to the Parliament, much of the detail of how the Parliament and Executive will work remains to be determined. In the political discussions on devolution much emphasis has been placed on the desire to create a Parliament which will work in a different way from that at Westminster, but it is only once the Parliament has met, determined and begun to operate its own procedures that it will be possible to say what its true character will be. Similarly, during the parliamentary debates on the Bill much was said about the relationship between the Scottish Parliament and its Executive and those of the United Kingdom. Again, it is only experience that will show whether this will be a truly co-operative and constructive relationship or one marred by tension and heavy reliance on the formal procedures provided in the Act. These issues will be hugely affected by the political situation at the time and it is practical politics rather than legal detail which will determine the future of devolution.

Each of the authors would like to say that all errors and omissions are attributable to the others, but honesty requires us to share full responsibility. The final product is very much a collective effort, but in the initial stages chapters 1, 2, 3 and 4 were drafted by Colin

Reid, chapters 5, 6 and 8 by Andrea Ross and chapters 7 and 9 by Alan Page.

Especially since the parliamentary timetable meant that much of our work on the final text of the Act had to be done in December and early January, our profound thanks go to all our families for putting up with us while we were occupied with this book. Thanks also go to all the staff at Butterworths, past and present, for their assistance in supplying us with materials as the Bill worked its way through Parliament and for their role in the production of the book in its final form.

Alan Page
Colin Reid
Andrea Ross

Department of Law, University of Dundee

8 January 1999

Contents

Table of Statutes

Table of Orders and Regulations

1 Introduction

1.1 'There shall be a Scottish Parliament.' This simple statement opens the first section of the Scotland Act 1998 and states the most obvious feature of the transformation of the constitutional position of Scotland within the United Kingdom. The remainder of the Act then deals with how the Parliament is elected and what powers it has, as well as providing for the appointment and powers of a First Minister and Scottish Executive. The Act also provides for the relationship between these new governmental structures in Scotland and the existing United Kingdom Parliament and Government, which retain a major say in governing Scotland. On some issues, the Act provides detailed rules, on others a bare framework to be supplemented by further provisions. Moreover, the Act allows for its own amendment, so that the initial position of the Scottish Parliament and Executive can be adjusted in the light of experience or political policy.

1.2 The Scottish Parliament is a creation of the United Kingdom Parliament and is legally subject to its wishes. At all stages the powers of the Scottish Parliament and Executive are subject to limitations which can be enforced through both judicial and political means. However, on major constitutional matters, the political reality is often more significant than the legal theory, and the people and politicians of Scotland will determine what the future will bring. The first few years of the Parliament's existence will be crucial in determining how it is to operate and whether the new arrangements are likely to provide a lasting settlement of the place of Scotland within the United Kingdom, or merely a staging-post to a wider separation.

BACKGROUND

1.3 The Scotland Act marks the culmination of a period of prolonged debate about the role of Scotland within the United

Kingdom. The union between the Scottish and English Parliaments in 1707[1] was a strange one when viewed through modern eyes, since whilst creating a single legislature it left intact two separate legal systems, each with its own judicial and administrative structures. The distinctiveness of Scotland was increasingly recognised during the nineteenth century (e g through the creation of the post of Secretary for Scotland in 1885[2]) and discussions about the position of Scotland continued into the twentieth century.

1 Union with Scotland Act 1706, Union with England Act 1707.
2 Secretary for Scotland Act 1885; the post became that of a Secretary of State under the Secretaries of State Act 1926.

1.4 The recent origins of the process which has culminated in the passing of the Scotland Act 1998 can be said to lie in the 1960s when electoral success for the Scottish National Party made the issue of Scotland's future one of concern to the main political parties[1]. A Royal Commission on the Constitution was set up in 1968 and reported in 1973[2], and devolution became the policy of the Labour governments in the 1970s[3]. The Scotland Act 1978 was enacted, proposing the creation of a Scottish Assembly, with law-making powers in those areas specifically devolved to it, but no tax-raising power. However, the government's weak position in Parliament allowed the Act to become subject to the requirement that it would come into force only if in a referendum in Scotland it gained the support of a majority of those voting and of at least 40% of those registered to vote in Scotland[4]. In the referendum in March 1979, the Act was supported by a narrow but clear majority of those actually voting, but failed to clear the '40% hurdle'[5], and consequently was repealed without ever coming into force[6].

1 See generally, J.G. Kellas, *The Scottish Political System* (4th edn, 1989), ch 8.
2 *Report of the Royal Commission on the Constitution* ('Kilbrandon Report'), Cmnd 5460 (1973).
3 *Democracy and Devolution: Proposals for Scotland and Wales*, Cmnd 5732 (1974); *Our Changing Democracy: Devolution to Scotland and Wales*, Cmnd 6348 (1975); *Devolution to Scotland and Wales: Supplementary Statement*, Cmnd 6585 (1976).
4 Scotland Act 1978, s 85.
5 At the referendum, 51.6% of those voting supported the Act coming into force (equivalent to 32.8% of the electorate).
6 Scotland Act 1978 (Repeal) Order 1979, SI 1979/928.

1.5 The Conservative governments in power from 1979 until 1997 were deeply opposed to any proposals for devolution to Scotland, but for the opposition parties, which in fact enjoyed majority support in Scotland, and for many individuals involved on a non-party basis, the issue remained an important one. The work of organisations such as the Campaign for a Scottish Assembly and the Scottish Constitutional Convention meant that not only was the issue kept alive but that progress was made towards an agreed form and structure for the proposed Parliament[1].

1 As well as representatives from the Labour and Liberal Democratic parties (the Conservative and Scottish National Parties declined to participate), the membership of the Constitutional Convention included representatives of other smaller political parties, local authorities, the trade union movement, churches, ethnic minorities and some business and commercial organisations. The consensus which they reached played a major part in the shaping of the devolution proposals presented by the Labour Party; see the Convention's paper *Towards Scotland's Parliament* (1990) and the Convention's final report, *Scotland's Parliament. Scotland's Right* published in November 1995.

1.6 The Labour party's victory in the general election of 1997 was followed rapidly by the publication of a White Paper, *Scotland's Parliament*[1], which formed the basis of the referendum on 11 September 1997, at which there were very large majorities in favour of the creation of the Scottish Parliament and for it to have tax-raising powers[2]. The Scotland Act 1998 received the Royal Assent in November 1998. While the Bill was passing through Parliament a Consultative Steering Group comprising politicians from all parties and representatives of other groups met to bring together views on and to consider the operational needs and working methods of the Parliament, developing proposals for the standing orders and rules of procedure which the Parliament might adopt[3]. The first general election for the Scottish Parliament is to be held on 6 May 1999, and the Parliament will be formally opened and assume its powers on 1 July 1999[4].

1 Cm 3658.
2 The votes in favour were 74.3% and 65.3% respectively.
3 The Consultative Steering Group's report, *Shaping Scotland's Parliament,* was produced in December 1998 and further papers are available on the Scottish Devolution Web-site: http://www.scottish-devolution.org.uk/.
4 Scotland Act 1998 (Commencement) Order 1998, SI 1998/3178.

1.7 Developments in Scotland are only part of a wider constitutional transformation affecting all of the United Kingdom. Under the Government of Wales Act 1998, an Assembly for Wales and a Welsh Executive are created, less powerful than their Scottish counterparts, e g the Assembly's legislative powers are limited to the making of subordinate legislation, and all primary legislation continues to be made by the United Kingdom Parliament. The Northern Ireland Act 1998 provides for a

Northern Ireland Assembly and Executive Committee, as part of the wider adjustment of governmental arrangements for Northern Ireland following the Good Friday Agreement of 1998[1]. Meanwhile throughout the United Kingdom, the Human Rights Act 1998 will give effect to the European Convention on Human Rights, although still not providing for the rights protected by the Convention an absolute guarantee capable of withstanding express legislation by the United Kingdom Parliament. Taken together these changes amount to a fundamental reshaping of the constitutional landscape of the United Kingdom.

1 *The Belfast Agreement: An Agreement Reached at the Multi-Party Talks on Northern Ireland*, Cm 3883 (1998).

NATURE OF THE SCOTTISH PARLIAMENT

1.8 The Scottish Parliament is a very different sort of body from the United Kingdom Parliament. The way in which it is elected, the extent to which it can control its own proceedings, the powers which it has to make laws, and the extent to which it can be challenged and overridden by other bodies are all issues on which there are important differences between the two Parliaments. There is a danger that by concentrating on the restrictions on the Scottish Parliament a negative impression of its powers and role may be given. The Scottish Parliament, and Executive, have wide powers and will be the leading players in the government of Scotland. Yet in a constitutional system which has been based on a United Kingdom Parliament with unlimited power, it is the restrictions which serve to mark out the unique nature of the new body which has been created. In all of the following ways (see paras 1.9–1.18 below) the Scottish Parliament differs from that of the United Kingdom.

1.9 The Parliament is elected by a system of proportional representation, combining constituency members with additional seats allocated on a regional basis[1]. This by itself will lead to a Parliament different in character from that at Westminster since it is unlikely that any one party will achieve the dominance which the 'first-past-the post' system gives to a party even when it falls a very long way short of obtaining an overall majority of the votes cast by the electorate. Coalitions and co-operation will be required if the Parliament is to complete any substantial achievements.

1 See paras 2.1–2.8 below.

1.10 The Parliament is subject to territorial limits on its powers. No laws can be made which apply beyond Scotland[1].

1 See para 5.4 below.

1.11 The Parliament has no power to make laws on certain matters. Whereas the Scotland Act 1978 operated on the basis of the express devolution of competence in certain listed areas to the Scottish Assembly, the Scotland Act 1998 operates on the opposite basis. The Scottish Parliament is thus competent to deal with all matters in Scotland other than those expressly reserved for the United Kingdom Parliament. The list of reserved matters is long and detailed[1]. The exercise in Scotland of certain functions within reserved matters can be transferred to Scottish Ministers[2].

1 See paras 5.5–5.6 and Chapter 6 below.
2 See para 7.22 below.

1.12 The Parliament is subject to a number of other limits on its powers. Most notably the Parliament cannot make any law which is incompatible with European Community law or with rights under the European Convention on Human Rights[1].

1 See para 5.21 below.

1.13 The Parliament can be overridden at any time by the United Kingdom Parliament. It is expressly stated that the Act does not affect the power of the Parliament of the United Kingdom to make laws for Scotland (s 28(7)), so that even where a matter is within the competence of the Scottish Parliament, legislation which is effective in Scotland can still be made at Westminster.

1.14 The Parliament is required to legislate on certain matters. For a number of issues the Act does not contain detailed rules but states that the Parliament must make provision[1] to address the issue, and sometimes states the effect which such provision must have, e g there must be a register of members' interests (s 39).

1 Sometimes by legislation and sometimes by standing orders.

1.15 The Parliament has tax-varying powers, but only to the very limited extent of altering the basic rate of income tax by no more than 3%[1]. The funding available for the Scottish Parliament and Executive will thus depend on that provided by the United Kingdom Parliament.

1 See paras 7.43–7.48 below.

1.16 The validity of an Act of the Scottish Parliament can be challenged in the courts. Legislation made in breach of the limits on the Parliament's competence is invalid, and provision is made for how such issues are to be dealt with in litigation throughout the United Kingdom (Sch 6)[1].

1 See Chapter 8 below.

1.17 The limits on the Parliament's powers can be enforced by political means. The Law Officers of both the Scottish and United Kingdom governments can intervene to prevent legislation receiving the Royal Assent if they consider that there is a doubt over its competence, and the Secretary of State (a member of the United Kingdom government) can similarly intervene on certain grounds[1].

1 See paras 5.29–5.35 below.

1.18 The Parliament has no inherent powers or privileges. Unlike the Westminster Parliament it has no immunities from the general law and no powers to punish those, both members and outsiders, who transgress against its privileges. It is therefore necessary for those immunities which are thought desirable (e g in relation to defamation and contempt of court)[1] to be expressly provided, and for the criminal law to be invoked as the means of enforcing prohibitions even on the members of the Parliament[2]. This contrasts with the situation at Westminster where such matters are exclusively in the hands of Parliament itself.

1 See paras 4.24–4.28 below.
2 E g in relation to breaches of the rules on the registration of interests or prohibiting paid lobbying (s 39).

KEY TERMS

1.19 In order to assist in understanding the provisions of the Act, it is useful if a few key terms are explained at this stage.

Advocate General: The Advocate General for Scotland is a new member of the United Kingdom Government, providing it with legal advice on matters relating to Scotland[1]. This role was previously filled by the Lord Advocate who is now a member of the Scottish Executive.
Devolved matters: In essence these are the areas in which the Scottish Parliament and Executive have the competence to act. These are not

expressly defined but cover all issues not included in reserved matters or otherwise excluded from the Parliament's competence[2].

Executive devolution: This is the process by which the exercise in Scotland of powers retained by the United Kingdom Government can be transferred to the Scottish Executive. The Scottish Executive can thus be authorised to exercise powers even though they fall within the area of reserved matters and lie beyond the competence of the Scottish Parliament.

First Minister: The First Minister, appointed by the Queen on the nomination of the Parliament, is effectively the Scottish Prime Minister and is responsible for appointing the other Scottish Ministers with the agreement of the Parliament[3].

Judicial Committee: The Judicial Committee of the Privy Council is the court which has the final say in legal disputes as to the competence of Acts of the Scottish Parliament and actions by the Scottish Executive. For devolution issues its membership is limited to those members from the United Kingdom, excluding those from elsewhere in the Commonwealth[4].

Law Officers: In Scotland, these are the Lord Advocate and the Solicitor General for Scotland[5].

Order in Council: Orders in Council, nominally made by the Queen, are the most formal and dignified form of subordinate legislation, but have no more or less legal effect than other forms.

Parliamentary Corporation: Because the Parliament is not itself a legal entity capable of owning property, entering contracts or being a party to legal proceedings, the Scottish Parliamentary Corporate Body is created to provide a vehicle for the legal relationships and transactions necessary for the Parliament to operate properly[6].

Presiding Officer: The Presiding Officer is the equivalent of the Speaker of the House of Commons and plays a key role in controlling the proceedings of the Parliament[7].

Reserved matters: These are the matters over which competence has been retained by the United Kingdom Parliament and Government. The Scottish Parliament and Executive have no power to make laws or exercise powers in relation to these matters, although some powers within the reserved areas can be expressly transferred to the Scottish Executive[8].

Retained functions: This term refers to those functions which must be exercised by the Lord Advocate and cannot be transferred to other members of the Scottish Executive[9].

Scottish Administration: This term refers to the office-holders of the Scottish Executive (i e Scottish Ministers) and their staff[10]. The members of the civil service which supports the Scottish Executive remain part of the United Kingdom civil service[11].

Scottish Executive: The holders of the main offices in the Scottish government form the Scottish Executive. These are the First Minister, the other Ministers and the Law Officers[12].

Secretary of State: In accordance with general constitutional practice, where the Act confers powers or functions on 'the Secretary of State', any of the Secretaries of State in the United Kingdom Government may act[13]. Many functions within Scotland are, and will continue to be, exercised by Secretaries of State other than the Secretary of State for Scotland, e g the administration of various benefits by the Secretary of State for Social Security.

Secretary of State for Scotland: The Secretary of State for Scotland remains a member of the United Kingdom Government. He or she may continue to exercise functions in Scotland in relation to reserved matters, as well as fulfilling a political role.

Standing Orders: The Act provides for the establishment of the Parliament and Executive, and for some key aspects of its operation, particularly in relation to finance, but most of the details of how the Parliament is to operate and conduct its business are to be determined by the Parliament itself by means of standing orders[14].

Subordinate legislation: Acts of Parliament (whether from the Scottish or United Kingdom Parliament) cannot provide all of the detailed rules necessary to regulate everything which it is thought necessary to regulate. Accordingly the Parliaments can delegate to Ministers or others the power to make law within the limits of the authorisation contained in an Act of Parliament. Such subordinate or delegated legislation may be subject to some parliamentary scrutiny, but the procedure will always be less onerous than that required for passing an Act of Parliament. Subordinate legislation has full legal effect but its validity can be challenged on the grounds that it goes beyond the terms set out in the Act which authorises its making.

1 See para 7.9 below.
2 See Chapter 5 below.
3 See paras 7.3–7.4 below.
4 See para 8.14 below.
5 See paras 7.6–7.8 below.
6 See paras 4.6–4.9 below.
7 See paras 4.2–4.3 below.
8 See 'executive devolution' below, and para 7.22 below.
9 See para 7.20 below.
10 See paras 7.15–7.17 below.
11 See para 7.17 below.
12 See para 7.2 below.
13 Interpretation Act 1978, Sch 1; *Agee v Lord Advocate* 1977 SLT (Notes) 54.
14 See paras 4.10–4.14 below.

2 Elections

2.1 Elections to the Scottish Parliament involve an element of proportional representation. This by itself will mean that the Parliament will operate in a different way from Westminster since there is unlikely to be the single party domination which is a feature of the House of Commons. The form of proportional representation which has been chosen is a version of the 'additional members' system, under which additional seats are allocated to parties whose share of the vote is not reflected in the number of individual constituencies won. There are many different ways in which such systems can operate, and the key elements of the Scottish system are:

1 each voter has two votes;
2 one vote counts to elect the member for the local constituency;
3 the second vote is used to elect regional members;
4 each region returns a number of regional members;
5 regional seats are allocated on the basis of the regional votes cast, taking into account the results of the constituency elections within the region;
6 the candidates for regional seats appear either on a party list or as individuals;
7 there is no opportunity for voters to express preferences between candidates on the party lists and the vote is given simply to the party.

2.2 This system is a major change from the existing electoral system, and indeed from the versions of proportional representation used previously in the United Kingdom[1], and has several significant features. The system does not attempt to provide representation exactly in proportion to the number of votes cast nationally[2]. Instead it maintains the idea of local representation, but through the additional members endeavours to remove the worst inequities of the 'first-past-the-post' system which has been used in British parliamentary elections. The additional members are elected on a regional, not national, basis, allowing differences within Scotland to be reflected. The fact that voters have two separate votes means that they can divide their votes between parties, perhaps voting for the constituency member on a personal basis but showing their party preference in the regional vote.

1 Eg in Northern Ireland and for the university constituencies before 1948 (Representation of the People Act 1918, ss 20,42).

2 Nevertheless, the system appears likely to produce results remarkably close to this outcome; see Appendix 1.

2.3 It is possible for individuals to stand for election as regional members without being on a party list, but voters have no opportunity to express preferences between the candidates on a party list. Seats are given to the party and filled simply by taking those placed highest on the list prepared by the party itself. Despite the earlier approval of this system for the Scottish Parliament (and the Welsh Assembly[1]), it was this 'closed list' aspect of similar proposals for elections to the European Parliament which led to conflict between the Lords and Commons at the end of the 1997–98 parliamentary session leading to the failure of the European Parliamentary Elections Bill.

1 Government of Wales Act 1998, ss 5–7.

VOTING SYSTEM

Constituency Seats

2.4 At an election there are two stages; the election of constituency members and then the allocation of regional seats[1]. The process for electing constituency members is exactly the same as is used for current parliamentary elections (s 1(2)). The election is based on individual constituencies, with voters casting a vote for named individual candidates and the seat being won by the candidate who wins most votes.

1 The constituency stage must be completed first (s 7(1)).

Regional Seats

2.5 The second stage takes place on a regional basis. In addition to the constituency vote, each voter has a second vote which can be used to vote either for a party which has submitted a regional list or for an individual who is standing as a candidate for the region (s 6).

These votes are counted on a regional basis, quite separately from the votes cast for the constituency members. The allocation of regional members is then determined by the repeated calculation of the 'regional figure' for each party or individual. Since this figure takes account of the number of constituency seats already won in the region, the party with the most regional votes may well not receive the most (or indeed any) regional seats if it has already been successful in winning constituencies.

2.6 The regional figure is calculated by taking the number of regional votes cast for a party or individual and dividing it by the number of constituency seats gained plus one (s 7). Thus for a party which won no constituency seats, the regional figure will be the total of regional votes cast for it, whereas for a party which has already won three constituencies the regional figure will be a quarter of the total of its regional votes. The first regional seat is then allocated to the party with the highest regional figure, and goes to the individual whose name comes highest on that party's list (or to an individual candidate if he or she has the highest regional figure) (s 8). The process is then repeated with the regional figures being recalculated at each stage, adding the regional seats already allocated to any constituency seats won. Once a party's list is exhausted or an individual candidate is allocated a seat, they drop out of the calculations.

2.7 The process becomes clearer when an example is followed. This example is based on the 1997 General Election and figures for the whole of Scotland are given in Appendix 1. The examples are illustrative only and are subject to the important qualifications noted in that Appendix.

Scotland North-East

	Labour	SNP	Conservative	Liberal Democrat
Party vote	118,162	115,950	98,366	72,880
Constituency seats	5	3	0	2
Stage 1: divide by	5+1= 6	3+1= 4	0+1= 1	2+1= 3
Stage 1 figure	19,694	28,988	**98,366**	24,293

	Labour	SNP	Conservative	Liberal Democrat
Stage 2: divide by	5+1= 6	3+1= 4	1+1= 2	2+1= 3
Stage 2 figure	19,694	28,988	**49,183**	24,293
Stage 3: divide by	5+1= 6	3+1= 4	2+1= 3	2+1= 3
Stage 3 figure	19,694	28,988	**32,789**	24,293
Stage 4: divide by	5+1= 6	3+1= 4	3+1= 4	2+1= 3
Stage 4 figure	19,694	**28,988**	24,592	24,293
Stage 5: divide by	5+1= 6	4+1= 5	3+1= 4	2+1= 3
Stage 5 figure	19,694	23,190	**24,592**	24,293
Stage 6: divide by	5+1= 6	4+1= 5	4+1= 5	2+1= 3
Stage 6 figure	19,694	23,190	19,673	**24,293**
Stage 7: divide by	5+1= 6	4+1= 5	4+1= 5	3+1= 4
Stage 7 figure	19,694	**23,190**	19,673	18,220
Constituency seats	5	3	0	2
Regional seats	0	2	4	1
Total seats	5	5	4	3

2.8 As can be seen, the regional seats go to those parties which are under-represented by the results at constituency level. A party that does well in winning constituency seats may get no regional seats; a party that has received a lot of votes but won few constituencies will be allocated several regional seats. Although this is not the express intention, in all of the calculations as detailed in Appendix 1 the system proves remarkably effective in giving each party a share of the number of seats very close indeed to its share of the overall vote.

CANDIDATES

2.9 For the constituency seats, candidates stand as individuals in the same way as occurs at present for parliamentary elections. In practice, of course, most candidates are selected by political parties and are designated as such on the ballot paper. At a general election no-one can be a candidate for more than one constituency (s 5(2)), but constituency candidates can also appear on the party list for the region where their constituency lies (see below). No-one can be a candidate for more than one by-election at a time (s 9(6)).

2.10 For the regional seats, candidates can stand either as individuals or through their inclusion in a party list. Party lists can be submitted by any registered political party (s 5(4)). The registration of political parties has been introduced both to enable the identification of parties eligible to submit lists at elections and to deal with the risk of confusion between parties with similar names[1]. The registration system is created by the Registration of Political Parties Act 1998 and is concerned wholly with the identification of parties, not their views. All parties which apply are entitled to be registered provided that they submit the relevant information on their senior officers and that their name is not too long, is not obscene or offensive, and is not liable to cause confusion with other registered parties; party emblems can also be registered. The system is administered by the companies registrar for England and Wales.

1 This follows the notorious case in 1994 where a candidate in the European Parliament Election in Devon and East Plymouth stood as a 'Literal Democrat' and won more votes than the difference between the successful Conservative candidate and the second-placed Liberal Democrat; *Sanders v Chichester, The Times* 2 December, 1994.

2.11 The party lists may include only one person, and are subject to a maximum of twelve (s 5(6)). There are only seven regional seats available in any region, but some of those on the list may win election as constituency members, since the rules allow for people on a party list also to stand as candidates for a constituency within the region (but only if they do so as representatives of the same party). Moreover, the list remains in operation throughout the duration of each Parliament to provide replacements if any of a party's regional members cease to be members of the Parliament (s 5(5)). As time passes, candidates on the list may no longer be available for some reason, and the longer list should ensure that a replacement can be found if required[1].

1 See paras 2.35–2.36 below.

2.12 Candidates cannot be included in the list if they are standing for a constituency outside the region, if they are individual candidates for any region, or if they are on any other party list, whether for the same region or any other (s 5(7)). These rules ensure that there must be completely separate lists for each party and region.

2.13 Individual (i e non-party) candidates for regional seats can stand both for a constituency and for the regional seat which includes that constituency, but they cannot be individual regional candidates if they are standing in a constituency as the representative of any registered party. Various other limitations apply to prevent multiple candidacy. Individuals are not allowed to stand if they are standing as an individual candidate in any constituency outside the region or for any other regional seat, nor if they appear on any party list for any region (s 5(8)).

2.14 There is no rule preventing members of the Westminster or European Parliaments from standing for election to the Scottish Parliament, although the salary of a member who is also a member of either of these Parliaments is reduced (s 82)[1]. The personal qualifications required by candidates are dealt with in paras 3.4–3.8 below.

1 See para 3.3 below.

ELECTORS

2.15 The right to vote at elections for the Parliament is governed by the same rules as apply to local government elections (s 11(1)). This means that two categories of people who cannot vote at elections for the United Kingdom Parliament are entitled to vote for the Scottish Parliament, namely peers and citizens of the European Union.

2.16 The rules for who qualifies as an elector are laid down in Part I of the Representation of the People Act 1983[1] and in essence grant the right to vote to British, Irish, Commonwealth and European Union citizens who are resident in a constituency and entered on the electoral register. Those under the age of 18 on the date of the election are not entitled to vote, nor are those detained in prison following conviction, nor those suffering from a legal incapacity, e g through severe mental illness.

1 As amended, most notably to allow European Union citizens the right to vote at local, and now Scottish Parliament, elections; Local Government Elections (Changes to the Franchise and Qualification of Members) Regulations 1995, SI 1995/1948. See 15 *Stair Memorial Encyclopaedia* paras 1075–1151.

2.17 Voters are not entitled to cast more than one constituency vote plus one regional vote. Although voters can legitimately be registered in more than one constituency, they cannot vote in more than one at a general election, although it appears possible for them to vote in more than one constituency when by-elections are being held (s 11(2)).

CONSTITUENCIES AND REGIONS

2.18 Elections to the Parliament are based on two sorts of geographical areas: constituencies and regions. The boundaries of these areas are to be kept under review by the Boundary Commission for Scotland[1] in the same way as those for the United Kingdom Parliament, and new rules introduced by the Scotland Act mean that there will be significant changes within the first few years of the Parliament's existence.

1 Parliamentary Constituencies Act 1986 (PCA 1986).

Constituencies

2.19 The constituencies are the same as those used for elections to the United Kingdom Parliament, except that the Orkney and Shetland Islands each form a separate constituency (as opposed to being united in a single constituency for Westminster) (Sch 1, para 1). This means that for the first election there will be 73 constituencies. This number will, however, be reduced within the lifetime of the first two Parliaments as a consequence of measures to deal with the numerical 'over-representation' of Scotland at Westminster.

2.20 Since the constituencies for the Scottish and Westminster Parliaments are the same (apart from Orkney and Shetland), the review and redistribution of constituencies is governed by the process which already exists for Westminster. This entrusts the task to the Boundary Commission for Scotland[1], which as well as carrying out minor adjustments on a continuous basis is under an obligation to carry out from time to time a general review of all constituencies. In that process the Commission is bound to have regard to several factors, in particular special geographical considerations (e g for remote or sparsely populated areas) and the desirability of all seats having as nearly as possible the same number of electors[2].

1 Governed by PCA 1986.
2 PCA 1986, Sch 2 paras 5–6.

2.21 The present constituencies are the result of the last review in 1994 for which the Commission was bound by two further rules which will not apply at the next review. The first was that there should be no fewer than 71 constituencies in Scotland[1], and the second was that the average size of each seat (the 'electoral quota') should be worked out separately for Scotland[2]. These two features combined to give Scotland considerably more constituencies than if seats were distributed evenly across the United Kingdom in strict proportion to population[3]. Under the Scotland Act, the requirement to have at least 71 seats in Scotland is removed, and it is provided that the electoral quota to be taken into account in future reviews is that for England (s 86)[4]. Together these changes will inevitably mean a considerable reduction in the number of Scottish constituencies at the next review, and therefore a reduction in both the number of seats in the Scottish Parliament and the number of MPs from Scotland in the Westminster Parliament.

1 PCA 1986, Sch 2 para 1(2).
2 PCA 1986, Sch 2 para 8(a).
3 The average number of electors per constituency was 55,339 in Scotland, 69,578 in England and 67,077 across the United Kingdom as a whole.
4 Orkney and Shetland are still treated separately; they must remain separate seats for the Scottish Parliament and cannot be joined with any area apart from each other for Westminster.

2.22 The next review must take place between eight and twelve years after the previous one[1], and thus is due between 2002 and 2006. Since the second general election for the Scottish Parliament will be held in May 2003[2], there will be at most two Parliaments of the present size and a smaller Parliament will meet either in 2003 or at the next general election in 2007.

1 PCA 1986, s 3(2), as amended by the Boundary Commissions Act 1992, s 2(3).
2 See para 2.28 below.

Regions

2.23 There are eight regions and each will return seven regional members (Sch 1, para 2). The regions are the areas defined as constituencies for the European Parliament under the European Parliamentary Constituencies (Scotland) Order 1996[1], and are detailed in Appendix 2. The 1996 Order ensured that the boundaries of the European constituencies would fit with those of the parliamentary constituencies as revised in the years after the last European election in 1994. These European constituencies may never actually be used for elections to the European Parliament, since for the elections from 1999 onwards the government's intention is to use a form of proportional representation, replacing the current system of electing single members for large constituencies on a 'first-past-the-post' basis. The system proposed for Great Britain[2] is essentially the same as that used for regional seats for the Scottish Parliament, with Scotland forming a single region of the United Kingdom returning eight members from party lists[3]. The European Parliamentary Elections Bill was rejected by the House of Lords amid much political controversy at the end of the 1997–98 parliamentary session, but the re-introduced Bill received the Royal Assent in time to take effect for the European Parliament elections in May 1999.

1 SI 1996/1926.
2 In Northern Ireland the single transferable vote system will continue to be employed; European Parliamentary Elections Act 1978, s 3A inserted by the European Parliamentary Elections Act 1999.
3 Individual candidates may also stand; European Parliamentary Elections Act 1978, s 3, as substituted by the European Parliamentary Elections Act 1999.

2.24 Although the number of regions is fixed by the Act, their definition and the number of members returned may be varied. When the Boundary Commission for Scotland carries out its general review of constituencies it must also review the regions and the number of members they return and either recommend changes or report that none are required (Sch 1 para 3). Since there will inevitably be considerable changes to the constituencies at the next general review, there will also have to be changes to the regions.

2.25 In reviewing the regions, the Commission is governed by a number of rules (Sch 1 para 7). The regions should all be as close to each other in size of electorate as is reasonably practicable, having regard to special geographical considerations, and no constituency can be split between regions. The number of regions is fixed at eight, but the number of regional members is subject to review and is to be determined, so far as reasonably practicable, by maintaining the existing ratio of regional seats to constituency seats, namely 56 regional seats to 73 constituency ones (Sch 1 para 7(3)). In other words once the number of constituency seats has been determined there should be just over three-quarters of that number of regional seats. Each region is then to be given one-eighth of the number of regional seats.

2.26 If the total number of regional seats is not exactly divisible by eight, a more complex allocation takes place (Sch 1 para 7(2)-(4)). First, as many seats as can be are divided equally between all of the regions. The seats left over, the 'residual seats', are then distributed by the Commission. No region may be allocated more than one residual seat, and the Commission is to be guided by the desirability of allocating the seats to those regions which are comparatively under-represented by the number of constituency seats and regional seats after the initial allocation. In order to identify which regions these are, the total electorate in the region is to be divided by the number of seats (constituency and regional) already determined for each region, and the residual seats are to go to those with the highest number of electors per seat.

Procedure for Review

2.27 The procedure for the review of constituencies is laid down in the Parliamentary Constituencies Act 1986, and similar measures are provided in the Scotland Act for the review of regions (Sch 1 paras 4–5). These include the advertisement of proposed changes and the potential to hold local inquiries, which must be held where local authorities or sizeable numbers of individuals object to the proposals. Under the 1986 Act, reports of the Boundary Commission are made to the Secretary of State[1], but any report proposing changes will also have to be laid before the Scottish Parliament (Sch 1 para 3(5)). Any changes to constituencies or regions are made by means of an Order in Council which must be approved in draft by both Houses of the United Kingdom Parliament[2].

1 PCA 1986, s 3.
2 PCA 1986, s 4.

TIMING OF ELECTIONS

2.28 General elections for the Scottish Parliament are to be held every four years. This differs from the position at Westminster where in effect the Prime Minister can choose the timing of the elections, provided only that no Parliament lasts beyond five years[1]. The Act expressly provides that general elections are to take place on the first Thursday in May every fourth year from the first election (s 2(2)), so that following the first general election in 1999, elections will take place in May 2003, 2007, 2011 and so on. Although the Act specifies the first Thursday in May as the date of the elections, the actual date can be altered by up to a month (earlier or later) on the recommendation of the Presiding Officer (s 2(5))[2]. Elections for the Scottish Parliament can be held on the same day as other elections (s 12(2)(d)).

1 Septennial Act 1715, as amended by the Parliament Act 1911, s 7.
2 The change of date is formally achieved by a royal proclamation (s 2(5)).

2.29 In two circumstances, though, general elections can be held outwith the normal timetable. The first is when the Parliament resolves to dissolve itself, thereby triggering a general election. Such a resolution requires a two-thirds majority, that is the number of votes in favour must be at least the same as two-thirds of the number of seats for members of the Parliament (not two-thirds of those actually voting, nor even two-thirds of the actual number of members at the time, allowing for vacancies) (s 3(1)(a)). The second is when the Parliament proves unable to nominate a First Minister within the 28–day period allowed[1] following either a general election or the First Minister leaving office (by resignation or other grounds) (s 3(1)(b)). The calling of an extraordinary election therefore requires either wide support in Parliament, or evidence that no Executive is able to command the support of the Parliament[2]. In either case the matter lies in the hands of the Parliament as opposed to the Executive so that, unlike the position at Westminster, the timing of elections is not something which can be manipulated for the benefit of a single party[3].

1 Section 46.
2 The dissolution of the Parliament and calling of an election are formally achieved by a royal proclamation made on the proposal of the Presiding Officer (s 3(2)).
3 Unless one party (or a coalition) dominates the Parliament to an extent unlikely given the element of proportional representation in the electoral system.

2.30 The fact that an extraordinary general election has taken place does not disrupt the timetable for elections, unless the extraordinary election falls within six months of the next scheduled general election, in which case the scheduled election is abandoned (s 3(3)). A Parliament elected at an extraordinary election will generally, therefore, last only until the end of the relevant four-year period. On the other hand, it is possible for a Parliament to last for slightly over the standard period of four years, if an extraordinary election comes within six months of the next general election, i e on or after the first Thursday in December during the final year of a Parliament's term.

2.31 The Parliament must meet within seven days of a general election being held (ss 2(3),(5), 3(2))[1].

1 In calculating the seven days no regard is had to Saturdays, Sundays, Christmas Eve, Christmas Day, Good Friday, bank holidays in Scotland or days appointed for public thanksgiving or mourning (s 4); the inclusion of the final possibility may be a consequence of the disruption to the campaigning in the devolution referendum in September 1997 resulting from the death of Princess Diana.

VACANCIES AND BY-ELECTIONS

2.32 Where a seat becomes vacant (through resignation or any other cause)[1] during the life of a Parliament, there are different consequences depending on whether the member was returned as a constituency member or a regional member.

1 See paras 3.1, 3.9–3.11 below.

Constituency Vacancies

2.33 If the member was elected as a constituency member, the seat is filled by means of a by-election in that constituency (s 9). The date of the by-election is determined by the Presiding Officer, and must be within three months of the vacancy occurring[1], or coming to the notice of the Presiding Officer. A by-election will not take place if the last day on which it could be held is within three months of the date for the next scheduled general election, and the seat will remain vacant until that election. This means that if a vacancy occurs (or comes to the Presiding Officer's notice) after the first Thursday in December in the last year of a Parliament the seat will remain unfilled until the general election in the following May.

1 The date when a vacancy is to be treated as occurring is to be determined by standing orders.

2.34 It is not permissible to be a candidate for more than one by-election at a time, nor can existing members stand as candidates (s 9(6)). This latter provision means that a member elected as a regional member cannot seek election as a constituency member during the life of a Parliament.

Regional Vacancies

2.35 Where the seat of a regional member becomes vacant, there is no by-election and the seat is filled in a different way or may remain vacant (s 10). If the member was returned from a party list, the seat is filled from the unsuccessful candidates on that party's list at the last general election. The regional returning officer must discover which of the unsuccessful candidates on the list are willing to serve as regional members[1] and the seat goes to the willing candidate whose name was highest on the party list. The returning officer must notify this name to the Presiding Officer, at which point that candidate is a member of the Parliament. This method of filling vacancies means that it is important for parties to ensure that they put forward lists which are long enough not only to fill the places won at the general election but also to ensure that a replacement is available if one of the successful regional members leaves the Parliament for whatever reason.

1 It may be that by the time a vacancy arises candidates have other commitments, or be subject to some disqualification.

2.36 If the member was returned as an individual candidate, then the seat remains vacant until the next general election (s 10(2)). The same applies if there is no-one from the party list who can take the seat, e g because all of the candidates on the list have already been elected or none is willing and able to serve.

OTHER ELECTORAL MATTERS

2.37 The Secretary of State has the power to make detailed rules governing the conduct of elections (s 12). These will cover such matters as limitations on the electoral expenses of individuals and parties, registration of electors, challenges to the results of elections and the designation of returning officers. Another issue which may be regulated is how the system for returning regional members is to operate if for some reason the election for all of the constituency seats in the region cannot be completed or if there is a tie for the final regional seat. In making such rules the Secretary of State can apply, with or without modification, the rules found in existing legislation for parliamentary, local or European elections.

2.38 The procedure for challenging the election of a member of the Parliament is that laid down in Part III of the Representation Act 1986, as applied by an order made by the Secretary of State under the above powers (s 12(5))[1].

1 See para 3.10 below.

3 Members of the Scottish Parliament

3.1 Although for election purposes there is a difference between constituency and regional members, once elected there is no differentiation between categories of Members of the Scottish Parliament (MSPs). Members enjoy that status from the date on which they are declared to be returned as the successful candidates at an election[1] until the Parliament is dissolved prior to an election (s 13). It is provided, though, that a member can resign at any time simply by giving notice in writing to the Presiding Officer (s 14). This is very different from the position at Westminster where there is no procedure for resignation and this result has to be achieved indirectly by MPs being appointed to a nominal post which disqualifies them from membership of the House of Commons.

1 Or in the case of filling a vacancy for a regional seat, from the date when the Presiding Officer is notified of this (s 10(6)).

3.2 Once elected, a member must take the oath of allegiance at a meeting of the Parliament (s 84). The form of the oath is prescribed in the Promissory Oaths Act 1868 and requires each member to swear that he or she will 'be faithful and bear true allegiance to Her Majesty Queen Elizabeth, her heirs and successors according to law'[1]. Until the oath is taken, a member cannot take part in proceedings of the Parliament (s 84(2)) and cannot receive any salary or allowances (s 83(2),(3)). If a member does not take the oath within two months of being elected (or any longer period provided by the Parliament) he or she ceases to be a member and the seat is declared vacant (s 84(3)). Standing orders may provide for withdrawing from a member the rights and privileges of that status (Sch 3 para 2). Members of the Scottish Parliament are entitled to be excused from jury service in Scotland and in England and Wales (s 85)[2].

1 Promissory Oaths Act 1868, ss 1, 10; an affirmation can be made in place of the oath (Oaths Act 1978, s 5).

2 Similar provision in relation to Northern Ireland will be made by amending the Juries (Northern Ireland) Order 1996, SI 1996/1141.

SALARIES

3.3 The Parliament must make provision for members to receive salaries and may make provision for pensions, gratuities or allowances to former members (s 81). These arrangements can be made through an Act of the Scottish Parliament or by resolution conferring functions to the Parliamentary corporation (s 81(5)), and different arrangements can be made for different cases (s 83(5)). The salary of members of the Scottish Parliament must be reduced if they are receiving salaries from either House of the United Kingdom Parliament or as members of the European Parliament[1] (s 82). The reduction can be by a particular amount or by a proportion of the normal salary, or calculated by reference to the salary payable from the other Parliament. Information relating to the salaries, allowances, pensions and gratuities must be published each financial year (s 83(1)).

1 By applying the European Parliament (Pay and Pensions) Act 1979, this applies to those MEPs representing constituencies in the United Kingdom; it is legally possible, but unlikely, for a member of the Scottish Parliament also to be a member of the European Parliament for a constituency outside the United Kingdom, and in that case it appears that no reduction in salary is required.

DISQUALIFICATIONS

3.4 The categories of people disqualified from being Members of the Scottish Parliament are largely the same as those for Westminster, but there are some differences. In particular, citizens of the European Union resident in the United Kingdom can be Members of the Scottish Parliament (s 16(2)) and there is no disqualification for peers or those who are ordained or are ministers of any religious denomination (s 16(1)). All of these groups are disqualified from membership of the House of Commons.

3.5 In the same way as for the rules on who is entitled to vote, this matter is dealt with in the Scotland Act primarily by applying (with some modifications) existing provisions rather than by legislating afresh (s 15). Accordingly, the main categories of disqualification are set out by applying parts of the House of Commons Disqualification Act 1975. The relevant provisions[1] disqualify the following groups:

(1) those holding judicial office[2];
(2) those employed in the civil service;
(3) members of the regular armed forces;
(4) members of the police; and
(5) members of a legislature outwith the Commonwealth.

1 House of Commons Disqualification Act 1975, s 1(1)(a)–(e).
2 This is defined by the list in Part I of Schedule 1 to the 1975 Act and includes judges of the Court of Session and sheriffs; the Law Lords (Lords of Appeal in Ordinary), who are not included in the list since their membership of the House of Lords already excludes them from the Commons, are expressly excluded from membership of the Scottish Parliament (Scotland Act 1998, s 15(1)(c)).

3.6 The 1975 Act includes the further category of those who hold any of the offices listed in Schedule 1 to that Act, which covers a wide range of public bodies. This Schedule does not apply directly, but provision is made for an Order in Council to be made listing office-holders who will be disqualified and it is likely that the list will be based on that Schedule (s 15(2)). However, given the division of responsibility between the two Parliaments, there will be instances where a post is incompatible with membership of one Parliament but not the other. The provision allows for the listing of office-holders who will be disqualified only in relation to a particular constituency or region[1].

1 For example, it has been suggested that lords-lieutenant might be disqualified but only in relation to the area of their lieutenancy.

3.7 The disqualifications listed above may be disregarded in individual cases if the Parliament so resolves (s 16(3)-(5)). The Parliament can only pass such a resolution when the ground for disqualification no longer exists and the Parliament considers that it is proper for the disqualification to be disregarded. This provision allows a person whose membership of the Parliament and holding of a disqualifying office have overlapped to continue as a member provided that the other office has been resigned. However, the Parliament cannot disregard a disqualification in this way if the disqualification has already been determined by the courts or is currently the subject of legal proceedings.

3.8 The disqualifications which apply to the House of Commons other than those in the 1975 Act also apply to the Scottish Parliament (s 15(1)(b)). This includes those who are less than 21 years of age, those disqualified following conviction of corrupt or illegal electoral practices[1], bankrupts[2], those suffering from severe mental illness[3] and certain convicted prisoners[4].

These disqualifications cannot be disregarded by the Parliament (s 16(3)).

1 Representation of the People Act 1983, ss 159–160, 173.
2 Insolvency Act 1986, s 427; members are suspended when the relevant court order is made and the seat declared vacant after six months, unless the order has been recalled (see para 3.9 below).
3 Mental Health Act 1983, s 141, which is amended to cover the Scottish Parliament by the Scotland Act 1998, Sch 8 para 19; the Presiding Officer has to arrange for medical examinations and disqualification takes effect if a member has been detained on the ground of mental illness and is still in that state after six months.
4 Those sentenced to more than one year in prison, during their sentence or while unlawfully on the run; Representation of the People Act 1981, s 1.

3.9 If a person who is disqualified is returned as a member of the Scottish Parliament, his or her return is void and the seat is vacant. Similarly if a sitting member becomes disqualified, he or she ceases to be a member and again the seat is vacant, to be filled as noted above (s 16(1)-(2))[1]. During the six-month period between a member being declared bankrupt or being detained on the grounds of mental illness and disqualification taking effect[2], the member cannot participate in proceedings and may have rights and privileges withdrawn by the Parliament (s 17(4)). The validity of proceedings in Parliament is not affected by the fact that a member is or becomes disqualified (s 17(5)).

1 See paras 2.32–2.36 above.
2 See para 3.8, notes 2 and 3 above.

3.10 There are two court procedures for determining claims that a member is subject to disqualification. At elections, the matter is dealt with by an election petition under Part III of the Representation of the People Act 1975 (s 12(5)). Such petitions must be made within 21 days of the election and are heard by the Election Court (two nominated judges of the Court of Session). Depending on the grounds of challenge, the respondent is either the member whose eligibility is questioned or the returning officer[1].

1 See 15 *Stair Memorial Encyclopaedia* paras 1436–1492.

3.11 At other times, any person claiming that a member is disqualified may apply to the Court of Session asking it to declare that this is indeed the case (s 18). The Court cannot make such a declarator if the Parliament has already resolved that the disqualification should be disregarded (s 18(3)(b)), but Parliament cannot disregard a disqualification which has been declared by the Court (s 16(5)). The Court of Session's decision on the matter is final, in other words there is no appeal to the House of Lords. In such proceedings the defender is the member whose status is challenged (not the returning officer or any other official). In both election proceedings and proceedings before the Court of Session the applicant must provide caution (i e security) of up to £5,000 for the expenses of the proceedings, in order to discourage frivolous or vexatious applications.

MEMBERS' INTERESTS

3.12 Recent events at Westminster have ensured that the issues of members' interests and 'cash for questions' are expressly addressed in the Act. Although the details of the rules will be contained in legislation made by the Parliament itself[1], a clear framework is laid down in the Act itself to ensure that members' interests are fully declared, conflicts of interest are limited and paid lobbying by members is prohibited[2].

1 The provisions must be in an Act of the Scottish Parliament or in subordinate legislation made under such an Act, not just in standing orders (s 39(8)).

2 Since they may be entitled to take part in proceedings of the Parliament (s 27(1)), the Lord Advocate and Solicitor General are bound by the rules discussed in this section, whether or not they are members of the Parliament (s 39(8)).

3.13 Following the pattern at Westminster, there is to be register of interests of members, which must be published and available for public inspection, and members are to be placed under an obligation to register financial interests (including benefits in kind) as defined for this purpose (s 39(1)-(2)). The register is then to be supported by provisions which must require members who have a financial interest in a matter to declare that interest before taking part in any proceedings relating to that matter (s 39(2)). Moreover, the provisions may require more than merely a declaration of interest, but may restrict or prevent members taking part in proceedings when they have an interest (s 39(3)). Given the current atmosphere created by the various 'sleaze' allegations of recent years, it can be expected that a fairly strict approach will be taken on these matters.

3.14 The related issue of 'cash for questions' is also expressly addressed (s 39(4)). Here there is little discretion for the Parliament since, although the details are left to future legislation, it is clearly provided that members must be prohibited from advocating or initiating any cause or matter on behalf of any person in return for any payment or benefit in kind. Similarly prohibited is urging any other member to raise an issue when this is done in consideration of any payment or benefit. It is thus clear that from the very beginning the Scottish Parliament will prohibit paid lobbying and attempt to ensure that members raise issues because of their personal concern, not as paid advocates of others.

3.15 The seriousness with which the issue is taken is demonstrated by the sanctions which can be imposed if these rules are breached. The legislation which is to be made must provide for members to be excluded from proceedings of the Parliament if they fail to comply with these rules (s 39(5))[1]. However, matters are not left just to the Parliament and it is a criminal offence for a member to take part in proceedings without registering or declaring an interest or to take part in paid lobbying in contravention of these rules (s 39(6)). This latter provision is particularly significant because it emphasises the status of the Scottish Parliament in comparison to Westminster. As one aspect of its constitutional supremacy, the United Kingdom Parliament enjoys complete privilege in relation to the regulation of its own affairs and matters such as these fall very firmly within the exclusive jurisdiction of Parliament, not within the scope of the ordinary criminal law.

1 Standing orders may also provide for the rights and privileges of a member to be withdrawn (Sch 3 para 2).

CORRUPTION

3.16 In addition to the rules noted above in relation to members' interests and the prohibition of paid lobbying, the Scottish Parliament is covered by rules in relation to bribery and corruption. This is achieved by classifying the Scottish Parliament as a public body for the purposes of the Prevention of Corruption Acts 1889–1916 (s 43). The Parliament and its staff are therefore covered by the same rules as apply to government departments, local authorities and other public bodies.

4 Administrative arrangements, privilege and procedure

4.1 The administrative framework for the Parliament rests on three main provisions; those authorising the election of the Presiding Officer, the appointment of the Clerk and the creation of the Scottish Parliamentary Corporate Body. Powers and functions are then allocated between these, although most of the details of how the Parliament is to operate are left to be determined by the Parliament itself, primarily by means of the standing orders to be made. The standing orders will also establish the procedure by which the Parliament will make laws, but some rules on procedure and legal privileges in relation to defamation and contempt of court are provided in the Act. The extent to which the courts can intervene in the parliament's affairs is also addressed. The Act also provides for the Parliament to establish a mechanism for investigating complaints of maladministration by the Scottish government.

PRESIDING OFFICER

4.2 The Presiding Officer (the equivalent of the Speaker of the House of Commons) plays a pivotal role in the workings of the Parliament. At its first meeting after a general election, the Parliament elects from among its members a Presiding Officer and two deputies (s 19); standing orders must provide that these do not all come from the same political party (Sch 3 para 5). Their term of office continues until the next time the Parliament holds such an election, so that they remain in office while the Parliament is dissolved for a general election and until the Parliament meets thereafter. They may resign or be removed from office by the Parliament, in which case a replacement will be elected. A deputy acts in place of the Presiding Officer if he or she is unable to act or that post is vacant, and the Presiding Officer can authorise deputies to act in his or her place, subject to standing orders. The extent to which the Presiding Officer and deputies may participate in the proceedings of Parliament (including their right to vote) may be regulated by standing orders.

4.3 The functions of the Presiding Officer set out in the Scotland Act include the following, and many more tasks will be entrusted to him or her under standing orders:

(1) recommending the date for a general election (ss 2(5), 3(1));
(2) receiving written notice when a member resigns (s 14); receiving notice of the mental illness or bankruptcy of members and declaring their seats vacant if their status does not change within six months[1];
(3) setting the date for by-elections (s 9(2));
(4) receiving notice when a regional vacancy is filled (s 10(6));
(5) membership of the Scottish Parliamentary Corporate Body, presiding at its meetings and the exercise of any functions delegated by it (s 21(2), Sch 2 para 5);
(6) administering oaths to witnesses before the Parliament (s 26);
(7) scrutiny of Bills to check that they are within the competence of the Parliament (s 31(2));
(8) submission of Bills for Royal Assent (s 32(3));
(9) receiving notification that the Law Officers or Secretary of State have no intention to question or delay a Bill (ss 33(3), 35(4));
(10) recommending to the Queen the Parliament's choice as First Minister (s 46(4));
(11) designating a member of the Parliament to exercise the functions of the First Minister if he or she is unable to act (s 45(4)).

1 Mental Health Act 1983, s 141 and Insolvency Act 1985, s 427, both as amended by the Scotland Act 1998, Sch 8 paras 19, 23 (see paras 3.8–3.9 above).

CLERK OF THE PARLIAMENT

4.4 The Act requires the appointment of a Clerk of the Parliament (s 20). The Clerk is appointed by the Scottish Parliamentary Corporate Body and provision is made for Assistant Clerks to exercise functions when the Clerk is for any reason unable to act. The Clerk may authorise Assistant Clerks or other members of the staff of the Parliament to exercise functions on his or her behalf.

4.5 The Act says little about the functions of the Clerk, although the Clerk is specified as the person who summons witnesses and documents (s 24) and who notes the date of Royal Assent on Acts of the Parliament (s 28(4)). Nevertheless, it is to be expected that, as at Westminster[1], the clerks will play a very major role in the day-to-day business of the Parliament as well as providing advice and guidance on the procedures to be followed.

1 See *Erskine May's Treatise on the Law, Privileges, Proceedings and Usages of Parliament* (22nd edn, 1997) pp 185–187, 197–198 and passim.

SCOTTISH PARLIAMENTARY CORPORATE BODY

4.6 The Scottish Parliament does not itself exist as a legal body capable of holding property, entering contracts, employing people or being a party to litigation. Instead a new body, the Scottish Parliamentary Corporate Body, is created to fulfil these functions (s 21); this follows the model used at Westminster[1]. This new body ('the corporation') enjoys full legal personality as a body corporate and as such can create, hold, transfer and exercise the full range of legal rights available to companies and other legal persons. The corporation will also represent the Parliament and its officers in legal proceedings[2].

1 House of Commons (Administration) Act 1978, Parliamentary Corporate Bodies Act 1992.
2 See paras 4.36–4.40 below.

4.7 The members of the corporation are the Presiding Officer (who presides at meetings (Sch 2 para 6)) and four members of the Parliament appointed in accordance with standing orders (s 21(2)). The members of the Parliament continue to hold office until they resign or cease to be members, and they remain in office when the Parliament is dissolved for a general election (Sch 2 para 1). The Parliament can give the corporation general or special directions in connection with the corporation's functions (s 21(4)), but otherwise the corporation may determine its own procedure, and may delegate functions to the Presiding Officer or Clerk (Sch 2 para 5).

4.8 The main statutory function of the corporation is to provide the Parliament with the property, staff and services which the

Parliament requires for its purposes (s 21(3)), and any property or liabilities to which the Parliament would be entitled or subject are treated as those of the corporation (s 21(5)). The expenses of the corporation are to be met by the Scottish Consolidated Fund, into which any sums received by the corporation are to be paid (s 21(6),(7))[1].

1 See para 7.35 below.

4.9 As well as the Clerk to the Parliament (s 20), the corporation must appoint Assistant Clerks and other staff, together known as the staff of the Parliament, and it is responsible for determining their terms and conditions of service, including the making of pension arrangements (Sch 2 para 3). The corporation may hold property and subordinate legislation may provide for the transfer to it of any property belonging to a Minister of the Crown which may be required for the corporation's functions (Sch 2 para 2). In order to allow the corporation to fulfil its functions, wide powers are given to enter contracts, to invest money, to accept gifts and to borrow money (with the Parliament's approval) (Sch 2 para 4). The corporation may be treated as a Crown body for certain purposes, especially to allow employment by the corporation to be treated as employment by a Crown body, and to enable land held or used by the corporation to be treated as held by a Crown body (Sch 2 para 7). This enables the corporation to be integrated into the broader arrangements for 'the public service'.

STANDING ORDERS

4.10 The detailed regulation of the proceedings of the Parliament is left to standing orders to be made by the Parliament itself (s 22). It is therefore the Parliament itself which will decide how it is to operate. There is no limit to the matters which can be governed by standing orders apart from the broad expression 'proceedings of the Parliament'[1] and the orders will cover all aspects of the procedure and conduct of business of the Parliament and rights and privileges of members of the Parliament. In the planning for devolution there has been much talk about the aim of creating a very different sort of Parliament from Westminster, with greater emphasis on accessibility and co-operation, with opportunities for wide participation before proposals enter the legislative stages and with a greater role for committees of the Parliament. These are all matters within the scope of the standing orders and way in which the Parliament operates will depend on the standing orders which it decides to make.

1 This expressly includes proceedings of any committee or sub-committee (s 126(1)).

4.11 No procedure is laid down in the Act for the making of standing orders, and this itself will be a matter for regulation by standing orders. Standing orders for the initial operation of the Parliament will be made by the Secretary of State under the general power to make transitory or transitional provisions in relation to the Act's coming into force (s 129). The procedure and operation of the Parliament (and hence the likely content of standing orders) have been the subject of consideration by the Consultative Steering Group[1], which has carried out wide consultation on how the Parliament should work. All final decisions will rest with the Parliament itself.

1 The report of the Group, *Shaping Scotland's Parliament*, was produced in December 1998 and further papers are available on the Scottish Devolution Web-site at http://www.scottish-devolution.org.uk/.

4.12 Throughout the Act there is reference to a number of matters which must be dealt with by standing orders, and others which it is expressly said may (and which inevitably will) be addressed.

4.13 Matters which must be provided for include:

(1) *the preservation of order*: the standing orders must provide for the preservation of order in the proceedings of the Parliament, including the prevention of conduct which would constitute a criminal offence; such orders may provide for the exclusion of members from proceedings (Sch 3 para 1);

(2) *sub judice rule*: the standing orders must make provision for the prevention of conduct which would be a contempt of court[1] as well as for a sub judice rule, which will presumably set wider restrictions on the discussion of matters which are before the courts (Sch 3 para 1);

(3) *meeting in public*: the proceedings of the Parliament are to be held in public, except when the standing orders prescribe otherwise; the orders may state the conditions on which members of the public are entitled to attend and provide for the exclusion of those who do not comply (Sch 3 para 3);

(4) *reporting*: provision must be made in the standing orders for reporting the proceedings of Parliament and for publishing the reports (Sch 3 para 4);

(5) *Presiding Officer and deputies*: provision must be made in standing orders to ensure that the Presiding Officer and deputies do not all represent the same political party (Sch 3 para 5);

(6) *committees*: in appointing members to committees and sub-committees, regard must be had to the balance of parties in the Parliament, and provision can be made to exclude members of the Parliament who are not members of a committee or sub-committee from its proceedings; standing orders providing for the appointment of committees may authorise these to appoint sub-committees (Sch 3 para 6);

(7) *vacancies*: the dates when constituency or regional vacancies are to be treated as occurring are to be determined by standing orders (ss 9(5), 10(7));

(8) *appointments to the Scottish Parliamentary Corporate Body*: the appointment of the four members of the Parliament to the corporation is governed by standing orders (s 21(2));

(9) *scrutiny of Bills*: standing orders must provide the form of statement to be made by the Presiding Officer following the scrutiny of a Bill prior to its introduction to the Parliament to ensure that it is within the competence of the Parliament (s 31(3));

(10) *progress of Bills*: the various stages of a Bill's passage through the Parliament, including the provision for general debate, consideration of details and final stage for approval or rejection must be provided by standing orders, as well as the opportunity for reconsideration once provisions have been held to be beyond the competence of the Parliament (s 36)[2];

(11) *Crown interests*: the standing orders must provide that a Bill containing provisions affecting the prerogative, hereditary revenues, personal property or interests of the Crown requires the consent of the Queen, the Prince or Steward of Scotland or the Duke of Cornwall as appropriate before it can be passed (Sch 3 para 7)[3];

(12) *financial reports*: standing orders must provide for the consideration of accounts and reports laid before the Parliament (s 70(3));

(13) *tax-varying resolutions*: the standing orders must provide that only a member of the Scottish Executive can move a motion for a tax-varying resolution (s 74(5)).

1 See paras 4.26–4.28 below.
2 See paras 4.32–4.35 below.
3 The matters covered are those which would require such consent at Westminster; see *Erskine May's Treatise on the Law, Privileges, Proceedings and Usage of Parliament* (22nd edn, 1997) pp 603–605.

4.14 The matters which the Act says may be addressed by standing orders include:

1 *participation of the Presiding Officer*: the Presiding Officer's power to authorise deputies to act in his or place and the extent to which the Presiding Officer and deputies may participate and vote in proceedings may be regulated (s 19(5),(6));
2 *withdrawal of rights*: standing orders may provide for the rights and privileges of a member to be withdrawn (Sch 3 para 2);
3 *witnesses*: in relation to people giving evidence in proceedings of Parliament (most likely to be before committees) or providing documents, the standing orders may provide for expenses and allowances and for the administration of oaths (s 26);
4 *Law Officers*: standing orders may allow for the Law Officers (Lord Advocate and Solicitor-General for Scotland) if they are not already members of the Parliament to participate (but not vote) in proceedings of the Parliament (s 27);
5 *progress of Bills*: as noted above, the standing orders regulating the progress of Bills must provide for certain stages, but they may also provide for different types of procedure for different types of Bill (s 36(2)).

WITNESSES AND DOCUMENTS

4.15 The Parliament is given wide powers to call people to give evidence and to require the production of documents. Although anyone can be invited to attend, the formal power to summon people can be exercised only in relation to matters within the Parliament's own competence[1]. The power can be exercised to require any person to attend the Parliament's proceedings for the purpose of giving evidence or to produce documents[2] which are in their custody or control (whether or not they own them) (s 23(1)). Committees and sub-committees can likewise summon witnesses and documents, but only when they have been expressly authorised to do so by standing orders or otherwise (e g by a special resolution of the Parliament) (s 23(8)).

1 See Chapter 5 below.

2 A 'document' includes anything in which information is recorded in any way (s 126(1)), and thus includes all forms of electronic storage of information; providing a copy of, or an extract of the relevant part of, the document suffices (s 26(5)).

4.16 The summons takes the form of notice in writing from the Clerk to the Parliament sent by registered post or recorded delivery (s 24). When a person appears to give evidence, the Presiding Officer or other member authorised by standing orders may administer an oath[1] and may require the witness to take the oath; failure to take the oath when required to do so is a criminal offence (s 26(1)–(3)). Provisions may be made in standing orders for the payment of allowances and expenses to those who attend the Parliament to give evidence or who produce documents when requested or required to do so (s 26(4)).

1 A solemn affirmation may be made in place of taking an oath; Oaths Act 1978, s 5.

4.17 Although the Parliament will be free to invite anyone to attend, the legal power to call witnesses and documents is restricted to issues within the competence of the Parliament. There is therefore a series of provisions designed to ensure that all matters within the powers of the Parliament and the Scottish Ministers are included but that the Parliament does not trespass onto matters reserved for Westminster and the government of the United Kingdom (s 23(1)–(6)). The power to call for witnesses and documents is therefore restricted to matters within the competence of the Parliament or in relation to which the Scottish Ministers exercise functions. A further limitation is that the power can be exercised in relation to people outwith Scotland only in connection with their discharge of functions relating to these matters. Ministers of the Crown (i e members of the United Kingdom government) and those in Crown employment[1] can be summoned only in relation to their discharge of functions relating to devolved matters or the functions of Scottish Ministers, but even in such circumstances they cannot be summoned if the function in question is one exercisable in Scotland by a Minister of the Crown as well as by Scottish Ministers or where Ministers of the Crown act with the agreement of or after consultation with the Scottish Ministers. The power cannot be exercised in relation to the discharge of functions relating only to reserved matters.

1 Defined by s 191(3) of the Employment Rights Act 1996.

4.18 The limitations described above endeavour to keep the Parliament within its constitutional bounds in relation to the United Kingdom Parliament and Executive. Further limitations endeavour to prevent the Parliament from straying across the boundary protecting the independence of the judiciary. The

Parliament cannot use its power to summon a judge of any court, nor members of any tribunal in connection with their discharge of their functions as such (s 23(7)).

4.19 In addition to the limitations described above, the power to seek evidence is restricted in two further ways. No person can be required to answer any question or produce any document if he or she would be entitled to refuse to answer or to produce it in court proceedings in Scotland (s 23(9)). The main areas in which witnesses will be permitted to refuse to answer are therefore those covered by the privilege against self-incrimination, the privileges to protect communications between husband and wife and between lawyer and client in relation to litigation, and 'public interest immunity', the at times controversial[1] area where public policy allows matters to be withheld in the public interest[2]. Since it is the courts, not the Parliament, which can impose sanctions for failing to answer questions or produce documents[3], it will be the courts which determine the extent of these restrictions.

1 As demonstrated in the 'Arms to Iraq' affair; *Report of the Inquiry into the Export of Defence Equipment and Dual-use Goods to Iraq and Related Prosecutions* (Scott Report) (HC Paper 115 (1995–96)).
2 See Field & Raitt, *Evidence* (2nd edn, 1996) ch 12.
3 See para 4.21 below.

4.20 The second restriction relates to the handling of specific criminal prosecutions. Procurators fiscal are entitled to refuse answers or documents relating to the operation of the criminal prosecution system in any particular case, where authorised by the Lord Advocate to do so on the basis that providing the answer or document might prejudice that case or would otherwise be contrary to the public interest (s 23(10))[1].

1 See paras 4.22–4.23 below.

4.21 The power to call witnesses and documents is enforced by means of a number of criminal offences (s 24). Again it is significant that these matters are addressed through the criminal law and that the Parliament does not enjoy any jurisdiction to impose sanctions itself (other than on members). Once properly called to do so by the Parliament, it is an offence for any person:

1 to refuse or fail to attend proceedings as required;
2 to refuse or fail to answer any questions relating to the matter specified in the notice; or
3 to refuse or fail to produce any document[1].

No crime is committed if there is a reasonable excuse for the refusal or failure. It is also a crime deliberately to alter, suppress, conceal or destroy any document which one has been called on to produce, and here it is not accepted that there can be a reasonable excuse to provide a defence. Where these offences are committed by a company or other body corporate, any director, manager, secretary or other similar officer[2] will be personally guilty and subject to punishment if it is proved that the offence was committed with his or her consent or connivance, or through his or her neglect. Provisions of this kind which make sure that the individuals responsible for wrong-doing cannot hide behind a corporate identity is increasingly common when statutory offences are being created.

1 'Document' includes any form of storing information (s 112(1)).
2 Or any person purporting to act in such capacity.

LAW OFFICERS

4.22 Special provision is made for the involvement in parliamentary proceedings of the Law Officers, namely the Lord Advocate and the Solicitor General for Scotland[1]. Unlike the other members of the Scottish Executive, these need not be members of the Parliament, but, given the importance of their role, particularly in relation to the system of criminal prosecution, it is considered appropriate that they should be able to contribute to, and be subject to scrutiny by, the Parliament. At the same time provision is made to protect their independence in dealing with individual criminal cases.

1 See paras 7.6–7.8.

4.23 The Law Officers may participate, but may not vote, in proceedings of the Parliament (s 27(1)). The extent of their participation is governed by standing orders, as is the extent to which they are bound by other rules applying to members, although they are automatically bound by the rules on members' interests and paid lobbying contained in the Act itself (s 39(8)). They may refuse to answer questions or produce documents in relation to particular criminal prosecutions if they consider that providing the answer or document might prejudice criminal proceedings in that case or otherwise be contrary to the public interest (s 27(3)).

DEFAMATION

4.24 In order to ensure freedom of debate, statements[1] made in proceedings of the Parliament enjoy absolute privilege in relation to the law of defamation (s 41). This means that whatever the accuracy of the statement or the intent with which it was made, no action for defamation can be based on it. 'Proceedings of the Parliament' is not defined, but certainly covers committee hearings where witnesses appear as well as debates in the Parliament itself. Publications made under the authority of the Parliament, e g the official reports of debates, committee papers and authorised radio or television broadcasts, are also protected in this way. It will, however, be possible to make use of what is said in the Parliament to support actions based on statements made elsewhere, e g to demonstrate the truth of the statement or to show that there is malice behind a statement which might otherwise enjoy qualified privilege[2].

1 A 'statement' means 'words, pictures, visual images, gestures or other method of signifying meaning'; Defamation Act 1996, s 17(1).

2 This contrasts with the position at Westminster where statements in Parliament cannot be relied on at all except to the extent that the person affected agrees to waive the rule normally excluding the courts from examining anything said or done within Parliament; Defamation Act 1996, s 13.

4.25 Reports of proceedings in Parliament also enjoy a degree of protection in relation to defamation. Protection is given under the general provision which grants privilege to a fair and accurate report of proceedings in public of a legislature anywhere in the world unless the publication is shown to have been made with malice[1]. Thus any standard reporting of what is said or done in public proceedings, including humorous 'Parliamentary Sketches'[2], will be protected, but the publication of a biased selection of parliamentary comments or their reproduction out of context may still form the basis of an action where the person responsible is motivated by malice.

1 Defamation Act 1996, s 15 and Sch 1 para 1.

2 *Cook v Alexander* [1974] QB 279.

CONTEMPT OF COURT

4.26 Since it does not share the general immunity from the ordinary law enjoyed by the Westminster Parliament, the

Scottish Parliament is subject to the general law on contempt of court. In order to avoid proceedings in Parliament having an undue effect on individual cases, the Parliament is required to adopt standing orders which include a sub judice rule restricting discussion of cases before the courts, and which prevent conduct constituting a contempt of court (Sch 3 para 1). As an additional measure, the Law Officers and procurators fiscal are entitled to refuse to answer questions or produce documents when that might prejudice criminal proceedings in any case (ss 23(10), 27(3)).

4.27 A full application of the rules on contempt might, however, interfere with the freedom of the Parliament to make laws, since statements in the Parliament, or even the consideration of certain matters at all, might be seen as having a prejudicial effect on litigation before the courts. Accordingly some immunity is granted, but the immunity is limited to proceedings in relation to a Bill or subordinate legislation and reports of such proceedings (s 42). It is provided that such proceedings are not covered by the 'strict liability rule' introduced by the Contempt of Court Act 1981. Under that rule any conduct which creates 'a substantial risk that the course of justice in proceedings[1] . . . will be seriously impeded or prejudiced' is a contempt of court[2], unless that risk is 'merely incidental' to 'a discussion in good faith of public affairs or other matters of general public interest'[3]. That qualification by itself may have protected all but the most exceptional proceedings on legislative matters, but any doubt is removed by the express immunity. It is only the strict liability rule which is disapplied, so that any deliberate attempt to prejudice legal proceedings is still punishable, even if made in the context of considering legislation.

1 The rules cover risks to 'active' proceedings as defined in the Contempt of Court Act 1981, Sch 1.
2 Contempt of Court Act 1981, s 2(2).
3 Contempt of Court Act 1981, s 5.

4.28 In other proceedings the standard rules of contempt will still apply. Thus not only is any deliberate contempt punishable by the courts, but also the strict liability rule applies. Again, the qualification protecting discussion of public affairs where there is only an incidental risk to cases before the courts will offer fairly wide protection, but not if the discussion strays into the details of particular cases.

MALADMINISTRATION

4.29 The Parliament is required to make provision for the investigation of complaints of maladministration against the actions of the Scottish Administration (s 91). In relation to the United Kingdom government, and a wide range of other public bodies, this is the responsibility of the Parliamentary Commissioner for Administration (the Parliamentary Ombudsman) created by the Parliamentary Commissioner Act 1967. The Scottish Parliament is required to pass legislation establishing a system to achieve the same purpose, and in doing so it must have regard to the provisions of the 1967 Act.

4.30 The system must allow for the investigation of complaints which would fall within the Parliamentary Commissioner's jurisdiction if made in relation to the United Kingdom government. These are complaints of 'injustice in consequence of maladministration[1], where there are no other means of redress by way of appeal or legal proceedings[2], and provided that the matter does not fall within one of the excluded areas, including personnel matters, the investigation of crime, the conduct of legal proceedings and commercial transactions[3]. The actions (or failures to act) which must be subject to investigation are those of office-holders in the Scottish Administration and of members of the Scottish Executive in the exercise of the functions of Scottish Ministers. The Parliament may also provide for the investigation of complaints against cross-border public authorities concerning Scotland, provided that no reserved matter is concerned.

1 Parliamentary Commissioner Act 1967, s 5(1).
2 Parliamentary Commissioner Act 1967, s 5(2).
3 Parliamentary Commissioner Act 1967, Sch 3.

4.31 The requirement merely to have regard to the provisions of the 1967 Act leaves it open to the Parliament to adopt different procedures from those for the Parliamentary Commissioner. Most notably, the requirement that complaints can be made to the Parliamentary Commissioner only through a Member of Parliament need not be repeated in the provisions for the Scottish Ombudsman.

LEGISLATIVE PROCEDURE

4.32 The Parliament makes law by enacting Acts of the Scottish Parliament, which shall be judicially noticed (s 28). The procedure by which such laws are made is largely regulated by standing orders, although a basic framework is provided by the Scotland Act and the issue is specifically addressed in *Shaping Scotland's Parliament*, the report of the Consultative Steering Group. A proposed Act is known as a Bill and becomes an Act when it has been passed by the Parliament and received the Royal Assent.

4.33 Standing orders must provide for a three-stage consideration of Bills: a general debate with an opportunity to vote on the Bill's general principles, consideration of and voting on the details of a Bill, and a final stage at which the Bill can be passed or rejected (s 36). Provision can be made for expediting proceedings in relation to particular Bills. Different forms of procedure can be introduced for consolidation Bills which merely restate the law, and for Bills which merely repeal spent enactments. Similarly, different procedure can be adopted for private legislation which will be competent where the subject matter falls wholly within the competence of the Parliament[1]. A Bill is presented for Royal Assent by the Presiding Officer (s 32(1)).

1 Where orders require parliamentary approval and fall within the legislative competence of the Parliament, the power to grant such approval is transferred to the Scottish Parliament by s 95 of the Act. The Private Legislation Procedure (Scotland) Act 1936 remains in force to govern Scottish private legislation at Westminster but cannot be used where the subject matter is wholly within the competence of the Scottish Parliament (Sch 8 para 5). Several of the matters for which private legislation is necessary, e g transport projects, may raise difficult issues on the boundaries of devolved and reserved matters.

4.34 There are also further procedures to deal with issues as to the competence of a Bill (see below)[1]. The Presiding Officer must give his opinion before a Bill is introduced whether its provisions will be within the legislative competence of the Parliament (s 31). A Bill cannot be presented for Royal Assent until the four week period for the Secretary of State to intervene or for referring any doubts over its competence has passed, or until any reference has been determined by the Judicial Committee of the Privy Council (s 32). Standing orders must provide that where the Judicial Committee decides that any provision in a Bill is outwith the Parliament's competence, there must be an opportunity for the Bill to be reconsidered (s 36). If a Bill is amended when it is reconsidered in this way, there must be a further final stage of consideration at which the Bill as a whole can be approved or rejected.

1 Fully discussed at paras 5.29–5.37 below.

4.35 The validity of an Act of the Scottish Parliament is not affected by any invalidity in the proceedings of Parliament leading to its enactment, which means that the making of an Act cannot be questioned in the courts on the grounds of procedural irregularities (s 28(7)). The validity of an Act can be challenged on the basis that it is outwith the competence of the Parliament[1].

1 See Chapter 8 below.

THE COURTS AND THE PARLIAMENT

4.36 Legal actions involving the Parliament and its officers may arise either from its formal business or from its day-to-day operations (e g contractual or employment disputes affecting its property or staff). The Act makes provision to ensure that the Parliament can be appropriately represented in such proceedings, and more significantly to ensure that the courts cannot be used as a means of disrupting the work of the Parliament.

4.37 On the simple technical issue of who can sue or be sued, it is the Parliamentary corporation which represents the Parliament, the Presiding Officer or any deputy, or any member of the staff of the Parliament in all legal proceedings (s 40(1)-(2)). This applies whether the action has been raised against the Parliament or its officers (e g the corporation will be the respondent if there is an attempt to seek judicial review of a decision by the Presiding Officer) or is brought by the Parliament (e g the corporation will be the pursuer if a firm supplying the Parliament with stationery or any other item fails to keep its contract).

4.38 The more important issue relates to the extent of the courts' powers to intervene in the workings of the Parliament. There was a fear that the courts could be used as a means of disrupting the Parliament, with legal challenges being used to delay measures progressing through the Parliament or otherwise interfere with its operation. Accordingly the courts are restricted in the remedies which they can order in any proceedings against the Parliament (s 40(3)–(5)). The only remedy which is available against the Parliament is a declarator, and it is not possible for the courts to make any order for suspension, interdict, reduction or specific performance. This restriction applies to interim orders as well as final ones, and cannot be circumvented by making orders against any member or officer of the Parliament if that would have the same effect as one of the prohibited remedies against the Parliament itself.

4.39 The effect of this is to ensure that although the courts can consider the legality of what is happening in the Parliament, they cannot interfere directly and cannot tell the Parliament what to do. The Parliament will have to decide how to respond to a declarator made against it, and although it will normally be expected to react by ensuring that the law is upheld, there may be situations where it decides that a minor infringement of the law should be overlooked. The validity of an Act of the Parliament is not affected by any invalidity in the proceedings of the Parliament leading to its enactment (s 28(5)).

4.40 The Parliament is therefore in an unusual position in relation to the courts. It does not have complete control over all of its own affairs in the same way as the United Kingdom Parliament does. The courts have an important role to play in enforcing the rules on several essentially internal matters, such as the giving of evidence to the Parliament[1], the registration of members' interests and paid lobbying[2]. Yet, at the same time the Parliament enjoys a number of privileges, in relation to contempt of court and defamation[3], in relation to the remedies available against it and as a result of the provision that Acts cannot be challenged on the basis of procedural flaws in their making. The courts, however, will play a major role in enforcing the limits of the legislative competence of the Parliament[4].

1 See para 4.21 above.
2 See para 3.15 above.
3 See paras 4.24–4.28 above.
4 See Chapter 8 below.

5 Legislative competence of the Scottish Parliament

5.1 The Scottish Parliament will have the power to make laws. Its laws will be every bit as much law as Acts of the United Kingdom Parliament. Not only will it be able to pass new laws in relation to devolved matters in Scotland, but it will be able to amend or repeal existing Acts of the United Kingdom Parliament in devolved areas[1]. However, unlike the United Kingdom Parliament, the legislative powers of the Scottish Parliament are not unlimited[2]. Its powers are set out and limited by the Scotland Act 1998. Under the Act it has no power to make laws which: would form part of the laws of another country or territory; relate to matters which have been reserved to the United Kingdom Parliament; are in breach of the restrictions on modifying enactments in Schedule 4; are incompatible with the European Convention on Human Rights or Community Law or would remove the Lord Advocate (s 29(1)).

1 The Scottish Parliament is also able to consider and pass private legislation, promoted by individuals or bodies such as local authorities in relation to devolved matters.

2 The United Kingdom Parliament is a sovereign body. It can make or unmake laws without restrictions. However, following the passage of the European Communities Act 1972, the United Kingdom Parliament has limited its own sovereignty by making its laws subject to those of the EC. For more information see: Bradley and Ewing *Constitutional and Administrative Law* (12th edn, 1997).

5.2 Since it is impossible to define precisely what is and what is not within the competence of the Scottish Parliament, the Act contains provisions which allow for a certain amount of overlap, set out certain rules of interpretation and permit modifications to the list of reserved matters. There are also provisions in the Act which are designed to ensure that both the Parliament and the Scottish Executive act within their respective powers, minimise potential conflicts and resolve disputes as early as possible.

LEGISLATIVE COMPETENCE

5.3 Section 29(1) provides that any Act of the Scottish Parliament is not law so far as any provision of the Act is outside the legislative competence of the Parliament. It then sets out five different instances where the Parliament cannot make laws. These are dealt with in turn below (see paras 5.4–5.22).

Laws of another country or territory (s 29(2)(a))

5.4 The Parliament cannot make laws which would form part of the law of another country or territory other than Scotland or which confer or remove functions exercisable otherwise than in Scotland. Thus, for example, the Parliament cannot legislate to regulate the teaching of mathematics in schools in Wales.

Reserved matters (s 29(2)(b))

5.5 In drafting the Scotland Act 1998, the Government chose a retaining model of devolution whereby the central authority devolves all of its powers to the local body except for certain powers which it specifically reserves to itself[1]. The list of matters which have been reserved to Westminster is set out in Schedule 5 of the Act[2]. These tend to be matters which the Government considers to be best dealt with on a United Kingdom-wide basis. For example, matters such as the Constitution and the public service which deal with integrity of the United Kingdom as a nation are reserved. Also reserved are certain services which are best provided at a United Kingdom level such as energy and transport, social security schemes, the post and broadcasting. Also reserved are the maintenance of certain standards such as product standards and those imposed for consumer protection. Furthermore, the United Kingdom as a whole has a strong voice in international policy. It is considered desirable not to dilute that voice by splitting it in two. As a result, the Act reserves defence, national security, interception of communications, official secrets, terrorism and foreign affairs. Also, the larger United Kingdom economic unit is perceived to benefit business and provide access to wider markets and investment. As a result matters such as fiscal, economic and monetary policy; the currency; financial markets; business associations;

competition; intellectual property and import and export control are reserved to Westminster[3].

1 The alternative approach, the transferring model, was the model used in the Scotland Act 1978. Under this approach, the central authority devolves to the local body certain specified areas of legislative or executive competence, while everything not specified is reserved to the centre. That Act was criticised as extremely complicated, requiring frequent updating to take account of new and amended legislation and likely to lead to many disputes over what matters were or were not within the proposed Assembly's powers.
2 Section 30(1) states that Schedule 5 shall have effect.
3 See Chapter 6 for details on reserved matters.

5.6 The list of reserved matters is the key element of a retaining model. However, in some respects it is what is not on the list that is most interesting. The role of the Scottish Parliament is to make laws in relation to devolved matters in Scotland, yet nowhere in the Scotland Act 1998 are the devolved powers listed. The White Paper *Scotland's Parliament*[1] provides a fairly extensive list of matters which may be considered to be devolved and over which the Scottish Parliament is intended to have legislative power. These tend to be matters which are local in nature and which affect individuals and regions more directly. The devolved matters include: the private law of Scotland; the criminal law of Scotland; home affairs; local government; social work; housing; education; health; agriculture; forestry; fishing; food standards; economic development; town and country planning; environment; natural and built heritage; sports and the arts; and voluntary sector. Broadly, these functions are similar to the responsibilities of the Scottish Office prior to devolution.

1 Cm 3658 (1997).

Enactments protected from modification under Schedule 4 (s 29(2)(c))

5.7 The Scottish Parliament may make laws which modify or revoke enactments of the United Kingdom Parliament in so far as they relate to devolved matters. Hence, the Scottish Parliament will be able to amend the Town and Country Planning (Scotland) Act 1997 when necessary as planning is a devolved matter. However, the Parliament cannot make laws which are in breach of the restrictions on modifying enactments set out in Schedule 4. There are three Parts to Schedule 4. Part I lists specific provisions of enactments which are protected from modification by the Scottish

Parliament. Part II lists the exceptions to Part I and Part III deals with consequential modifications to sections 53 and 54 which deal with the transfer of functions to the Scottish Ministers.

Part I – Protected provisions

5.8 Paragraph 1 provides that an Act of the Scottish Parliament cannot modify (or confer power by subordinate legislation to modify)[1] any of the following provisions:

(1) articles 4 and 6 of the Union with Scotland Act 1706 and the Union with England Act 1707 so far as they relate to freedom of trade;
(2) the Private Legislation Procedure (Scotland) Act 1936;
(3) certain provisions of the European Communities Act 1972 which contain the relevant definitions and recognise EC law as part of United Kingdom law[2];
(4) certain provisions of Schedule 32 to the Local Government, Planning and Land Act 1980 which deal with the designation of enterprise zones[3];
(5) sections 140A to 140G of the Social Security Administration Act 1992 which deal with rent rebate and rent allowance subsidy and council tax benefit; and
(6) the Human Rights Act 1998.

1 For the remainder of the discussion of Schedule 4 'modify' shall include 'confer power to modify by subordinate legislation'.
2 Specifically, section 1 and Schedule 1, section 2 other than subsection (2), the words following 'such Community obligation' in subsection (3) and the words 'subject to Schedule 2 to this Act' in subsection (4).
3 Paras 5(3)(b) and 15(4)(b).

5.9 Paragraph 2 protects the law on reserved matters against modification by Acts of the Scottish Parliament. For the purposes of this paragraph, the phrase 'the law on reserved matters' is defined to mean any enactment the subject-matter of which is a reserved matter and which is comprised in an Act of Parliament (not this Act)[1] or subordinate legislation under an Act of Parliament and any rule of law which is not contained in an enactment and the subject-matter of which is a reserved matter. It is the law 'about' reserved matters. Thus, the Scottish Parliament cannot modify the Energy Act 1976 since energy is a reserved matter.

1 Power to amend the Scotland Act 1998 itself is dealt with separately, see below at para 5.13.

5.10 Rules of Scots private law or Scots criminal law (whether or not contained in an enactment) are subject to this restriction only to the extent that the rule in question is *special to* a reserved matter (para 2(3)). Thus, the Scottish Parliament is able to legislate on the rules of Scots private and criminal law which are of general application and which distinguish Scots law as a separate system of law. However, the Parliament cannot modify those rules of Scots private or criminal law which are special to reserved matters. For example, it could not modify those provisions in the Proceeds of Crime (Scotland) Act 1995 which deal with confiscating the proceeds of drug trafficking (a reserved matter)[1].

1 592 HL Official Report (5th series) col 821, 21 July 1998.

5.11 There are also two specific reservations. These are where the subject-matter of the rule is: interest on sums due in respect of taxes or excise duties and refunds of such taxes or duties; and the obligations, in relation to occupational or personal pension schemes, of the trustees or managers (para 2(3)). This latter application of the general rule extends to cases where liabilities under orders made in matrimonial proceedings or agreements made between the parties to a marriage are to be satisfied out of the assets of the scheme (para 2(4)).

5.12 Paragraph 3 sets out an exception to the law on reserved matters. Changes to Scots private or criminal law may make incidental or consequential modifications to the law on reserved matters (whether by virtue of the Act in question or another enactment) however, the rule must not have a greater effect on reserved matters than is necessary to give effect to the purpose of the provision (para 3(1)). Thus, the Scottish Parliament may be able to legislate on devolved matters such as health and safety which incidentally may affect the energy sector (a reserved matter). However, if there is a means of completing the legislative task without making modifications which affect reserved matters or which affect reserved matters to a lesser extent then the Parliament should choose this approach. To do otherwise would risk acting outwith its competence.

5.13 Paragraph 4 protects the Scotland Act 1998 itself from modification by Acts of the Scottish Parliament (para 4(1). Certain specific provisions are excepted from this general rule (para 4(2)). Most of these provisions relate to the validity of certain acts or proceedings including those of: the Parliament, the Presiding Officer, the Auditor General and the Scottish Parliamentary Corporate Body. The rest set out certain notice requirements, offences and other legal issues[1]. The Scottish Parliament may also modify any provisions which involve making charges on or requiring payments from or to the Scottish Consolidated Fund (para 4(3)). Similarly, the Parliament may modify Part III of this Act in regard to the establishment of a new fund out of which loans may be made to the Scottish Ministers (para 4(4)). Finally, the general rule does not prevent the Scottish Parliament from modifying provisions to the Scotland Act which have ceased to have effect as a consequence of an Act of the Scottish Parliament. This consequential measure allows the Scottish Parliament to update this Act. For instance, it could possibly repeal s 39(1) which requires the setting up of a register of members' interests once the Scottish Parliament has legislated to this effect.

1 Sections 1(4), 17(5), 19(7), 21(5), 24(2), 28(5), 39(7), 40–43, 50, 69(3), 85 and 93 and paragraphs 4(1) to (3) and 6(1) of Schedule 2.

5.14 Paragraph 5 prohibits Acts of the Scottish Parliament from modifying certain enactments which have been modified by the 1998 Act. Specifically, these are:

(1) the effect of section 119(3) (charges on the Consolidated Fund) in relation to any provision of an Act of Parliament relating to judicial salaries;
(2) that part of any enactment as is amended by Sch 8 paras 2, 7, or 32 and relates to the Advocate General[1]; and
(3) that part of any enactment as is amended by Sch 8 paras 9(b) or 29[2].

1 These paragraphs add references to the Advocate General to the Crown Suits (Scotland) Act 1857, the Crown Proceedings Act 1947 and the Criminal Procedure (Scotland) Act 1995.
2 These paragraphs relate to provisions of the Lands Tribunal Act 1949 and the Scottish Land Court Act 1993.

5.15 Finally, paragraph 6 provides that an Act of the Scottish Parliament cannot modify any enactment so far as the enactment relates to powers exercisable by a Minister of the Crown by virtue of section 56 (shared powers).

Part II – Exceptions to Part I

5.16 Nothing in Schedule 4 prevents an Act of the Scottish Parliament from restating the law or repealing any spent enactment (para 7). Furthermore, an Act of the Scottish Parliament may amend any enactment by changing the titles of *inter alia* courts, tribunals, judges, court officers, non ministerial posts in the Scottish Administration, any member of staff of the Scottish Administration or any register (para 9). Any reference to a declarator in any enactment is also capable of being amended (para 9).

5.17 The Scottish Parliament may also modify any enactment for or in connection with the purposes of sections 70 (financial control, accounts and audit) or 91 (maladministration) (para 10).

5.18 Finally, provision is made in paragraph 11 of Schedule 4 to give the Parliament flexibility in the making of subordinate legislation. Specifically, this paragraph permits the Scottish Parliament to modify an enactment for or in connection with any of the following purposes:

(1) making different provision in respect of the document[1] by which a power to make subordinate legislation is to be exercised[2];
(2) making different provision (or no provision) for the procedure, in relation to the Parliament, to which legislation made in the exercise of such a power (or the instrument or other document in which it is contained) is to be subject;
(3) applying any enactment comprised in or made under an Act of the Scottish Parliament relating to the document by which such powers may be exercised.

1 'Document' is defined in s 126 (1) of the Act to mean anything in which information is recorded in any form (and references to producing a document are to be read accordingly).

2 The power to make subordinate legislation or a power to confirm or approve the legislation must be exercisable by either: a member of the Scottish Executive, any Scottish public authority with mixed functions or no reserved functions or any other person (not being a Minister of the Crown) within devolved competence (para 11(3)).

Part III – Consequential modification of sections 53 and 54

5.19 Paragraph 12(2) provides that if, because of anything in Part I of Schedule 4, a provision of an Act of the Scottish Parliament modifying an enactment so as to provide for the function to be exercisable by a different person would be outside the legislative competence of the Parliament the function is not so transferred[1]. This provision is designed to prevent the modification of powers which the United Kingdom Ministers share with the Scottish Ministers by virtue of section 53. It ensures that ministerial functions such as the funding of council tax benefit and housing benefit will remain with the United Kingdom Government rather than being caught by the general devolution of the funding of local authorities and Scottish Homes[2].

1 For the purposes of determining whether any function under any of the provisions referred to in para 12(1) is transferred to the Scottish Ministers by virtue of section 53 and the extent to which any such function (other than a function of making, confirming or approving subordinate legislation) is exercisable by them, the references in section 54 to the legislative competence of the Parliament are to be read as if section 29(2)(c) which deals with provisions which are in breach of the restrictions of this Schedule, were omitted (para 13(2)).
2 594 HL Official Report col 127, 2 November 1998.

5.20 Finally, if any pre-commencement enactment or prerogative instrument is modified by subordinate legislation under section 105[1], a function under that enactment or instrument is not transferred by virtue of section 53 if the subordinate legislation provides that it is not to be transferred.

1 See para 7.57 below.

Incompatibility with any Convention rights or Community law (s 29(2)(d))

5.21 The Scottish Parliament cannot make laws which are incompatible with Convention rights or with Community Law[1]. 'Convention rights' are defined in the Act with a reference to section 1 of the Human Rights Act 1998 and are most of the rights set out in the European Convention on Human Rights[2]. The United Kingdom, as a member of the European Community, has agreed to be subject to Community law[3] and as a result it is important that the Scottish Parliament be obliged to implement, enforce and follow Community law.

1 'Community law' is defined in s 126(9) to include all those rights, powers, liabilities, obligations and restrictions from time to time created or arising by or under Community Treaties and all those remedies and procedures from time to time provided for by or under the Community Treaties.
2 These include *inter alia* the right to life, freedom from torture or degrading treatment, freedom from slavery, the right to liberty and security of the person, the right to a fair trial, the prohibition of retroactive criminal laws, the right to respect for a person's private and family life, freedom of thought, conscience and religion, freedom of peaceful assembly and association and the right to marry and found a family. Note: Article 13 is excluded.
3 See European Communities Act 1972 s 2(1) and (4) and *Factortame v Secretary of State for Transport (No. 2)* [1991] 1 AC 603.

Removal of the Lord Advocate (s 29(2)(e))

5.22 The Parliament cannot make laws which would remove the Lord Advocate from his position as head of the systems of criminal prosecution and investigation of deaths in Scotland. This is one of a number of provisions in the Act which safeguard the independence of the Lord Advocate and the Solicitor General in exercising their prosecution and related functions[1].

1 See paras 7.6–7.8 below.

BOUNDARY ISSUES

5.23 There is a great deal of overlap between the devolved and reserved competences. Aspects of many of the devolved matters are actually reserved to Westminster under Schedule 5. For example, while the protection of animals broadly[1] is devolved to the Scottish Parliament, the protection of animals used for scientific purposes is reserved under B7 of Schedule 5 to Westminster. The Act recognises that the boundary between heads of reserved matters and the boundary between reserved and devolved competences is not clear cut and attempts to deal with difficult circumstances.

1 Including protection against cruelty to domestic, captive and wild animals, zoo licensing, controlling dangerous wild animals and game.

Interpretation provisions

5.24 In addition to the provisions relating to the law on reserved matters set out in Schedule 4 and discussed above[1], section 29(3) provides that the question of whether a provision of an Act of the Scottish Parliament relates to a reserved matter is to be determined, by reference to the purpose of the provision, having regard (among other things) to its effect in all circumstances[2]. This subsection is subject to section 29(4) which provides that a provision which:

1 would otherwise not relate to reserved matters; but
2 makes modifications of Scots private law, or Scots criminal law, as it applies to reserved matters,

is to be treated as relating to reserved matters unless the purpose of the provision is to make the law in question apply consistently to reserved matters and otherwise[3]. A change to the law relating to criminal responsibility which would affect both reserved (i e drug trafficking) and devolved matters would fall under this section.

1 See para 5.12 above.
2 Courts are to consider whether the 'pith and substance' of the statute as a whole falls within the express powers of the particular legislature (*Gallagher v Lynn* [1937] AC 863). Section 29(3) is to protect Acts of the Scottish Parliament from a literal approach to interpretation. 592 HL Official Report (5th series) col 819, 21 July 1998.
3 See also paras 5.9–5.12 above.

5.25 In order to reduce the scope for practical problems arising from a declaration that an apparently valid Bill or Act of the Scottish Parliament is outside its competence, section 101(2) provides that such provisions are to read as narrowly as is required for them to be within competence, if such a reading is possible and is to have effect accordingly. This is known as the principle of efficacy and is considered to be the normal rule of construction which courts apply in construing legislation from parliaments with limited powers. Under this principle, the courts would seek to give effect to legislation rather than to invalidate it[1].

1 Section 101 also applies to the competence of subordinate legislation, see para 8.4 below.

The power to modify Schedules 4 and 5

5.26 The boundary of reserved matters is not static and Her Majesty may by Order in Council make any modifications to Schedules 4 or 5 which are considered necessary or expedient (s 30(2)). Orders in Council may also be used to specify functions which are to be treated as being or not being functions which are exercisable in or as regards Scotland (s 30(3)). This provision may be useful in clarifying ongoing issues as to when a function is being exercised in Scotland and when it is being exercised on a United Kingdom-wide basis. Furthermore, an Order in Council made under this section may also modify any enactment or prerogative instrument (including any enactment comprised in or made under this Act) or any other instrument or document as Her Majesty considers necessary or expedient in connection with other provision made by the Order. Note that the use of this power requires the agreement of both Parliaments[1].

1 Schedule 7 of the Act provides that for Orders in Council made under s 30, a draft instrument must have been laid before, and approved by resolution of, each House of Parliament and must have been laid before and approved by resolution of, the [Scottish] Parliament.

Sovereignty of the United Kingdom Parliament

5.27 Section 28(7) provides that nothing in the Scotland Act affects the United Kingdom Parliament's power to make laws for Scotland. Indeed there may be instances where it would be more convenient for legislation on a devolved matter to be passed by the United Kingdom Parliament. It is likely that a convention will be established that Westminster will not normally legislate on devolved matters in Scotland without the consent of the Scottish Parliament[1]. Where problems do arise it is for the Scottish Executive and Whitehall to resolve the matter through negotiation rather than to participate in some form of legislative ping pong. If the situation appears to be at an impasse, the solution would be for the United Kingdom Parliament to enact primary legislation adjusting the boundary between reserved and devolved matters[2].

1 As happened in Northern Ireland earlier this century, 592 HL Official Report (5th series) col 791, 21 July 1998.
2 592 HL Official Report (5th series) col 791, 21 July 1998.

5.28 The Union with Scotland Act 1706 and the Union with England Act 1707 have effect subject to the Scotland Act 1998 (s 37).

PRE-LEGISLATIVE SCRUTINY

5.29 In any system of government where powers are shared, the possibility of one level of government encroaching into the others' territory must be foreseen as a likely occurrence. While every attempt has been made to ensure the boundaries are clearly set out in the Scotland Act, it is also necessary to include provisions which are designed to minimise potential conflicts and resolve disputes as early as possible. It is essential that extensive checks are carried out in regard to the competence of a Bill before it starts its passage through the Scottish Parliament to eliminate, as far as possible, later challenges to its competency. The Act introduces five opportunities for Bills to be scrutinised to ensure they are within the legislative competence of Parliament.

Statement by a member of the Scottish Executive

5.30 The member of the Scottish Executive in charge of a Bill must, on or before the introduction of the Bill in Parliament, state that in his view the provisions of the Bill are within the legislative competence of the Parliament (s 31(1))[1].

1 The form of any statement is to be set out by standing orders (s 31(3)).

Statement by the Presiding Officer

5.31 The Presiding Officer is to decide, on or before the introduction of a Bill in the Parliament, whether or not in his view the provisions of the Bill would be within the legislative competence of the Parliament and state his decision (s 31(2))[1]. It is likely that a decision by the Presiding Officer that the provisions of a Bill were outside the competence of the Parliament would trigger some of the other scrutiny procedures set out below.

1 The form of any statement is to be set out by standing orders (s 31(3)).

Reference by Law Officers to the Judicial Committee

5.32 The Advocate General, the Lord Advocate or the Attorney General may refer the question of whether a Bill or any provision of a Bill would be within the legislative competence of the Parliament to the Judicial Committee of the Privy Council[1] for decision (s 33(1))[2]. This can occur at any time during the four weeks from the passing of the Bill or any subsequent approval of the Bill (s 33(2)). No such reference is to be made once the officer in question has notified the Presiding Officer that he does not intend to make a reference in relation to the Bill unless the Bill has been subsequently approved following reconsideration by Parliament by virtue of section 36(5) (s 33(3)). A reference under this section (hereafter a 'section 33 reference'), requires the Judicial Committee to decide the competence issue on hypothetical facts, not yet the subject of litigation. Judgements relating to hypotheses are generally considered to be *obiter* in United Kingdom courts and therefore not of binding authority. Section 103(1) provides that any decision of the Judicial Committee in proceedings under the Scotland Act is to be binding in all legal proceedings other than proceedings before the Judicial Committee itself. Thus, a Bill which is ruled to be within the competence of the Scottish Parliament is protected from any post-assent devolution challenges in a lower court based on actual facts.

1 See para 8.14 below.
2 Although a member of the Scottish Executive, the Lord Advocate is expected to form an independent view. If the Lord Advocate's views as to the competence of a Bill were not shared by his or her colleagues, he or she could, in theory, institute proceedings although resignation is more likely.

Reference by the Judicial Committee to the European Court of Justice

5.33 Where a reference has been made by one of the Law Officers under section 33 and the Judicial Committee has in turn, referred the reference to the ECJ[1] for a preliminary ruling and neither of these references has been decided or otherwise disposed of, the Parliament may resolve that it wishes to reconsider the Bill (s 34(1)(2)). In such a case, the Presiding Officer must notify the Law Officers of this fact and the person who made the section 33 reference must request the withdrawal of the reference. This section is designed to ensure Bills are not unnecessarily held up by references to the ECJ and gives the Parliament an opportunity to reconsider the Bill in terms of its competence.

1 Such references are made where the decision of the European Court of Justice is required on an issue of EC law; Article 177 (or new Art 234) of the Treaty establishing the European Community, Article 41 of the Treaty establishing the European Coal and Steel Community or Article 150 of the Treaty establishing the European Atomic Energy Community.

Intervention by the Secretary of State

5.34 The Secretary of State for Scotland may intervene to prevent the passage of a Bill in the Parliament by making an order prohibiting the Presiding Officer from submitting the Bill for Royal Assent (s 35). There are two grounds for such an order. First, an order may be made if the Bill contains provisions which the Secretary of State has reasonable grounds to believe would be incompatible with any international obligations or the interests of defence or national security. An order may also be made if the Bill contains provisions which make modifications to the law as it applies to reserved matters (see s 29(3) (4) and Sch 4 para 2) and which the Secretary of State has reasonable grounds to believe would have an adverse effect on the operation of law as it applies to reserved matters. The order must identify the Bill and the provisions in question and state the reasons for making the order. There is no need for the Secretary of State to seek an order from the Judicial Committee.

5.35 An order under section 35 can be made at any time during the four weeks from the passing of the Bill or any subsequent approval of the Bill. If a section 33 reference has been made in relation to the Bill the period of four weeks begins with the reference being decided or otherwise disposed of by the Judicial Committee (s 35(3)). The Secretary of State is barred from making such a order once he has notified the Presiding Officer that he does not intend to do so, unless the Bill has been subject to a subsequent reconsideration under section 36(5) (s 35 (4)). An order in force under this section at a time when approval is given after such reconsideration shall cease to have effect (s 35(5)). In this situation, if the Secretary of State believes that the problem still exists then he must make a new order within the requisite time limits.

THE EFFECT OF THE SCRUTINY PROVISIONS

5.36 The Presiding Officer must not submit a Bill for Royal Assent at any time:

1 when the Advocate General, the Lord Advocate or the Attorney General is entitled to refer the Bill to the Judicial Committee for a determination of the Bill's competence under section 33; or
2 when such a reference has been made but has not yet been decided or otherwise disposed of by the Judicial Committee or where an order may be made by the Secretary of State under his power to intervene in section 35 (s 32(2)).

5.37 The Presiding Officer is also prohibited from submitting a Bill for Royal Assent in its unamended form if the Judicial Committee have decided that the Bill or any provision of it would not be within the legislative competence of the Parliament, or if a section 33 reference has been withdrawn following a request from the Parliament for withdrawal of the reference under s 34(2)(b).

6 Reserved matters

6.1 Chapter 5 provided a brief introduction to the matters which the Scotland Act 1998 reserves to the United Kingdom Parliament. This chapter looks at Schedule 5 which sets out the reserved matters in much more detail.

INTRODUCTION TO SCHEDULE 5

6.2 Schedule 5 is in three parts. Part I defines general overarching reservations. Part II sets out specific subject-related reservations by Sections grouped under Heads. Part III and the preliminary Section of Part II contain explanatory and interpretative provisions. The titles of the Heads and Sections in Part II are merely to assist the reader and do not form part of the definitions of reserved matters. The Schedule must be read as a whole. The effect is that even though a matter is excepted from a reservation in one Section, it could be reserved at least in part by others. For example, Section D5 reserves the subject-matter of the Energy Act 1976 other than section 9 . This Act enables the Secretary of State to make orders regulating or prohibiting the use of various fuels or electricity for the purposes of energy conservation. Section 9 of the Act deals with the use and liquidation of offshore natural gas and is covered by a separate reservation under Oil and Gas at Section D2.

6.3 Much of Schedule 5 defines reserved matters by reference to the subject-matter of particular enactments. Unless express provision is made to the contrary, these are to be read as references to that enactment as it has effect on the principal appointed day (the day devolution becomes fully effective, namely 1 July 1999) or, where it ceased to have effect before that day, as it had effect immediately prior to when it ceased to have effect (Sch 3 Part III para 5). Such references only include amendments made on or before the principal appointed day and do not include references to that enactment as extended or applied by other enactments.

EXECUTIVE DEVOLUTION

6.4 It is important to recognise that the list of reserved matters refer to legislative competence. In some instances, however, certain executive powers relating to reserved matters will be devolved to the Scottish Executive. For example, while the power to make laws in regard to road transport is reserved to Westminster, it is proposed that certain Ministerial functions such as the authorisation of traffic signs, the setting of some speed limits, the regulation of competitions on roads using motor vehicles or cycles, the rehabilitation of drunk drivers and the granting of permits for the use of minibuses be executively devolved to the Scottish Ministers by way of an Order under section 63[1].

1 Road Traffic Regulation Act 1984 s 17, Parts V and VI; Road Traffic Act 1988; Road Traffic Offenders Act ss 34A–34C; Transport Act 1985.

6.5 Section 63 permits the United Kingdom Parliament to transfer certain executive functions exercisable by a Minister of the Crown in regard to Scotland to the Scottish Ministers by an Order in Council[2]. The Order may provide for the function to be exercised wholly by the Scottish Ministers, to be exercised concurrently by the Scottish Ministers and a Minister of the Crown or to be exercised by the Minister of the Crown only with the agreement of, or after consultation with the Scottish Ministers. Schedule 5 specifies only what is reserved with respect to legislative competence. However, some proposals have been made in relation to what additional executive powers may or may not be devolved to the Scottish Executive in continually updated draft Orders in Council published by the Scottish Office[3]. Any executive devolution which is expected in a reserved area is highlighted in the discussion of Schedule 5 below.

1 See also para 7.22 below.
2 Scottish Office Draft Order in Council June 1998.

6.6 In order to preserve certain powers in the hands of the United Kingdom government following devolution, certain functions which are currently exercised by the Lord Advocate will be transferred by order to the Secretary of State. This is because the Lord Advocate following devolution will cease to be a member of the United Kingdom government and become instead part of the

Scottish Executive. Any functions which are to be executively devolved to the Scottish Ministers will then in turn be transferred by an order under section 63[1].

1 See for example, para 6.16 below.

6.7 Finally, the fact that the legislative authority to deal with a certain matter is reserved to Westminster, does not prevent the Scottish Parliament from discussing and debating the matter. Indeed, it is very likely that certain reserved matters such as oil and gas and broadcasting will continue to be of great interest to the Parliament. However, the Parliament's powers to summon witnesses to appear before it or to produce documents can be exercised only in relation to matters within its legislative competence[1]. In relation to reserved matters, therefore, witnesses can be invited, but not compelled, to give evidence to the Parliament.

1 See paras 4.15–4.21 above.

PART I – GENERAL RESERVATIONS

The Constitution

Scope

6.8 The general reservation states that the following aspects of the constitution are reserved: the Crown including succession to the Crown and a regency, the Union of the Kingdoms of England and Scotland, the Parliament of the United Kingdom, and the continued existence of the High Court of Justiciary and the Court of Session (para 1). Thus, matters relating to, for instance, the powers, membership and privileges of the United Kingdom Parliament are all reserved.

The Act sets out some specific matters which are covered by the general reservation and which are not affected by the exceptions listed below. These are:

1 the functions of the Lord Lyon King of Arms with regard to the granting of arms (but not those functions in his judicial capacity);
2 honours and dignities (para 2(2));

3 hereditary revenues of the Crown (para 3(3));
4 the royal arms and standard (para 3(3));
5 the management of the Crown Estate (para 2(3));
6 the subject-matter of the Crown Private Estates Acts 1800 to 1873 which regulate matters relating to the private estates such as how they may be held or disposed (para 4(2));
7 the compulsory acquisition of property held or used by a Minster of the Crown or government department (para 3(3));
8 the functions of the Security Service, the Secret Intelligence Service and the Government Communications Headquarters (para 2(4)).

Exceptions

The general reservation does not cover Her Majesty's prerogative, the functions exercised by persons acting on behalf of the Crown and any office of the Scottish Administration. These exceptions ensure that the Scottish Parliament is able to legislate about those functions which do not relate to other reserved matters and will enable the transfer of functions from a Minister of the Crown to the Scottish Ministers under section 53 where appropriate (para 2(1)).

Crown property is not a reserved matter (para 3(1)). Crown property is defined as property belonging to her Majesty in right of the Crown or belonging to any person acting on behalf of the Crown. This includes property which the Crown can sell and alienate such as the foreshore and rights and obligations over such property which are vested in the Crown as trustee for certain public rights which cannot be alienated such as the right of public navigation in waters over the seabed. This property forms part of the Crown Estate and is managed by the Crown Estate Commissioners. Also included is property held in trust for Her Majesty for the purposes of any person acting on behalf of the Crown such as a Government Department. These provisions ensure, for example, that the Scottish Parliament can apply its planning legislation to Crown property and pass legislation for a new harbour to extinguish any public rights over the foreshore which might be affected. Furthermore, even though the public service is a reserved matter under paragraph 8, the Scottish Parliament is able to legislate to acquire land for the public service. It also ensures that Ministerial powers to acquire land can be transferred to the Scottish Ministers under section 53.

Property the Queen holds in her private capacity such as Balmoral is not reserved (para 4). The Scottish Parliament will be able to legislate to affect the Queen's private estates in Scotland however, any such provision in a Scottish Bill will require the Queen's consent under standing orders (Sch 3 para 7).

Paragraph 1 does not reserve the use of the Scottish Seal (para 5) nor does it reserve the position of the Crown as the ultimate superior of all land in Scotland. This means that the Scottish Parliament would be able to abolish the feudal system of land tenure, should it ever so desire (para 3(2)).

Executive devolution

Nothing specific proposed.

Political parties

Scope

6.9 The registration and funding of political parties is reserved (para 6).

Exception

None.

Executive devolution

Nothing specific proposed.

Foreign Affairs, etc

Scope

6.10 This reservation covers international relations including relations with territories outside the United Kingdom, with the European Union and its institutions and with other international organisations, the regulation of international trade and international development assistance and co-operation (para 7). Thus, the conduct of international relations, including relations with the EU is a matter reserved to the United Kingdom Government. However, this reservation is not intended to preclude Scottish Ministers and officials from communicating with other countries, regions or international institutions so long as the representatives of the Scottish Parliament or Scottish Ministers do not purport to speak for the United Kingdom or reach agreements which commit the United Kingdom.

Exceptions

There are two exceptions to this reservation. First the Scottish Parliament is expected to observe and implement international obligations including those under the European Convention on Human Rights and under European Community law. Thus, the Scottish Parliament is able and required to legislate for the purpose of observing and implementing those obligations so far as they relate to devolved matters. Furthermore, any obligations on Ministers of the Crown to observe and implement international obligations in relation to devolved matters will be passed to the Scottish Ministers under section 53. Section 57(2) makes it beyond the competence of a Scottish Minister to make subordinate legislation or to do any act which is incompatible with any of the Convention rights or with EC law. Under section 58 the Secretary of State has the power to intervene where he has reasonable grounds to believe that any action, proposed action or failure to act by a member of the Scottish Executive would be incompatible with any international obligations[1].

The second exception permits the Scottish Ministers and officials to assist the United Kingdom Government in the conduct of international relations so far as they relate to devolved matters. Scottish Ministers are to be included in the discussion within the United Kingdom Government about the formulation of the United Kingdom's position on all issues which touch on devolved matters (e g fishing). This provision also permits participation where appropriate by Scottish Ministers and officials in the relevant European Council meetings and other negotiations at EU and international level.

Executive devolution

Nothing specific proposed.

1 See paras 5.34–5.35 above and paras 8.23–8.26 below.

Public Service

Scope

6.11 The Civil Service including the Home Civil Service and the Diplomatic Service is a reserved matter (para 8). Most of the staff of the Scottish Office, the Scottish Courts Administration and their executive agencies, the Crown Office, the Lord Advocate's Department and the Procurator Fiscal Service will be transferred to the Scottish Administration. Section 51 provides for the staff of the Scottish Ministers and the Lord Advocate to be members of the Home Civil Service as will be the statutory office holders who head the Scottish Record Office, the General Register Office and the Department of the Registers of Scotland and their staff. The Scottish Parliament will not be able to legislate about matters relating to Civil Servants in Scotland including their recruitment, selection, grading and conditions of service. The Home Civil Service is ultimately regulated by the royal prerogative and its management has been delegated to the Minister for the Civil Service[1] who has further delegated certain management functions such as the authority to prescribe qualifications for appointment and the determination of the number and grading of posts to Ministers and office holders in charge of Departments.

Exceptions

There are certain specialities of appointment and terms of conditions of service of certain court staff which distinguish them from other civil servants and which are peculiarly Scottish. As such, Part I of the Sheriff Courts and Legal Officers (Scotland) Act 1927 which deals with the appointment of sheriff clerks and procurators fiscal and Part III of the Administration of Justice (Scotland) Act 1933 which deals with the appointment and terms and conditions of service of officers are not reserved.

Executive devolution

It is proposed that those functions currently delegated to the Secretary of State for Scotland in respect of staff who become staff of the Scottish Executive should be delegated to the Scottish Ministers as set out in section 51(4).

1 Civil Services (Management Functions) Act 1992.

Defence

Scope

6.12 All matters relating to defence and the armed forces are reserved (para 9). Defence includes matters relating to the armed forces (including for example, their equipment, resources and deployment), defence policy, strategy, planning and intelligence and plans for the maintenance of essential supplies and services in case of war. Specifically reserved are visiting forces, international headquarters and defence organisations and powers relating to trading with the enemy.

Exceptions

The Scottish Parliament may pass legislation about civil defence. It may also confer powers on the armed forces, notably the Navy or the Air Force, in relation to sea fishing, in particular to enforce offences created under Scottish sea fisheries legislation.

Executive devolution

It is proposed that the power of appointment to the appeals tribunal established under the Reserve Forces Act 1996 currently exercisable by the Lord Advocate will be executively devolved to the Scottish Ministers.

Treason

Scope

6.13 Treason including the crime of treason (under the Treason Act 1351), constructive treason, treason felony, misprision of treason and the issue of who can commit those crimes, is reserved to the United Kingdom Parliament (para 10).

Exceptions

None.

Executive devolution

Nothing specific proposed.

PART II SPECIFIC RESERVATIONS

Head A Financial and economic matters

A1 Fiscal, economic and monetary policy

Scope

6.14 This reservation covers all matters relating to the issue and circulation of money, taxes and excise duties (and the bodies which administer them), government borrowing and lending (including the issue of Government Securities), the exchange rate, the Bank of England and control over United Kingdom public expenditure. The Scottish Parliament does however, have the power to allocate resources, whether as part of its assigned budget or raised through its tax-varying powers.

Furthermore, under Schedule 4, the legislative authority concerning any interest due on any taxes or excise duties is reserved[1].

Exception

Local taxes to fund local authority expenditure such as the council tax and non-domestic rates are not reserved.

Executive devolution

It is proposed that certain functions relating to the appointment and procedures of the Special and General Commissioners of Income Tax and the President of the Value Added Tax Tribunals be executively devolved to the Scottish Ministers[2].

1 See para 5.11 above.
2 Taxes Management Act 1970 ss 2–3.

A2 The currency

Scope

6.15 Coinage, legal tender and bank notes are reserved. This includes the denominations of money in the currency and the coins or notes which will constitute legal tender and what coins and bank notes may be issued. Thus, any decision regarding whether or not to join the European currency will be made at Westminster.

Exception

None.

Executive devolution

Nothing specific proposed.

A3 Financial services

Scope

6.16 All matters relating to financial services are reserved. The reservation includes investment business (as defined in the Financial Services Act 1986), banking and deposit-taking (as in the Banking Act 1987), collective investment schemes (such as unit trusts) and insurance. Other financial services are also included such as those provided by building societies and friendly societies.

Exception

The subject-matter of section 1 of the Banking and Financial Dealings Act 1971 (the fixing of bank holidays) is the one exception to this reservation.

Executive devolution

In line with the devolution of responsibility for the judicial system in Scotland, it is proposed that a number of functions currently exercised by the Lord Advocate or the Treasury in relation to tribunals concerned with these matters will be executively devolved to the Scottish Ministers or exercised after consultation with them[1].

1 See Banking Act 1987, Building Societies Act 1986, Financial Services Act 1986 and the Friendly Societies Act 1992 in regard to the appointment of the Chairman and other members of the respective Appeal Tribunals.

A4 Financial markets

Scope

6.17 In order to ensure a common market across the United Kingdom in securities and other instruments for investors and traders, financial markets, such as money markets and investment exchanges, are reserved. Expressly reserved are the listing and public offers of securities and investments, the transfer of securities (both certified and uncertified), and insider dealing and its consequences.

Exception

None.

Executive devolution

Nothing specific proposed.

A5 Money laundering

Scope

6.18 The subject-matter of the Money Laundering Regulations 1993[1] is reserved. These provide a scheme of rules to regulate certain financial businesses so as to prevent money laundering. However, this reservation is not limited to financial businesses and extends to include the regulation of the same matters in other contexts.

Exception

None listed, although the Scottish Parliament will be able to legislate on the general criminal law relating to money laundering except where it pertains to the proceeds of drug trafficking as this is reserved under B1 below.

Executive devolution

None.

1 SI 1993/1933.

Head B Home affairs

B1 Misuse of drugs

Scope

6.19 The criminal law in respect of the misuse of drugs and the proceeds of drug trafficking is reserved. Specifically, this reservation covers the subject-matter of the following enactments:

1 the Misuse of Drugs Act 1971 which provides for criminal offences in respect of the cultivation, possession, production, supply, import and export of 'controlled drugs' (as defined in the Act), authorises certain activities in relation to such drugs, confers special powers on the police and establishes the Advisory Council on the Misuse of Drugs;
2 sections 12 to 14 of the Criminal Justice (International Co-operation) Act 1990 which make it an offence to manufacture or supply certain substances knowing or suspecting that the substance is to be used in or for the unlawful production of a controlled drug and make it an offence to conceal, disguise, transfer, convert or remove from the jurisdiction the proceeds of drug trafficking for the purpose of avoiding (or assisting someone to avoid) prosecution for a drug trafficking offence or the making or enforcement of an enforcement order;
3 Part V of the Criminal Law (Consolidation) (Scotland) Act 1995, which confers powers of search and investigation and creates offences in respect of drug trafficking, and the Proceeds of Crime (Scotland) Act 1995 as it relates to drug trafficking. The latter Act makes general provision for the forfeiture of

things used in the commission of crime and special provision for the confiscation of the proceeds of crime.

Exception

None listed, however the Scottish Parliament will have competence in relation to other matters relevant to the misuse of drugs under its powers relating to education, health, social work, police and the criminal prosecution system.

Executive devolution

It is proposed that the appointment of members to, making procedural rules for and referring cases to the Misuse of Drugs Tribunal will be executively devolved to the Scottish Ministers with a requirement for the consent of the Home Secretary in the case of procedural rules[1].

1 Under the Misuse of Drugs Act 1971 these functions are currently exercised in Scotland by the Secretary of State for Scotland.

B2 Data protection

Scope

6.20 The protection of personal data is reserved. Specifically, legislative competence is reserved in relation to the subject-matter of the Data Protection Act 1998 and Council and European Parliament Directive (EC) 95/46[1] which deal with the obtaining, holding, processing and disclosure of personal data and the free movement of such data.

Exception

None

Executive devolution

It is proposed that the Lord Chancellor will consult the Scottish Ministers before appointing the Chairman and Deputy Chairman of the Data Protection Tribunal.

1 OJ L281 23.11.95 p31.

B3 Elections

Scope

6.21 All matters concerning elections to the House of Commons, the Scottish Parliament and the European Parliament are reserved including the subject-matter of the European Parliamentary Elections Act 1978, the Representation of the People Acts 1983 and 1985, and the Parliamentary Constituencies Act 1986.

The franchise at local government elections is also specifically reserved.

Specific provisions relating to elections to the Scottish Parliament, as they are governed by the Act itself, are also outwith the legislative competence of the Scottish Parliament[1].

Exception

None listed, although the Scottish Parliament is able to legislate on *inter alia* the frequency of elections, terms of office, ward boundaries, direct elections to specific offices and procedures for local elections.

Executive devolution

It is expected that certain functions for Westminster and European Parliamentary elections which are currently carried out by the Secretary of State will be transferred to the Scottish Ministers[2].

1 See Chapter 2 and para 5.13 above.
2 See the Representation of the People Act 1983, ss 18(5), 25(1), 29(4)–(7), 47(1), 52(1); the Representation of the People (Scotland) Regulations 1986 (SI 1986/1111) Regs 51(2), 55(2); and the European Parliamentary Elections Act 1978 Schedule 1 paras 4(2)(b), 6(4).

B4 Firearms

Scope

6.22 The subject-matter of the Firearms Acts 1968 to 1997 is reserved. These Acts *inter alia* make it a criminal offence in certain circumstances and without authority to possess, handle, purchase, sell, distribute or transfer certain firearms and imitation firearms and provide for the regulation of firearm dealers and provide for the licensing of pistol clubs.

Exception

None.

Executive devolution

It is expected that three executive functions currently exercised by the Secretary of State will be devolved to the Scottish Ministers. These functions are the power under section 5 of the 1968 Act to allow people to possess prohibited weapons and ammunition, the powers in relation to Museum Firearms Licences[1] and the power to approve and give guidance to rifle clubs[2].

1 Firearms (Amendment) Act 1988.
2 Section 15 of the 1988 Act, as amended by the Firearms Act 1997.

B5 Entertainment

Scope

6.23 This Section reserves the subject-matter of the following enactments:

1 the Video Recordings Act 1984 which regulates the distribution and classification of video recordings;
2 sections 1 to 3 and 5 to 16 of the Cinemas Act 1985 which deal with the licensing of premises for film exhibition.

In addition, the legislative competence for the classification of films for public exhibition is reserved. This last function is carried out at present by the British Board of Film Classification.

Exception

None listed, however, under section 4 of the Cinemas Act 1985 the Scottish Parliament will have the power to make regulations in respect of safety at film exhibitions and in respect of the health and welfare of children in relation to attendance at film exhibitions.

Executive devolution

It is anticipated that the power to give and revoke certificates to certain kinds of organisations under section 6(6) and (7) of the 1985 Act will be devolved to the Scottish Ministers by an order under section 63.

B6 Immigration and nationality

Scope

6.24 Immigration and nationality are reserved matters. A range of matters is covered by this reservation including: entry to the United Kingdom; the granting of political or other forms of asylum; the status and capacity in the United Kingdom of non-British citizens; the grant of work permits; the free movement of persons within the European Economic Area; and the issue of passports and other travel documents[1].

Exception

None

Executive devolution

It is expected that the statutory function of appointing medical inspectors under the Immigration Act 1971 will be transferred to a Scottish Minister by an order under section 63.

1 Immigration control is now largely a matter of statute, the principal controlling statute being the Immigration Act 1971 as amended. Passports are issued under the royal prerogative.

B7 Scientific procedures on live animals

Scope

6.25 This reservation covers the use of live animals for experimental or other scientific purposes. Specifically, it reserves the subject-matter of the Animals (Scientific Procedures) Act 1986 which makes it an offence for a person to carry out a procedure on an animal which may cause the animal pain, suffering, distress or lasting harm unless the procedure is carried out by a licensed person and is carried out as part of a programme of work that is subject to a project licence.

Exception

None listed, however, general matters relating to animal health and welfare are not reserved.

Executive devolution

Nothing specific proposed.

B8 National security, interception of communications, official secrets and terrorism

Scope

6.26 This Section reserves national security (including safeguarding the well-being of the United Kingdom) and the interception of communications subject to the exceptions listed below. It also reserves the subject-matter of the Official Secrets Acts 1911 and 1920 which deal with spying and the protection of prohibited places and of the Official Secrets Act 1989 which makes provision for the lawful and unlawful disclosure of official information. The Section also reserves special powers and provisions for dealing with terrorism.

Exception

An exception applies to information, documents or other articles protected against disclosure by section 4(2) of the Official Secrets Act 1989. This section prevents the disclosure of information which may result in the commission of a crime, impedes the prevention or detection of crime or impedes the prosecution of suspected offenders.

The subject-matter of Part III of the Police Act 1997 is not reserved. Part III empowers senior police officers to authorise entry to and interference with property mainly for the purposes of surveillance. Also excepted is surveillance not involving interference with property. These exceptions are in line with the general devolution of the criminal law.

Executive devolution

It is expected that the power to issue warrants for the interception of communications for the purposes of detecting or preventing serious crime in Scotland will be devolved to the Scottish Ministers. Further executive devolution is proposed under section 63 to transfer certain Ministerial functions under the Official Secrets Act and other Acts[1] to the Scottish Ministers.

The tribunal established by the Interception of Communications Act 1985 will be a cross-border body as described in sections 83–85[2].

1 Sections 7, 8 and 12 of the Official Secrets Act 1989; s 32A of the Police (Scotland) Act 1967 and s 117(1)(a) of the Local Government etc (Scotland) Act 1994.
2 See paras 7.49–7.51 below.

B9 Betting, gaming and lotteries

Scope

6.27 Betting, gaming and lotteries (including the National Lottery) are reserved matters. This includes the granting of betting office licences, betting at horse racecourses and dog racecourses, the constitution of the Horserace Totalisator Board (the Tote), the regulation of pool betting, games of chance, the taxation of the proceeds from such activities, the running of the National Lottery and the distribution of its proceeds to good causes[1].

Exception

None.

Executive devolution

It is intended that a number of functions relating to betting, gaming and lotteries will be devolved to the Scottish Ministers. Much of this is in line with the general devolution of judicial procedures. For example, it is proposed that the power to appoint members to the Horserace Betting Levy Appeal Tribunal for Scotland under section 29 of the Betting, Gaming and Lotteries Act 1963 will be passed from the Secretary of State to the Scottish Ministers by an order under section 63.

It is also anticipated that the powers relating to how National Lottery money is distributed in Scotland, its management, restrictions on distribution etc[2] will be transferred to Scottish Ministers.

1 See for example the Betting, Gaming and Lotteries Act 1963, the Gaming Act 1986, the Lotteries and Amusements Act 1976 and the National Lottery etc Act 1993.
2 See the National Lottery etc Act 1993, ss 26, 27, 29, 35.

B10 Emergency powers

Scope

6.28 All matters relating to emergency powers are reserved including the circumstances in which such powers can be exercised, what the powers should be and any ancillary provision such as compensation for loss arising from their exercise. More specifically, the reservation includes the main statutory provisions set out in the Emergency Powers Act 1920 which gives Her Majesty the power to declare a state of emergency and to make regulations by Order in Council for securing the essentials of life to the community.

Exception

No exception is stated, however, the civil authorities are entitled to plan for emergencies and it is proposed that section 2 of the Emergency Powers Act 1920 be amended to allow Her Majesty, by Order in Council, to confer powers or impose duties on the Scottish Ministers in the same way as she can upon the Secretary of State.

Executive devolution

It is proposed that the powers under the section 117(1)(b) of the Local Government etc (Scotland) Act 1994 to give directions to a Scottish water authority for the purposes of mitigating the effects of a civil emergency be devolved to the Scottish Ministers by an order under section 63.

B11 Extradition

Scope

6.29 All matters relating to extradition are reserved. Specifically, this covers the Extradition Act 1989 which provides the procedures for extraditing persons to states other than the Republic of Ireland. It also covers the Backing of Warrants Act 1965 which sets out the procedure for extraditing persons to the Republic of Ireland. In a very limited sense the law relating to extradition to the United Kingdom is also covered, although this is mainly a matter of international law and the law of the state in question.

Exception

None.

Executive devolution

It is anticipated that many of the executive functions currently exercised in Scotland by the Secretary of State will transfer to the Scottish Ministers by an order under section 63. These functions relate to extradition both to and from the United Kingdom and include an order for return and arranging for a person to be sent back to a foreign state. It is proposed that the extradition court proceedings continue to be arranged by the Crown Office.

B12 Lieutenancies

Scope

6.30 The subject-matter of the Lieutenancies Act 1997 is reserved. This makes provision for the division of Scotland into areas for lieutenancy purposes (now largely ceremonial), for the appointment and removal of lords-lieutenant, lieutenants, deputy lieutenants, vice lords-lieutenant and clerks of lieutenancies and about the functions and privileges of each office.

Exception

None.

Executive devolution

It is proposed that the statutory duty to inform the Lord-Lieutenant that Her Majesty does not disapprove of the granting of a commission of deputy Lieutenant should be transferred from the Prime Minister or Secretary of State to the Scottish Ministers. Other functions derived from common law such as advising Her Majesty on appointments may be transferred to the First Minister.

Head C Trade and industry

C1 Business associations

Scope

6.31 The reservation covers the creation, operation, regulation and dissolution of types of business association. It is designed to preserve a level playing field for business within the United Kingdom. 'Business association' is defined as any person (other than an individual) established for the purpose of carrying on any kind of business, whether or not for profit. 'Business' is defined as including the provision of benefits to the members of an association. The definition covers *inter alia* both registered and unregistered companies, partnerships, building societies, friendly societies and European economic interest groupings.

More specifically, the reservation covers matters such as:

1 the creation of types of business associations such as the manner in which limited liability companies are incorporated by registration under the Companies Act 1985;
2 the operation of types of business associations including matters relating to the internal structure and organs of the type of business association such as the appointment and powers and liabilities of members, officers or boards of directors;
3 the regulation of types of business associations including the authorisation, registration, supervision and investigation of business associations and their relationships, and the imposition of civil or criminal sanctions; and
4 the dissolution of types of business associations.

The reservation does not restrict the Scottish Parliament from establishing business associations for devolved purposes but any such association would have to comply with the relevant Act of the United Kingdom Parliament. Furthermore, the Scottish Parliament may legislate on Scots private law matters such as the law of contract or damages which may apply to business associations. The law in this case must affect devolved and reserved matters consistently as set out in section 29(4) of the Act[1].

Exceptions

Particular public bodies established by or under any enactment are excepted from this reservation. This allows the Scottish Parliament by enactment to create and provide for the operation, regulation and dissolution of any public body for devolved purposes. This covers statutory bodies such as Scottish Homes or types of statutory bodies such as local authorities or other bodies required to carry out activities within devolved areas such as the arts, sports, education, health or the environment.

Also excepted are charities, which otherwise fall within the definition of business association. It is intended that the Scottish Parliament should be able to legislate with regard to the creation, operation, regulation and dissolution of charities under Scots law.

Executive devolution

Nothing specific proposed.

1 Note that the Secretary of State under s 33(1) may prevent the Bill from being submitted for Royal Assent if he or she considers such legislation will have an adverse affect on the operation of an enactment as it relates to reserved matters (e g companies legislation); paras 5.12 and 5.34 above.

C2 Insolvency

Scope

6.32 Most matters relating to insolvency and winding up of business associations are reserved.

In general the winding up of business associations is reserved. The term 'winding up' includes the winding up of solvent as well as insolvent business associations.

Specifically reserved are:

1 the modes of, grounds for and general legal effect of winding up and the persons who may initiate the winding up;
2 liability to contribute to assets on winding up;
3 powers of courts in relation to proceedings for winding up, other that the power to sist proceedings;
4 arrangements with creditors; and
5 procedures giving protection from creditors.

These reservations ensure that, so far as possible, the law relating to winding up in Scotland will be consistent with that in England and Wales.

This Section also reserves matters relating to preferred or preferential debts for the purpose of the Bankruptcy (Scotland) Act 1985, the Insolvency Act 1986 and any other enactment relating to the sequestration of the estate of any person or to the winding up of business associations, the preference of such debts against other such debts and the extent of their preference over other types of debt. Also reserved are matters relating to the regulation of insolvency practitioners and matters relating to the co-operation of the insolvency courts.

Exception

There are some substantial exceptions largely due to the differences between insolvency law and practice in England and Wales and the law and practice in Scotland. Excepted from this reservation in relation to business associations are the process of winding up, the effect of winding up on diligence and the avoidance and adjustment of prior transactions on winding up.

Matters relating to floating charges and receivers are also not reserved except in relation to preferential debts, the regulation of insolvency practitioners and the co-operation of insolvency courts. Thus, the circumstances in which receivers are appointed and the effect of their appointment are not reserved.

Executive devolution

Nothing specific proposed.

C3 Competition

Scope

6.33 This Section reserves the regulation of anti-competitive practices and agreements, abuse of dominant position and monopolies and mergers. This includes the powers to investigate any body or person for the purposes of competition law and the administration of competition law. Thus, responsibility for competition policy will remain with the President of the Board of Trade. The Director of Fair Trading will be responsible for enforcement of the prohibitions on anti-competitive agreements with rights of appeal to the tribunal within the new Competition Commission set up under the Competition Act 1998.

Exception

The existing situation whereby the Scottish Office is responsible for regulating the legal profession and the provision of legal services will continue as an exception to this reservation. This type of regulation can affect competition in the provision of legal services, for instance through rules of conduct. The legal profession is defined to include not only advocates and solicitors but also qualified conveyancers and licensed executry practitioners. The exception will not, however, enable the Scottish Parliament to legislate generally about the regulation of anti-competitive practices in the legal profession in Scotland. Also, the power of the United Kingdom competition authorities to investigate anti-competitive practices concerning the Scottish legal profession and apply competition legislation to members of the profession is not affected by this exception.

Executive devolution

It is expected that the Scottish Ministers, in agreement with the Secretary of State for Trade and Industry, will be responsible for the making of orders relating to unfair contract terms in arbitration agreements. It is also likely that the functions of the Secretary of

State under the Multi-lateral Investment Guarantee Agency Act 1988 relating to the development of legal procedures for certain arbitration proceedings will be devolved to the Scottish Ministers. The Scottish Ministers are also likely to be consulted by the Lord Chancellor in making rules in relation to Scottish proceedings under the Industry Act 1975.

C4 Intellectual property

Scope

6.34 All matters relating to existing and future intellectual property and ancillary matters are reserved, including patents, design rights, trade marks and copyright and all other existing and future analogous rights and matters such as design registration, publication rights, rights in performances and semi-conductor topographies, technical measures for the protection of works and rights management information, moral rights and the law on passing off, trade secrets and database rights. It also includes the registration of patent and trademark agents.

Exception

Excepted from this reservation is the subject-matter of Parts I and II of the Plant Varieties Act 1997 which deals with plant breeders' rights, including the licensing of the use of plant varieties, and establishes the Plant Varieties and Seeds Tribunal. The Scottish Parliament has the authority to legislate about plant breeders' rights in view of the devolution of agricultural matters generally.

Executive devolution

In line with the devolution of responsibility for judicial appointments generally, it is proposed that the Lord Chancellor will consult the Scottish Ministers before exercising his appointing and rule-making functions under the applicable intellectual property legislation[1].

1 Copyright, Designs and Patents Act 1988, Trade Marks Act 1994.

C5 Import and export control

Scope

6.35 The subject-matter of the Import, Export and Customs Powers (Defence) Act 1939 is reserved. This Act provides for controlling (through prohibition and regulation) the import, export and carriage of goods and for the enforcement of the law relating to these matters. Also reserved is the prohibition and regulation of the import and export of endangered animals and plants[1].

Exception

The control of movement of food, animals, plants and other items into and out of Scotland for the purposes of protecting human, animal or plant health, or to safeguard animal welfare, to protect the environment or to meet EC obligations under the Common Agricultural Policy is not reserved. This is consistent with the general devolution of agricultural, fisheries, food and related matters. Also excepted is the control of movement into and out of Scotland of animal feeding stuffs, fertilisers and pesticides for the purposes of protecting human, animal or plant health or the environment.

Executive devolution

Nothing specific proposed.

1 Plants and animals do not fall within the controls of 'goods'. The basis of the current law pertaining to this reservation comes from the Convention on International Trade in Endangered Species (CITES, 1973) (Cmnd 6647).

C7 Sea fishing

Scope

6.36 The regulation of sea fishing outside the Scottish zone (except in relation to Scottish fishing boats) is reserved. This means that the United Kingdom Government will remain responsible for its obligations under various international and EC laws for the control of sea fishing.

'The Scottish zone' is defined in section 126(1) of the Act to mean the sea within British fishery limits (that is, the limits set by or under section 1 of the Fishery Limits Act 1976) which is adjacent to Scotland. This limit is currently set at 200 nautical miles from the coast.

Exception

The control of Scottish fishing boats is excepted from this reservation. A Scottish fishing boat is defined in the Schedule as a fishing vessel which is registered in the register maintained under section 8 of the Merchant Shipping Act 1995 and whose entry in the register specifies a port in Scotland as the port to which the vessel is to be treated as belonging. Also excepted is sea fishing within the Scottish zone but in practice, this is largely already regulated by the European Community.

Executive devolution

Nothing specific proposed.

C7 Consumer protection

Scope

6.37 This reservation falls into three main sections.

The first section reserves the regulation of the following matters:

1 the sale and supply of goods and services to consumers[1];
2 guarantees in relation to such goods and services including commercial guarantees;
3 hire purchase, including the subject-matter of Part III of the Hire Purchase Act 1964;
4 trade descriptions, except in relation to food (this is not limited to the protection of consumers);
5 misleading and comparative advertising, except regulation specifically in relation to food, tobacco and tobacco products;
6 price indications, including relevant provisions in the Consumer Protection Act 1987;
7 trading stamps, including the issue, use and redemption of trading stamps and the rights of holders;
8 auctions and mock auctions of goods and services; and

9 hallmarking and gun barrel proofing - this covers the hallmarks applied to precious metals and the process of testing a gun for safety (a statutory requirement for small arms).

The second section reserves all matters relating to the safety of and liability for services to consumers.

The third section reserves the subject-matter of the following enactments:

1 the Hearing Aid Council Act 1968 which establishes the Hearing Aid Council which regulates hearing aid dispensers;
2 the Unsolicited Goods and Services Acts 1971 and 1975 which provide protection for those who receive unsolicited goods or who are charged for unsolicited directory entries;
3 Parts I to III and XI of the Fair Trading Act 1973 which *inter alia* establish the Office of the Director General of Fair Trading and the Consumer Protection Advisory Committee, set out the powers of the Director General to deal with certain traders and provide for the regulation of pyramid selling;
4 the Consumer Credit Act 1974 which regulates the advertising and provision of credit arrangements to individuals;
5 the Estate Agents Act 1979 which regulates the estate agency industry;
6 the Timeshare Act 1992 which imposes minimum information requirements and cooling off periods on the sale of timeshares;
7 the Package Travel, Package Holiday and Package Tours Regulations 1992[2] which amongst other things cover the information in brochures and form of contracts in the area; and
8 the Commercial Agents (Council Directive) Regulations 1993[3] which amongst other things set out the rights and duties of principals and their agents in relation to each other.

Exception

Specifically excepted from all of these reservations is the subject-matter of section 16 of the Food Safety Act 1990 which provides for regulations to be made in regard to the fitness of food, hygiene conditions and practices in food premises, food advertising and labelling.

Executive devolution

Nothing specific proposed.

1 A substantial amount of legislation is affected by this reservation, most notably the Sale of Goods Act 1979, the Supply of Goods and Services Act 1982, the Unfair Contract Terms Act 1977, the Unfair Terms in Consumer Contracts Regulations 1994 (SI 1994/3159). Most of this legislation goes beyond the strict terms of this reservation and the Scottish Parliament is able to legislate on these wider matters.
2 SI 1992/3288.
3 SI 1993/3053.

C8 Product standards, safety and liability

Scope

6.38 This reservation covers the technical standards and requirements in relation to products in pursuance of an obligation under European Community law. An example of relevant EC law is the directive concerned with the suitability of packaging for reuse or recycling[1]. This Section also reserves product safety and product liability and the labelling of products.

Exception

Specifically excepted from this reservation are: food (including drinks) and in relation to food safety, material which comes into contact with food (i e packaging); agricultural and horticultural produce; fish and fish products; seeds; animal feeding stuffs; fertilisers; and pesticides. These exceptions are consistent with the general devolution of agriculture, fisheries and food.

Executive devolution

Nothing specific proposed.

1 Council Directive (EC) 94/62, OJ L365 31.12.94 p10.

C9 Weights and measures

Scope

6.39 This Section reserves weights and measures including the units and standards of weight and measurement, and the regulation of trade as it involves weighing, measuring and quantities.

Exception

None.

Executive devolution

Nothing specific proposed.

C10 Telecommunications and wireless telegraphy

Scope

6.40 This reservation covers all matters relating to telecommunications and wireless telegraphy. In particular, this includes the subject-matter of the Telecommunications Act 1984 which sets out the regulatory and licensing regime for telecommunications systems. Telecommunications includes telephone systems and all forms of data transmission through electric, magnetic, electro-magnetic, electro-chemical or electro-mechanical means. The subject-matter of Part II of the Wireless Telegraphy Act 1949 which covers the prevention of interference is also reserved.

The internet services and electronic encryption are also reserved matters.

Exception

The subject-matter of Part III of the Police Act 1997 which deals with authorised interference with property mainly for the purposes of surveillance is not covered by this reservation.

Executive devolution

Nothing specific proposed.

C11 Post Office, posts and postal services

Scope

6.41 This Section reserves the Post Office and its subsidiaries, posts and the regulation of postal services. Specifically, it reserves all matters relating to the Post Office and its subsidiaries, including

Post Office Counters Ltd (which runs post offices) and Subscription Services Ltd (which issues TV licences) and the Post Office Users Council for Scotland[1]. The law relating to posts[2] (postage stamps, postal orders and postal packets) is also reserved. As postal services may be provided by operators other than the Post Office, the regulation of these services is also reserved.

Exception

None.

Executive devolution

Nothing specific proposed.

1 The relevant legislation is the Post Office Act 1969 and Part II of the Telecommunications Act 1981.
2 See the Post Office Act 1953.

C12 Research councils

Scope

6.42 This Section reserves research councils within the meaning of the Science and Technology Act 1965. It covers the establishment of and appointments to the research councils, the functions, powers and duties of such bodies and the provision of expenses and funds for distribution by them.

The Section also reserves the subject-matter of section 5 of the 1965 Act so far as it relates to Research Councils. The result is that the power to fund scientific research through the research councils is reserved to United Kingdom Ministers.

The United Kingdom Research Councils will continue to provide funds for research in Scotland in the same way as they have in the past. The Scottish Parliament will be able to legislate for the funding of research including scientific research and to establish bodies to carry out, administer or fund such research. This reservation simply precludes the Scottish Parliament from establishing Research Councils within the meaning of the 1965 Act or exercising any direct control over such Councils.

Exception

None.

Executive devolution

Nothing specific proposed.

C13 Designation of assisted areas

Scope

6.43 The subject-matter of section 1 of the Industrial Development Act 1982 is reserved. This gives the Secretary of State the power to designate areas within Great Britain as assisted areas (development areas and intermediate areas) where for economic, social or other reasons of regional policy, additional measures to promote their economic development are considered appropriate. Section 1 also provides for the preferential treatment of these areas.

Exception

None.

Executive devolution

Nothing specific proposed.

C14 Industrial Development Advisory Board

Scope

6.44 This section reserves all matters relating to the Industrial Development Advisory Board which is responsible for advising the Secretary of State in regard to financial assistance to industry.

Exception

None.

Executive devolution

Nothing specific proposed.

C15 Protection of trading and economic interests

Scope

6.45 The protection of trading and economic interests is reserved to the United Kingdom Parliament. This type of legislation is intended to protect individuals and businesses from the laws of other states where they purport to have effect outside the country where the laws are made. For example, legislation may be enacted to prevent the enforcement in the United Kingdom of foreign judgements or provide remedies in United Kingdom courts for persons adversely affected by the application of objectionable foreign laws.

Specifically, this Section reserves the subject-matter of the following enactments:

1 section 2 of the Emergency Laws (Re-enactments and Repeals) Act 1964 which gives the Treasury the power to block transfers of funds, gold or securities where that action is likely to be taken by a person or Government outside the United Kingdom to the detriment for the economic position of the United Kingdom;
2 Part II of the Industry Act 1975 which deals with the powers relating to the transfer of control of important manufacturing undertakings and is intended to cover cases where it is undesirable on wider policy grounds for assets of wider national importance to fall into the hands of non-residents; and
3 the Protection of Trading Interests Act 1980 which sets out the main provision concerning protection of trading or other business interests of persons in the United Kingdom from requirements, prohibitions or judgements imposed or made under the laws of other states.

Exception

None.

Executive devolution

Consistent with the general devolution of judicial procedures, it is proposed that the functions relating to the determination of procedural rules for the arbitral tribunal established under the Industry Act 1975 and the Aircraft and Shipbuilding Industries Tribunal established under the Aircraft and Shipbuilding Industries Act 1977 will be exercisable by respectively the Lord Chancellor or the Secretary of State for Trade and Industry after consultation with the Scottish Ministers. This would be achieved by an order under section 63.

Head D Energy

D1 Electricity

Scope

6.46 This reservation covers the generation, transmission, distribution and supply of electricity in Scotland. This is currently the subject-matter of Part I of the Electricity Act 1989. The reservation also specifically covers the subject-matter of Part II of the 1989 Act which deals with the re-organisation of the industry by privatisation.

Exception

The subject-matter of Part I of the Environmental Protection Act 1990 which deals with the authorisation of certain processes in regard to integrated pollution control is excepted from this reservation.

Executive devolution

Most of the current functions exercised by the Secretary of State in regard to the supply of electricity in Scotland will be executively devolved to the Scottish Ministers. These functions are generally related to the regulation of the industry in Scotland and include powers: to promote renewable energy; to levy electricity suppliers to pay for the promotion of renewable energy; to grant consent for new power stations, and for new or upgraded overhead power lines; to make orders relating to the felling and lopping of trees; to authorise persons to abstract and use water and to make regulations on environmental assessment of electricity applications. It is also likely that functions in respect of environmental assessment of electricity applications under the relevant regulations will be transferred to the Scottish Ministers along with the duty to exercise all functions in a manner best calculated to achieve certain ends set out in the Electricity Act 1989 (e g the protection of rural consumers, the environment) and duties relating to amenity considerations and the protection of fisheries. The Scottish Ministers may also need to be consulted in regard to the grant of licences.

D2 Oil and gas

Scope

6.47 This Section reserves to the United Kingdom Parliament the power to legislate about oil and gas. More specifically, the following subjects are reserved:

1 the ownership of, exploration for and exploitation of deposits of oil and natural gas[1];
2 the subject-matter of section 1 of the Minerals Exploration and Investment Grants Act 1972 which deals with contributions for mineral exploration, so far as it relates to the exploration for oil and gas;
3 offshore installations and pipelines;
4 the subject-matter of the Pipelines Act 1962 (including section 5 (deemed planning permission)) so far as relating to pipelines within the meaning of section 65 of that Act. The 1962 Act grants authorisation for the laying of pipelines on land and applies mainly to oil and gas pipelines. Section 5 is specifically reserved since many other forms of deemed planning permission are not reserved;
5 the application of Scots law and the jurisdiction of the Scottish courts in relation to offshore activities[2];
6 pollution relating to oil and gas exploration and exploitation, but only outside controlled waters (within the meaning of the Control of Pollution Act 1974)[3];
7 the subject-matter of Part II of the Food and Environment Protection Act 1985 so far as relating to oil and gas exploration and exploitation, but only in relation to activities outside such controlled waters;
8 restrictions on navigation, fishing and other activities in connection with offshore activities[4];
9 liquefaction of natural gas[5];
10 the conveyance, shipping and supply of natural gas through pipes.

Exception

The subject-matter of the following enactments is excepted from this reservation:

1 sections 10–12 of the Industry Act 1972 which deal with credits and grants for the construction of ships and offshore installations;

2 the Offshore Petroleum Development (Scotland) Act 1975 other than sections 3 to 7. This ensures that the Scottish Parliament has the authority to provide assistance for onshore activities in support of offshore activities; and
3 Part I of the Environmental Protection Act 1990 which deals with the authorisation of certain processes in regard to integrated pollution control.

Also excepted is the manufacture of gas, and the conveyance, shipping and supply of gas other than through pipes.

Executive devolution

It is proposed that many of the Secretary of State's functions in relation to pipelines beginning and ending in Scotland be transferred to the Scottish Ministers by an order under section 63. Certain other functions relating to the licensing of certain categories of operations, the declaration of part of the sea surrounding Scotland as a designated area and the approval of in situ abandonment and disposal of redundant oil installations are likely to be exercised only after consultation with the Scottish Ministers[6].

1 See for example the subject-matter of the Petroleum (Production) Act 1934.
2 See Part IV of the Oil and Gas (Enterprise) Act 1982 which provides for the application in relation to oil and gas installations on the Continental Shelf of the civil and criminal laws of the different parts of the United Kingdom.
3 See the Prevention of Oil Pollution Act 1971. Pollution into controlled waters (relevant territorial, coastal, inland and ground waters) is not reserved.
4 See ss 3–7 of the Offshore Petroleum Development (Scotland) Act 1975, and Part III of the Petroleum Act 1987.
5 See the Energy Act 1976.
6 See the Food and Environment Protection Act 1985, the Petroleum Act 1998 Part IV and the Offshore Petroleum Development (Scotland) Act 1975.

D3 Coal

Scope

6.48 This Section reserves all legislation relating to coal. In particular it reserves the law relating to the ownership and exploitation of coal, deep and opencast mining and subsidence. Policy in regard to the coal industry in the United Kingdom remains the responsibility of the Department of Trade and Industry, in consultation with the Scottish Ministers when appropriate. Operational matters in relation to coal will continue to fall within the remit of the Coal Authority.

Exception

Environmental duties in relation to planning approvals and restoration of land affected by coal-mining operations under sections 53 and 54 of the Coal Industry Act 1994 are not reserved. Also excepted is Part I of the Environmental Protection Act 1990 which deals with environmental authorisation for prescribed processes under integrated pollution control.

Executive devolution

Nothing specific proposed.

D4 Nuclear energy

Scope

6.49 This reservation covers all matters relating to nuclear energy and nuclear installations, including nuclear safety, nuclear security and safeguards, and liability for nuclear occurrences. The areas covered by the reservation include the development, production and use of nuclear energy, nuclear site licensing, nuclear safety, nuclear security, liability for nuclear occurrences and insurance in respect of such liability, nuclear safeguards required under international treaties and the United Kingdom Atomic Energy Authority.

Exception

The duties of the Scottish Environment Protection Agency under Part I of the Environmental Protection Act 1990 dealing with integrated pollution control are excepted from this reservation. Also excepted is the subject-matter of the Radioactive Substances Act 1993 which provides for the regulation of the keeping, use, disposal or accumulation of radioactive material including waste and the regulation of non-nuclear activities at nuclear installations.

Executive devolution

It is anticipated that all functions (including those relating to nuclear site licences, compensation and inspectors) of the 'Minister' under the Nuclear Installations Act 1965 currently exercised by the Secretary of State for Scotland (other than the making of orders and regulations) will be executively devolved to the Scottish Ministers. The functions relating to the making of orders and regulations will be exercised by the Secretary of State for Trade and Industry after consultation with the Scottish Ministers.

D5 Energy conservation

Scope

6.50 This reservation covers the subject-matter of the Energy Act 1976 other than section 9. This Act enables the Secretary of State to make orders regulating or prohibiting the use of various fuels or electricity for the purposes of energy conservation. It also enables him to make orders regulating or prohibiting the production, supply or acquisition of various fuels or electricity while an Order of Council is in force (which may give him further powers to implement an international obligation or to deal with an emergency). Section 9 deals with the use and liquidation of offshore natural gas and is covered by the reservation of Oil and Gas at D2.

Exception

Specifically excepted is the encouragement of energy efficiency other than by prohibition or regulation. As a result, the Scottish Parliament can legislate to encourage energy efficiency through the use of advice, publicity, grants and loans and other positive incentives.

Executive devolution

Nothing specific proposed.

Head E Transport

E1 Road transport

Scope

6.51 This Section reserves certain matters relating to road traffic and transport. Specifically reserved is the subject-matter of the following Acts:

1 the Motor Vehicles (International Circulation) Act 1952 which deals with the issue of international driving permits and the recognition of foreign permits;
2 the Public Passenger Vehicles Act 1981 and the Transport Act 1985 so far as relating to the system of public service vehicle operator licensing;
3 sections 17 and 25 and Parts V and VI of the Road Traffic Regulation Act 1984 which cover pedestrian crossings, what traffic can use special roads, the regulation of traffic signs and speed limits;
4 the Road Traffic Act 1988 and the Road Traffic Offenders Act 1988 which deal with road safety, construction and use of vehicles, licensing of drivers of vehicles, driving instruction, third party liability and compulsory insurance and the prosecution and punishment of road traffic offences;
5 the Vehicle Excise and Registration Act 1994 which deals with the licensing and registration of vehicles;
6 the Road Traffic (New Drivers) Act 1995 which deals with the revocation of driving licences during the licence holder's probationary period; and
7 the Goods Vehicle (Licensing of Operators) Act 1995.

The regulation of proper hours or periods of work by persons engaged in the carriage of passengers or goods by road, the conditions under which international and transport services for passengers or goods may be undertaken and the regulation of motor vehicle driving instructors are also reserved matters.

Exception

Two main exceptions exist to this Section. The subject-matter of sections 39 and 40 of the Road Traffic Act 1988 which deal with road safety and training is excepted from this reservation. The Scottish Parliament will be able to legislate about matters concerned with the promotion of road safety and to subsidise bodies other than local authorities to give road safety advice and training. However, since road safety is included on the list of concurrent powers set out in section 56, United Kingdom Ministers also have functions exercisable in regards to road safety in Scotland. The second exception covers sections 157 to 163 of the 1988 Act and gives the Scottish Parliament the power to legislate about payments for the hospital treatment of road traffic casualties. This is in line with the general devolution of health matters.

Executive devolution

It is proposed that certain Ministerial functions be executively devolved to the Scottish Ministers in regard to road traffic by way of an order under section 63. These functions include: the power to make regulations in respect to what traffic can use special roads in Scotland; the authorisation of traffic signs; certain functions relating to the setting of speed limits; the regulation of competitions on roads using motor vehicles or cycles; certain functions relating to rehabilitation courses for drunk drivers; and the granting of permits for the use of mini-buses. In addition it is proposed that the Lord Chancellor will consult the Scottish Ministers before appointing or removing judicial members of the Transport Tribunal[1].

1 Road Traffic Regulation Act 1984 s 17 and Parts V and VI; Road Traffic Act 1988; Road Traffic Offenders Act ss 34A–34C; Transport Act 1985.

E2 Rail transport

Scope

6.52 This Section reserves the provision and regulation of railways[1], rail transport security, the subject-matter of the Channel Tunnel Act 1987 and the subject-matter of the Railways Heritage Act 1996 which provides powers to make a railway heritage scheme.

Exception

Most grants relating to railway services are excepted from this reservation. The Scottish Parliament can legislate about capital and revenue grants for services relating to the carriage of passengers, stations, maintenance facilities and the rail network itself. Certain grant provisions, however, are reserved through an exception to the general exception. These reserved matters relate to government financial assistance where railway administration orders are made[2], to grants in relation to the carriage of goods by railway[3] and to the compensation payable to a passenger service operator who is required to run a passenger service which would not be commercially viable in accordance with a public service obligation under Community law[4].

Executive devolution

It is expected that several functions under the Railways Act 1993 will be transferred to the Scottish Ministers as they apply in Scotland by an order made under section 63. These include receiving the annual reports of the Rail Regulator, the Director of Passenger Rail Franchising and the Central Rail Users' Consultative Committee, laying these reports before Parliament and arranging for their publication, making grants for improved track access and the making of grants for improved facilities for freight haulage by railway.

These latter two grant making functions will be held concurrently with the United Kingdom Minister and the criteria for making such grants will be agreed by the Scottish Ministers and the United Kingdom Minister. Similarly, the Rail Users' Consultative Committee for Scotland deals with both devolved and reserved matters. As such appropriate arrangements will need to be made under the cross-border public bodies provisions in sections 88 and 89

1 Defined in s 82(1) of the Railways Act 1993 but excluding the wider definition of railway in s 81(2) of that Act.
2 The subject-matter of s 63 of the Railways Act 1993.
3 Section 82(1)(b) of the Railways Act 1993.
4 Section 136 of the Railways Act 1993 as required under Council Regulation (EEC) 1191/69 (as amended), OJ L156 28.6.69 p1.

E3 Marine transport

Scope

6.53 This reservation refers only to the subject-matter of specific Acts. Broadly, it appears that marine transport matters are reserved where there is a need for the consistent provision across the United Kingdom or for practical reasons. For example, the employment of seafarers is a reserved matter as are the activities of the coastguard.

The Section provides that the subject-matter of the following Acts are reserved matters:

1 the Coastguard Act 1925 which sets out the activities and powers of HM Coastguard;
2 the Hovercraft Act 1968 except so far as it relates to the regulation of noise and vibration caused by hovercraft;

3 the Carriage of Goods by Sea Act 1971 which incorporates into United Kingdom law certain international agreements dealing with the liability for the loss or damage of goods at sea;
4 section 2 of the Protection of Wrecks Act 1973 which prohibits approaching dangerous wrecks;
5 the Merchant Shipping (Liner Conferences) Act 1982 which exempts 'liner conferences'[1] and incorporates into United Kingdom law the UN Convention on a Code of Conduct for Liner Conferences;
6 the Dangerous Vessels Act 1985;
7 the Aviation and Maritime Security Act 1990 other than Part I (aviation security);
8 the Carriage of Goods by Sea Act 1992 which provides for bills of lading and deals with rights and liabilities under shipping contracts;
9 the Merchant Shipping Act 1995 which includes matters such as what constitutes a British ship, registration of ships, masters and seamen on seagoing ships, marine safety, fishing vessels, marine pollution from ships, lighthouse, salvage and wreck and enforcement officers;
10 the Shipping and Trading Interests (Protection) Act 1995 which deals with the response to discriminatory foreign action against United Kingdom shipping and trade interests;
11 sections 24 and 26–28 of the Merchant Shipping and Maritime Security Act 1997 which make provision for the protection of wrecks, piracy and international bodies.

Also reserved are navigational rights and freedoms as set out in international law and financial assistance for shipping services which start or finish or both outside Scotland. The Scottish Parliament will be able to legislate about financial assistance to shipping services operating wholly within Scotland.

Exception

Certain maritime transport matters are excepted. The Scottish Parliament will be able to legislate on matters regarding ports, harbours, piers and marine works[2] unless they relate to the reserved matters set out in 4, 6, 7, or 9 above. Legislative competence is also vested in the Scottish Parliament for the regulation of works which may obstruct or endanger navigation. Exceptions to this exception are works relating to oil and gas and telecommunications where consents for these industries will be reserved matters. Finally the subject-matter of the Highlands and Islands Shipping Services Act

1960 in relation to financial assistance for bulk freight services is excepted. This means that the Scottish Parliament can continue the subsidies to the bulk freight shipping services between the Highlands and Islands and locations outside Scotland which are necessary for the social and economic well-being of remote and island communities.

Executive devolution

Certain executive functions are likely to be devolved to the Scottish Ministers. These include powers to appoint assessors to inquire into the conduct or fitness of seamen and powers relating to the registration of fishing vessels as a British ship under the Merchant Shipping Act 1965. Other functions may require prior consultation with the Scottish Ministers such as the provision of regulations in relation to the marking of ships.

1 Cartels of deep sea container shipping operators concerned with the prevention of over-capacity and damaging price competition on certain routes.
2 'Marine work' has the same definition as in s 57(1) of the Harbours Act 1964 which is a harbour or boatslip used or required principally for the fishing industry or, where it is located in the Highlands or Islands areas, is used or required principally for the fishing or agricultural industries or for the maintenance of communications.

E4 Air transport

Scope

6.54 The regulation of aviation and air transport is a reserved matter. Specifically, reserved is the subject-matter of the following enactments:

1 the Carriage by Air Act 1961;
2 the Carriage by Air (Supplementary Provisions)Act 1962;
3 the Carriage by Air and Road Act 1979 (so far as it relates to carriage by air);

(These three Acts implement the Warsaw Convention (as amended) which deals with international carriage by aircraft of persons, baggage or cargo for reward.)

4 the Civil Aviation Act 1982 which *inter alia* provides for the Civil Aviation Authority, the regulation of aerodromes, civil aviation and aircraft;

5 the Aviation Security Act 1982 with deals with offences against the safety of aircraft and the protection of aircraft, aerodromes and air navigation installations against acts of violence;
6 the Airports Act 1986 which deals with the transfer of airport undertakings of local authorities, the regulation of the use of airports etc; and
7 sections 1 and 48 of the Aviation and Maritime Security Act 1990 which relate to endangering safety at aerodromes and powers in relation to certain aircraft.

Arrangements to compensate and repatriate passengers where an air operator becomes insolvent are also reserved.

Exception

Several sections of the Civil Aviation Act 1982 are excepted from the reservation. These include the power to provide aerodromes, the provision of aerodromes by local authorities, financial assistance for certain aerodromes, health controls at certain aerodromes and certain powers where land is required for airport development or expansion[1]. Also excepted is the subject-matter of Part II and sections 63, 64 and 66 of the Airports Act 1986 which relate to the transfer of airport undertakings of local authorities, airport bylaws and functions of operators of designated airports in regard to abandoned vehicles. Sections 59 and 60 of the 1986 Act which relate to the acquisition of land and the disposal of compulsorily acquired land are also excepted where land is to be or was acquired for the purpose of an airport development or expansion.

Executive devolution

It is anticipated that several functions relating to air transport currently exercised by the Secretary of State will be executively devolved to the Scottish Ministers by an order under section 63. These include several sections of the Civil Aviation Act 1982 including: the power to direct an aerodrome authority to fix charges in relation to aircraft noise; the power to authorise the Civil Aviation Authority to acquire land compulsorily in Scotland; the power to authorise any person to enter land in Scotland to make a survey; and various functions in relation to the publication of notices and the giving of directions in connection with the mitigation of noise and vibration from aircraft. Several functions under the Airports Act 1986 may also be devolved including the release of an airport from economic regulation after consultation with the Civil Aviation

Authority, the power, after consultation, to direct that the road traffic enactments should apply to a designated airport subject to modifications and the power to require an airport operator to monitor aircraft movements in relation to the regulation of noise and vibration from aircraft.

1 Civil Aviation Act 1982, ss 25, 30, 31, 34–36, 41–43, 50.

E5 Other matters

Scope

6.55 This Section reserves the transport of radioactive material[1] and the regulation of the carriage of dangerous goods. Also reserved are the technical specifications for public passenger transport including the subject-matter of section 125(7) and (8) of the Transport Act 1985 and Part V of the Disability Discrimination Act 1995 (public transport).

Exception

None

Executive devolution

It is proposed that several related executive functions be devolved to the Scottish Ministers by an order under section 63. These relate mainly to accessibility requirements and the carriage of disabled passengers in taxis and hire cars contracted out in a designated port, airport, railway station or bus station[2].

1 As defined in s 1(1) of the Radioactive Material (Road Transport) Act 1991 – material having a specific activity in excess of 70 kilobecquerels per kilogram or any lesser specific activity specified in an order made by the Secretary of State.
2 Disability Discrimination Act 1995 ss 33(2), 10(4) and s 20(2A) of the Civic Government (Scotland) Act 1982.

Head F Social security

F1 Social security schemes

Scope

6.56 This reservation is cast in a very broad way to allow for changes over time in the exact scope and coverage of the United

Kingdom-wide social security system and in the way in which benefits are delivered. The reservation itself describes social security not in terms of benefits for specific purposes but in terms of the power and responsibilities which underlie any type of social security provision.

There are four specific reservations. First, the establishment and financing from central or local government funds of schemes which provide assistance for social security purposes by way of benefits (i e pensions, allowances, grants and loans) to individuals is reserved. Second, the Section reserves the power to require persons (such as employers or local authorities) to establish or administer schemes providing assistance for social security purposes or to make payments in respect of such schemes and to keep records and supply information in connection with such schemes. Third, the Section reserves the establishment of a liability for a person to maintain himself or another for social security and child support purposes[1]. Finally, the subject-matter of the Vaccine Damage Payment Scheme is reserved.

Providing assistance for social security purposes are defined to include providing assistance to individuals or in respect of individuals due to old age, survivorship, disability, sickness, incapacity, injury, unemployment, maternity and the care of children or others needing care, low income and in relation to their housing costs or liabilities for local taxes.

Uniquely, this Section provides specific illustrations of what is covered by this reservation. These include National Insurance, the Social Fund, the administration and funding of housing benefit, the recovery of benefits paid because of accident injury or disease from persons paying damages and the sharing of information between government departments for the purposes of social security legislation.

Exception

The subject-matter of certain legislative provisions is specifically excepted from this reservation including: Part II of the Social Work (Scotland) Act 1968; section 2 of the Chronically Sick and Disabled Persons Act 1970; section 50 of the Children Act 1975; section 15 of the Enterprise and New Towns (Scotland) Act 1990; and sections 22, and 29–30 of the Children (Scotland) Act 1995. These provisions relate *inter alia* to the promotion of social welfare by local authorities including provision for exceptional payments to persons in need, the making of payments towards maintenance for children, assistance to children and their families, certain payments paid by local authorities to disabled people and other people.

Executive devolution

It is proposed that the appointments and procedures of the Social Security Commissioners will be made following consultation with the Scottish Ministers.

1 As set out in the Child Support Acts 1991 and 1995.

F2 Child support

Scope

6.57 This reservation covers the subject-matter of the Child Support Acts 1991 and 1995 which give the Secretary of State for Social Security the power to determine, regulate and enforce the payment of maintenance in respect of a child not living with both parents. The Acts limit the jurisdiction of the courts to make individual decisions on child maintenance in circumstances covered by the Acts.

The reservation includes an interpretation section which provides that if section 30(2) of the Child Support Act 1991 relating to the collection of payments other than child support maintenance, is not in force on the principal appointed day (1 July 1999), it is to be treated for the purposes of this reservation as if it were.

Exception

The subject-matter of sections 1 to 7 of the Family Law (Scotland) Act 1985 which deal with aliment is excepted from this reservation.

Executive devolution

It is suggested that by way of an order under section 63, the Scottish Ministers be consulted about appointments of deputy Child Support Commissioners and on the making of procedural regulations in respect of such Commissioners.

F3 Occupational and personal pensions

Scope

6.58 This Section reserves matters relating to occupational and personal pensions including the obligations of the trustees or managers of such schemes. The Act defines 'pension' to include gratuities and allowances. Personal pension schemes are established by financial institutions and are essentially contracts between individuals and pension providers. They attract a range of tax concessions. Occupational pensions are usually payable under trusts set up by employers in respect of their employees. The rules set out in the trust deed must comply with legislative requirements and can be overridden when a conflict arises.

The reservation covers provisions about pensions payable to or in respect of any persons except those listed in the exception (see below). It also covers the subject-matter of the Pensions (Increase) Act 1971 and covers the schemes for the payment of pensions listed in Schedule 2 of that Act except those mentioned in paragraphs 38A and 38AB.

For public service pensions, the reservation also covers the statutory provision for compensation for loss of office or employment, for loss or diminution of emoluments or where employment has been affected by constitutional changes in an overseas territory, as well as provisions for death or injury benefit. For example, the reservation will cover the statutory compensation scheme which exists where teachers are made redundant.

Exception

The exceptions to this reservation ensure that the Scottish Parliament will have the legislative competence to deal with the pensions of former members of the Scottish Parliament or the Scottish Executive and others under section 81(3) of the Act, for pensions of staff of the Scottish Parliament and for pensions of members and staff of public bodies with functions in devolved or mixed areas. However, these schemes must still comply with the codes set out in the Pensions Acts.

Executive devolution

It is likely that orders under section 63 of the Act will provide for widespread devolution in the area of public service pensions reflecting the present responsibility of the Secretary of State for Scotland for such pensions. These functions include the power to make regulations establishing and maintaining certain public service pensions and to provide compensation to certain public service employees[1].

1 See for example executive powers set out in the Superannuation Act 1972, Fire Services Act 1947 and Police Pensions Act 1976.

F4 War pensions

Scope

6.59 This Section reserves schemes for the payment of pensions (which includes grants, allowances, supplements and gratuities) for or in respect of persons who have a disablement or who have died as a consequence of service as members of the armed forces of the Crown. This reservation includes the establishment and regulation of public bodies such as the Pensions Appeal Tribunal, the Central Advisory Committee on War Pensions and the local War Pensions Committees.

The Section also reserves the subject-matter of a number of particular schemes which enable provision to be made which is analogous to war pensions in respect of persons other than ex-service men. These enactments are the Personal Injuries (Emergency Provisions) Act 1939 which provides for payments for civil defence volunteers and civilians during World War II, sections 3–5 and 7 of the Pensions (Navy, Army, Air Force and Mercantile Marine) Act 1939 which make payment provisions for mariners, pilots, lighthouse crews etc who suffered war related injury or detention and section 1 of the Polish Resettlement Act 1947 which makes payment provisions for Polish naval and armed forces under British command during World War II and Polish resettlement forces and their dependants.

Exception

None.

Executive devolution

Nothing specific proposed.

Head G Regulation of the professions

G1 Architects

Scope

6.60 This reservation covers all matters relating to the regulation of the profession of architect including professional qualifications, eligibility to practise, and control over professional competence and conduct of architects.

Exception

None.

Executive devolution

Nothing specific proposed.

G2 Health professions

Scope

6.61 This reservation covers all matters relating to the regulation of the health professions including professional qualifications, eligibility to practise, and control over professional competence and conduct. It does not reserve matters such as the pay and conditions of service of the health professions within the National Health Service in Scotland nor their deployment and management.

The term 'health professions' means professions regulated by the following regulatory enactments:

1 the Pharmacy Act 1954;
2 the Professions Supplementary to Medicine Act 1960;

3 the Veterinary Surgeons Act 1966;
4 the Medical Act 1983;
5 the Dentists Act 1984;
6 the Opticians Act 1989;
7 the Osteopaths Act 1993;
8 the Chiropractors Act 1994; and
9 the Nurses, Midwives and Health Visitors Act 1997.

It thus includes *inter alia* pharmacists, dieticians, physiotherapists, medical laboratory scientific officers, prosthetists and orthotists, occupational therapists, radiographers, chiropodists, veterinary surgeons, doctors, dentists, dental auxiliaries, opticians, osteopaths, chiropractors, nurses, midwives and health visitors.

Exception

The subject-matter of sections 21 and 25 of the National Health Service (Scotland) Act 1978 is excepted from this reservation leaving the Scottish Parliament with the power to legislate about what vocational training and experience is required of doctors, dentists and dental auxiliaries before they can provide general medical or dental services in the NHS. This is in line with the overall devolution of health service matters.

Executive devolution

Nothing specific proposed.

G3 Auditors

Scope

6.62 This reservation covers all matters relating to the regulation of the profession of auditor, including professional qualifications, eligibility to practise, and control over professional competence and conduct of auditors.

Exception

None.

Executive devolution

Nothing specific proposed.

Head H Employment

H1 Employment and industrial relations

Scope

6.63 Employment rights and duties and industrial relations are reserved. This includes the subject-matter of the following enactments:

1 the Employers' Liability (Compulsory Insurance) Act 1969 which requires employers to insure against liability for injury or disease sustained by their employees and arising out of or in the course of their employment;
2 the Employment Agencies Act 1973 which regulates employment agencies and employment businesses;
3 the Pneumoconiosis etc (Workers' Compensation) Act 1979 which provides for the payment of lump sums by the State to or in respect of persons disabled by industrial lung diseases caused by various kinds of noxious dust at work;
4 the Transfer of Undertakings (Protection of Employment) Regulations 1981[1] which provide for the protection of employees' rights on the transfer of an undertaking, such as the sale of a business;
5 the Trade Union and Labour Relations (Consolidation) Act 1992 which covers a wide range of matters including employers' associations, collective bargaining, industrial action, and procedures for handling redundancies;
6 the Industrial Tribunals Act 1996 which deals with industrial tribunals and the Employment Appeal Tribunal;
7 the Employment Rights Act 1996 which covers the protection of wages, suspension from work, rights to time off work, maternity rights, unfair dismissal and employees' rights on the insolvency of an employer; and
8 the National Minimum Wage Act 1998.

Exception

Excepted from this reservation is the subject-matter of the Agricultural Wages (Scotland) Act 1949 which establishes the

Scottish Agricultural Wages Board which is responsible for fixing minimum wages, holiday entitlements and other terms and conditions of employment for agricultural workers.

Executive devolution

It is likely that the power of the Secretary of State for Scotland to issue certificates exempting a body from the requirement to insure against employers' liability risks will be transferred to the Scottish Ministers by a section 63 order. Also proposed is that the power to make an order providing that certain proceedings which could be heard by a court in Scotland be brought before an industrial tribunal be executively devolved so that it is exercisable by the Scottish Ministers with the consent of the Secretary of State for Trade and Industry[2].

1 SI 1981/1794.
2 See Reg 2(a) of the Employers' Liability (Compulsory Insurance)(Amendment) Regulations 1974 (SI 1974/208) and s 3 of the Industrial Tribunals Act 1996 respectively.

H2 Health and safety

Scope

6.64 This reservation covers the health and safety of workers including the control of certain hazardous substances. Its scope is determined by reference to the subject-matter of Parts I and II of the Health and Safety at Work etc Act 1974. Part I of the 1974 Act[1] makes provisions for the general purposes of securing the health, safety and welfare of persons at work, protecting persons other than persons at work against the risks to health or safety arising out of or in connection with the activities of persons at work, controlling the keeping and use of explosive or highly flammable or otherwise dangerous substances etc. It also provides for health and safety regulations, imposes a range of statutory duties, establishes the Health and Safety Commission and the Health and Safety Executive and sets out their functions. Part II makes provision for an employment medical advisory service and confers certain functions relating to that service on the Commission and Executive.

Exception

Public safety in relation to non-reserved matters is excepted. As such, the Scottish Parliament has legislative competence to deal with matters such as food safety and safety at sporting venues.

Executive devolution

Nothing specific proposed.

1 As extended or applied by s 36 of the Consumer Protection Act 1987 (fairgrounds), ss 1–2 of the Offshore Safety Act 1992 (offshore and gas safety), s 117(7) of the Railways Act 1993 (in relation to railway safety).

H3 Job search and support

Scope

6.65 This reservation covers matters relating to the provision of advice and support, including financial support, to assist people to select, obtain training for and obtain and retain employment or to assist people to obtain suitable employees. It does so by reference to the subject-matter of the Disabled Persons (Employment) Act 1944 and the Employment and Training Act 1973 except as it relates to training for employment. As a result, the Employment Service continues to be responsible for training and assisting potential employees and employers.

Exception

Sections 8 to 10A of the 1973 Act which relate to career services are excepted from this reservation. These sections confer a duty on the Secretary of State to secure the provision of career services for school and certain college students and a power to arrange the provision of such services for others. This duty is devolved to the Scottish Ministers and the Scottish Parliament has the power to legislate on careers guidance services.

Also excepted is the subject-matter of sections 2(3)(c) and 12 of Part I of the Enterprise and New Towns (Scotland) Act 1990 which give Scottish Enterprise and Highlands and Islands Enterprise duties relating to providing assistance to people seeking work. In order to ensure that the Scottish Parliament has legislative competence over these activities and in accordance with the general devolution of economic development and training matters, the provision of schemes for giving job support and training by bodies carrying on activities only in Scotland is excepted from the reservation.

Executive devolution

Nothing specific proposed.

Head J Health and medicines

J1 Abortion

Scope

6.66 Legislative competence relating to abortion is reserved. The Scottish Parliament cannot make statutory provisions to alter the criminal law relating to abortion in Scotland or any provision in the Abortion Act 1967, such as to alter the circumstances in which an abortion may lawfully be carried out.

Exception

None listed[1].

Executive devolution

It is likely that two of the executive functions exercised by the Secretary of State under the 1967 Act will be devolved to the Scottish Ministers. These are the power to approve places where a termination of pregnancy may be carried out and the power to make regulations in regard to the certification of medical opinions, notice to the Chief Medical Officer in Scotland and restricting the disclosure of patient information.

1 Note however, that under Schedule 4, the Parliament can legislate to modify Scots private law and this in turn can affect a reserved matter such as abortion so long as the law is not special to a reserved matter and applies consistently to reserved and devolved matters. An example would be a law relating to the date of acquisition of human personality. If however, the Secretary of State believed that the provision would adversely affect the law relating to abortion (for example the Abortion Act 1967) he would have the power to intervene under s 35 and prevent the Bill from becoming law.

J2 Xenotransplantation

Scope

6.67 Xenotransplantation is the transplantation of viable organs or other tissues (e g bone marrow) from animals to humans or the use of viable animal tissue extra-corporeally, perhaps as part of a medical device. All matters pertaining to xenotransplantation are reserved to the United Kingdom Parliament.

Exception

None.

Executive devolution

Nothing specific proposed.

J3 Embryology, surrogacy and genetics

Scope

6.68 This Section actually sets out three separate reserved matters. The first reservation covers surrogacy arrangements as defined by the Surrogacy Arrangements Act 1985 and the subject-matter of that Act. A surrogate mother under the 1985 Act is a woman who carries a child in pursuance of an arrangement made before she began to carry the child and made with a view to handing that child over, with the parental rights being exercised by another person. The arrangement is a surrogacy arrangement if, were a woman to whom the arrangement relates to carry a child in pursuance of it, she would be a surrogate mother. The Act prohibits third parties from initiating or negotiating surrogacy arrangements on a commercial basis and provides for related matters. It does not deal with the legality under common law of surrogacy arrangements. Surrogacy is not an offence in the criminal law of Scotland, but section 36(1) of the Human Fertilisation and Embryology Act 1990 amended the 1985 Act to the effect that no surrogacy arrangement is enforceable. The 1990 Act also makes provision as to the parentage of children born as the result of surrogacy arrangements; these confer a power on the courts to make an order providing for a child born as a result of a surrogacy arrangement to be treated in law as the child of the couple who commissioned the surrogate mother to carry the child. Thus, this aspect of parentage, which is normally a matter for Scots private law, is not devolved to the Scottish Parliament.

The second reservation covers the subject-matter of the Human Fertilisation and Embryology Act 1990 which deals principally with: the regulation of the creation, keeping or using of human embryos or gametes outside the body; the regulation of any activities relating to the above including research or the provision of infertility treatment services; and the definition of parents of any child being or having been carried by a woman as the result of the placing in her an embryo or of eggs and sperm or her artificial insemination. The Act also establishes the Human Fertilisation and Embryology Authority which regulates such research and treatment.

The third reservation covers all remaining matters relating to human genetics. This includes research, testing or treatment concerning the human genome, or genetic disorders including gene therapy research and all matters relating to the social, ethical and economic consequences of human genetics such as providing genetic testing for insurance or employment purposes.

Exception

None.

Executive devolution

It is suggested that the power to make regulations under section 30(9) of the 1990 Act in connection with parental orders in favour of sperm and egg donors (applying provisions relating to adoption) be transferred to the Scottish Ministers[1].

1 The Parental Orders (Human Fertilisation and Embryology) (Scotland) Regulations 1994 (SI 1994/2804) currently cover these matters.

J4 Medicines, medical supplies and poisons

Scope

6.69 This reservation pertains to the control and safety of medicines and medical supplies. Specifically, the subject-matter of the following enactments is reserved:

1 the Medicines Act 1968, the Marketing Authorisations for Veterinary Medicinal Products Regulations 1994 and the Medicines for Human Use (Marketing Authorisations Etc) Regulations 1994[1] which together regulate the manufacture, distribution, importation, marketing, sale and supply of medicines and medical supplies for both human and animal use. Various bodies are established to regulate and advise Ministers on the safety of medicinal products such as the Medicines Commission, the Committee on Safety of Medicines and the Veterinary Products Committee;
2 the Poisons Act 1972 which provides for the regulation of the sale and storage of non-medicinal poisons within Great Britain, the categorisation of poisons and determination of who may sell certain poisons; and
3 the Biological Standards Act 1975 which establishes the National Biological Standards Board whose main duties are to set standards for and to test the purity and potency of biological substances such as vaccines, anti-bodies, hormones and blood products.

Also reserved is the regulation of prices charged for medical supplies or medicinal products which are supplied for the purposes of the National Health Service in Scotland[2].

Exception

None.

Executive devolution

It is proposed that by an order under section 63, the Scottish Ministers be given the duty to enforce or secure the enforcement of any provisions in the 1968 Act and of any regulations or orders made in relation to it; and the power to make regulations to grant the Pharmaceutical Society of Great Britain or a local authority the power to enforce any regulations dealing with medicinal products[3].

1 SIs 1994/3142 and 1994/3144.
2 As established under s 1 of the National Health Service (Scotland) Act 1978.
3 These powers are set out in s 109(1)(2) and s 109(3) of the 1968 Act respectively.

J5 Welfare foods

Scope

6.70 This Section reserves schemes for the distribution of welfare foods set out in regulations made under section 13 of the Social Security Act 1988. For example, nutritional supplements, such as liquid cow's milk, dried milk and vitamins, are provided to expectant and breast-feeding mothers and children under the age of five. Eligibility for the scheme is dependent upon entitlement to certain income-related benefits and so is closely linked to social security schemes. Other schemes exist for children under 5 in day care and for children aged between 5 and 15 who are unable because of a physical or mental disability to attend school.

Exception

None.

Executive devolution

Nothing specific proposed.

Head K Media and culture

K1 Broadcasting

Scope

6.71 This Section reserves the subject-matter of the Broadcasting Acts 1990 and 1996. The result is that all regulatory responsibilities relating to television and radio broadcasting are reserved including the functions of regulatory bodies such as the Independent Television Commission, the Radio Authority and the Broadcasting Standards Commission.

The Section also reserves the British Broadcasting Corporation which operates under its Royal Charter and is also subject to some of the provisions of the Broadcasting Acts.

Exception

None listed.

Executive devolution

It is anticipated that section 63 orders will be used to ensure that the power of the Secretary of State for Culture, Media and Sport to appoint those members of the ITC, the Radio Authority and the Broadcasting Standards Commission who make the interests of Scotland their special care will be exercisable only after consultation with the Scottish Ministers and that certain functions which relate to the funding of Gaelic broadcasting will be transferred to the Scottish Ministers[1]. Administrative arrangements are likely to be made to ensure that Scottish Ministers are consulted on future appointments of the National Governor for Scotland of the BBC.

1 See para 1 of Schedule 1 to the 1990 Act and s 183 of the 1990 Act respectively.

K2 Public lending right

Scope

6.72 This Section reserves the public lending right by reference to the subject-matter of the Public Lending Right Act 1979 which establishes the framework for a scheme whereby payments are made to authors in respect of copies of their books which are lent out to the public by public libraries. Annual payments to authors are based on loans of their books in a sample of United Kingdom library authorities. The 1979 Act also provides for the appointment of the Registrar of Public Lending Right who administers the scheme.

Exception

None.

Executive devolution

Nothing specific proposed.

K3 Government Indemnity Scheme

Scope

6.73 The Government Indemnity Scheme is set out in sections 16 and 16A of the National Heritage Act 1980 and is designed to encourage public access to works of art and other objects on loan, by relieving museums, galleries, libraries etc of the cost of commercial insurance. This is achieved through an undertaking to indemnify the lender for the loss of or damage to the object loaned. Legislative competence in respect of the subject-matter of these provisions in the 1980 Act is reserved to the Westminster Parliament.

Exception

None.

Executive devolution

It is proposed that the executive powers conferred on the Secretary of State to undertake to indemnify under section 16 of the 1980 Act be transferred to a Scottish Minister insofar as they relate to institutions or bodies in Scotland and that an amendment be made to section 16A of the 1980 Act so as to require a Scottish Minister to make a report to the Scottish Parliament in respect of the working of the scheme in Scotland. All of this will be achieved by an order under section 63 of the Scotland Act.

K4 Property accepted in satisfaction of tax

Scope

6.74 This reservation ensures that the Commissioners of Inland Revenue under the Inheritance Act 1984 will continue to be able to accept land, books, works of art and other items in satisfaction of liability to inheritance tax or interest thereon. This Section reserves the subject-matter of sections 8 and 9 of the National Heritage Act 1980 which set out the powers of Ministers to direct how certain property or works of art accepted by the Inland Revenue should be disposed of and to pay the Commissioners of the Inland Revenue sums equal to the amounts of tax concerned.

Exception

None.

Executive devolution

Despite this reservation it is proposed that the existing Ministerial powers in regard to directing how property accepted by the Inland Revenue should be disposed of and determining whether a particular item of property should be accepted by the Inland Revenue[1] will be executively devolved to the Scottish Ministers in so far as they are exercisable in or as regards Scotland.

1 See s 9 of the National Heritage Act 1980 and s 230 of the Inheritance Tax Act 1984.

Head L Miscellaneous

L1 Judicial remuneration

Scope

6.75 This Section reserves the determination of the salaries of Judges of the Court of Session, Sheriffs Principal and Sheriffs, members of the Lands Tribunal for Scotland and the Chairman of the Scottish Land Court. This Section reserves only the determination of the level of salaries of the holders of these specified judicial appointments. The Scottish Ministers are responsible for paying the salaries from the Scottish Consolidated Fund. The determination and payment of judicial pensions is reserved as a consequence of the reservation of occupational and personal pensions in Section F3 of this Schedule.

Exception

None.

Executive devolution

Nothing specific proposed.

L2 Equal opportunities

Scope

6.76 This Section reserves equal opportunities including the subject-matter of the following enactments:

1 the Equal Pay Act 1970 which makes provisions for the elimination of discrimination on the grounds of sex in relation to the terms and conditions of employment including pay;
2 the Sex Discrimination Act 1975 which makes provisions for the prevention or elimination of discrimination on the grounds of sex (women, men, transsexuals) or marital status and establishes the Equal Opportunities Commission;
3 the Race Relations Act 1976 which provides for the elimination of discrimination on racial grounds and establishes the Commission for Racial Equality; and
4 the Disability Discrimination Act 1995 which provides for the elimination of discrimination against disabled persons in connection with employment and the provision of goods, facilities, and services and the disposal or management of premises. It also establishes the National Disability Council.

The interpretation provision at the end of the Section defines 'equal opportunities' to be the prevention, elimination or regulation of discrimination between persons on grounds of sex, or marital status, on racial grounds, or on grounds of disability, age, sexual orientation, language or social origin or of other personal attributes, including beliefs or opinions such as religious beliefs or political opinions[1].

Exception

Two exceptions exist to this reservation. First, the Scottish Parliament can legislate on matters to encourage the observance of equal opportunity requirements. However, it cannot use prohibition or regulation to do so. The Parliament can allocate financial and other resources to the encouragement of equal opportunities.

Secondly, the Scottish Parliament may legislate to impose duties on any office-holder of the Scottish Administration or any Scottish public authorities with functions relating to mixed or devolved matters to make arrangements with a view to securing that their functions are carried out with due regard to the need to meet the equal opportunity requirements[2]. The Parliament may also impose similar duties on cross-border public authorities in regard to their Scottish functions[3]. Under this exception the Parliament could develop schemes to secure better provision of services to certain groups who may be the subject of discrimination.

Executive devolution

It is anticipated that the power of the Secretary of State under the Education (Scotland) Act 1980 including the powers to enforce duties under the 1976 Act and to call for a local inquiry will be transferred to the Scottish Ministers by an order under section 63. Also one member of each of the Equal Opportunities Commission, the Commission for Racial Equality and the National Disability Council is to be appointed with the agreement of the Scottish Ministers.

1 Note that the subject-matter of Part V of the 1995 Act which deals with standards for public passenger transport of disabled people is also expressly reserved under E5 (Transport – Other Matters).
2 'Equal opportunity requirements' are defined in the interpretation provisions of this section to mean the requirements of the law for the time being relating to equal opportunities.
3 'Scottish functions' are defined in the interpretation provisions of this Section to mean functions which are exercisable in or as regards Scotland and which do not relate to reserved matters.

L3 Control of weapons

Scope

6.77 This Section reserves the control of nuclear, biological, chemical and any other weapon of mass destruction as distinct from other weapons, such as firearms[1].

Exception

None.

Executive devolution

Nothing specific proposed.

1 See for example matters covered under the Biological Weapons Act 1974 and the Chemical Weapons Act 1996.

L4 Ordnance Survey

Scope

6.78 This Section reserves the Ordnance Survey (OS), the national mapping organisation for Great Britain and the Isle of Man. Specifically, legislative competence is reserved by reference to the subject-matter of the Ordnance Survey Act 1841 which confers functions on the Secretary of State (for Environment, Transport and the Regions) in respect of the survey of Great Britain and the Isle of Man by virtue of which the OS Department prepares the OS maps.

Exception

None.

Executive devolution

Nothing specific proposed.

L5 Time

Scope

6.79 This Section reserves: the designation of the time scale and time zones used in the United Kingdom and matters related to them, such as Greenwich Mean Time; the determination of units of time such as minutes, hours, days and years and the calendar generally; the determination of the date of Easter pursuant to the Easter Act 1928; and the determination of summer time under the Summer Time Act 1972.

Exception

The computation of periods of time for any purpose is excepted from this reservation. For example, the Scottish Parliament has legislative competence to deal with the calculation and determination of when obligations expire or become unenforceable for the purposes of the civil law.

Also excepted is the subject-matter of section 1 of the Banking and Financial Dealings Act 1971 which provides for the setting of dates for bank holidays and the Term and Quarter Days (Scotland) Act 1990 which sets out for Scotland the dates of term days used in legal documents made under Scots law such as leases. The term days are Whitsunday and Martinmas: 28 May and 28 November respectively and the quarter days are Candlemas and Lammas: 28 February and 28 August.

Executive devolution

Nothing specific proposed.

L6 Outer space

Scope

6.80 This reservation extends to all matters related to the regulation of activities in outer space[1]. In addition, the negotiation of international agreements relating to outer space would fall within the reservation of foreign affairs under Part I, Paragraph 7 of this Schedule.

Exception

None.

Executive devolution

Nothing specific proposed.

1 See for example the Outer Space Act 1986.

7 The Scottish Administration

INTRODUCTION

7.1 Part II of the Act creates a Scottish Administration which will constitute the government of Scotland in respect of devolved matters. It will assume the functions of the Scottish Office and associated departments. The Scottish Administration will be under the direction and control of a Scottish Executive, drawn mainly from the Scottish Parliament on the Westminster model, and responsible to it for the devolved government of Scotland. The accountability of the Executive to the Parliament is underpinned by sections 45(2), 47(3) and 48(2) of the Act, which require members of the Executive to resign in the event of a motion of no confidence in it being passed by the Parliament. The enforced resignation of the Scottish Executive will lead to an extraordinary general election and the formation of a new Executive unless a new governing coalition can be found from within the Parliament.

THE SCOTTISH EXECUTIVE

7.2 The Scottish Executive will be made up of a First Minister, Ministers appointed by the First Minister, and the Lord Advocate and Solicitor General for Scotland (s 44(1)). Collectively they are referred to as 'the Scottish Ministers' (s 44(2)). The Act also makes provision for the appointment of junior Scottish Ministers, who are members of the Scottish Administration but not of the Scottish Executive. The Act prohibits members of the Scottish Executive, including junior Scottish Ministers, from holding office in the United Kingdom Government (s 44(3)).

The First Minister

7.3 The First Minister will be to all intents and purposes the Scottish Prime Minister. Under the Act the First Minister is nominated by the Parliament and appointed by the Queen on the recommendation of the Presiding Officer (ss 45(1), 46(4)). The person nominated will normally be the leader of the party able to command the support of a majority in the Parliament. Since no one party is likely to secure an outright majority of seats in the Parliament this will in all probability be based on some form of coalition. The Act makes provision for the nomination by the Parliament of one of its members for appointment as First Minister in a number of circumstances:

1 following the holding of a poll at a general election;
2 the First Minister tendering his resignation;
3 the office of the First Minister becoming vacant otherwise than in consequence of his resignation, e g in consequence of his death; and
4 the First Minister ceasing to be a member of the Parliament otherwise than by virtue of a dissolution (s 46(2)).

Once a nomination has been made, the Presiding Officer recommends to the Queen the appointment of the member nominated (s 46(4)). If a nomination is not made within the permitted period, which is normally 28 days, an extraordinary general election must be held (s 3(1)(b)). A First Minister may resign at any time, and must do so if the Parliament passes a vote of no confidence in the Scottish Executive (s 45(2)). A forced resignation will almost certainly lead to a extraordinary general election unless the majority forcing the resignation is sufficiently cohesive to form an alternative government. A voluntary resignation on the other hand need not lead to an election unless it is impossible to appoint a successor from the ruling coalition or party. Where the office is vacant or the First Minister is unable to act, the Presiding Officer may designate a member to exercise the First Minister's functions (s 45(4)). The office of First Minister is held at Her Majesty's pleasure (s 45(1)). In theory therefore the First Minister may be dismissed.

Functions of the First Minister

7.4 The responsibilities of the First Minister include:

1 the appointment and dismissal of Ministers (s 47);

2 recommending the appointment and dismissal of the Law Officers (s 48);
3 the appointment and dismissal of junior Scottish Ministers (s 49);
4 nominating the Lord President of the Court of Session and the Lord Justice Clerk (s 95(2));
5 recommending the appointment of other Court of Session judges, sheriffs and sheriffs principal (s 95(4));
6 recommending the removal of Court of Session judges and the Chairman of the Scottish Land Court (s 95(6)).

The First Minister is also the Keeper of the Scottish Seal (s 45(7))[1].

1 The Scottish Seal is the Seal appointed by the Treaty of Union to be used in place of the Great Seal of Scotland (s 2(6)).

Ministers

7.5 Ministers are appointed by the First Minister from among the members of the Parliament with the approval of the Queen and the agreement of the Parliament (s 47(1), (2)). There is no obligation on the First Minister to appoint Ministers and it would be possible therefore to have a Scottish Executive which consisted only of the First Minister and the Law Officers. Nor does the Act set any limit on the number of Ministers who may be appointed. Ministerial offices are at the disposal of the First Minister who may remove Ministers without, for example, the need to secure the Parliament's agreement (s 47(3)(b)). Together with the First Minister, Ministers must resign if the Parliament passes a vote of no confidence in the Scottish Executive (s 47(3)(c)). Since they hold office at Her Majesty's pleasure, they are also in theory liable to be dismissed by the Queen (s 47(3)(a)).

The Scottish Law Officers

7.6 Whereas Ministers are appointed by the First Minister with the approval of the Queen and the agreement of the Parliament, the Law Officers are appointed by the Queen on the recommendation of the First Minister after obtaining the agreement of the Parliament (s 48(1)). The fact that the Law Officers are appointed directly by the Queen rather than by the First Minister is not entirely without significance. Under the Act, as we have seen, the position of the Lord Advocate is entrenched: the Scottish Parliament has no power to remove the Lord Advocate from his position as head of the systems of criminal prosecution and investigation of deaths in Scotland (s 29(2)(e)). The Act also expressly provides that decisions taken by the Lord Advocate in his capacity as head of the systems of criminal prosecution and investigation of deaths in Scotland must continue to be taken by him independently of any other person (s 48(5)). These guarantees of the Lord Advocate's traditional independence are further buttressed by restrictions on his removal. The Law Officers may be removed from office, but only by the Queen acting on a recommendation from the First Minister made with the agreement of the Parliament. They thus occupy a position which is in several respects different from that of other members of the Executive.

7.7 In contrast to the other members of the Scottish Executive, there is also no requirement for the Law Officers to be drawn from among the members of the Scottish Parliament, continuing a tradition whereby they may be drawn from sympathetic members of the Scottish Bar[1]. Where they are not MSPs, they may participate in proceedings to the extent permitted by standing orders, but not vote (s 27(1))[2]. They are also subject to the same rules on the registration and declaration of interests as members of the Parliament (s 39(8)). The intention is that they should be accountable to the Scottish Parliament for their decisions, including those relating to individual cases. They may decline, however, to provide documents or to answer questions about particular criminal cases, if they consider that doing so might prejudice the proceedings in that case or would otherwise be contrary to the public interest (s 27(3)).

1 During the parliamentary proceedings on the Bill it was conceded by the Lord Advocate that there was no reason why appointments should continue to be confined to the Faculty of Advocates: 593 HL Official Report (5th series) col 2032, 28 October 1998.

2 See paras 4.22–4.23 above.

7.8 In common with other members of the Scottish Executive, the Law Officers must resign if the Parliament passes a vote of no confidence in the Scottish Executive (s 48(2)). The Act however makes provision for the Lord Advocate to remain in office until such time as he is replaced by the incoming administration, but only for the purpose of exercising his 'retained functions', i e those functions which are exercisable by the Lord Advocate alone and not by his ministerial colleagues (s 48(3)). This will secure continuity in the exercise of his retained functions during a possible change in government[1].

1 Continuity in criminal proceedings is secured by the Criminal Procedure (Scotland) Act 1995, s 287, which continues to have effect (s 48(4)). The saving is therefore for the Lord Advocate's functions in relation to civil proceedings and his other Law Officer functions.

The Advocate General for Scotland

7.9 The United Kingdom Government will continue to need constitutional and legal advice on Scottish affairs after devolution. The Act makes provision, therefore, for the appointment of an Advocate General for Scotland as the Scottish Law Officer to the United Kingdom Government (s 87). The Law Officer functions of the Lord Advocate in relation to reserved matters will be transferred to the holder of that post by a transfer of functions order made under the Ministers of the Crown Act 1975.

Junior Ministers

7.10 The Act also makes provision for the appointment of junior Scottish Ministers from among the members of the Scottish Parliament 'to assist the Scottish Ministers in the exercise of their functions' (s 49(1)). In contrast to Ministers, junior Scottish Ministers are not members of the Scottish Executive. This means that they are unable to exercise functions conferred on the Scottish Ministers. Like Ministers, junior Ministers are appointed by the First Minister with the approval of the Queen and the agreement of the Parliament (s 49(1), (3)). They may be removed from office by the First Minister, and they must resign if the Parliament passes a vote of no confidence in the Scottish Executive. Since they hold office at Her Majesty's pleasure they are also in theory liable to be dismissed by the Queen (s 49(4)).

Defects in appointment

7.11 The Act provides that the validity of acts of members of the Scottish Executive, including junior Scottish Ministers, is not affected by any defect in the parliamentary proceedings relating to their appointment (s 50). This will prevent arguments being raised before the courts about whether, for example, Parliament did or did not agree to a particular appointment. In this respect as in others the Act evinces an intention that the Parliament should have the final say in matters of its own procedure.

Remuneration

7.12 The remuneration (salaries, allowances and pension arrangements) of members of the Scottish Executive, including junior Scottish Ministers, is a matter for the Scottish Parliament (s 81). Section 83 of the Act requires information about the sums paid to members of the Scottish Executive to be published for each financial year.

Oaths

7.13 A member of the Scottish Executive is required to take the official oath in the form provided by the Promissory Oaths Act 1868 and to take the oath of allegiance (s 84(4))[1]. The official oath is the same oath as is sworn by Ministers of the Crown: 'I do swear that I will well and truly serve Her Majesty Queen Elizabeth in the Office of . . . so help me God'. The oath of allegiance is the same as is used in the Westminster Parliament: 'I do swear that I will be faithful and bear true allegiance to Her Majesty Queen Elizabeth, her heirs and successors, according to law. So help me God'. Junior Scottish Ministers must take the oath of allegiance (s 84(5)). The Scottish Ministers including the Lord Advocate, the Solicitor General and the junior Scottish Ministers are not required to take the oath of allegiance on their appointment if they have already taken it as MSPs. The Lord Advocate and the Solicitor General will have to take the oath if they are not members of the Scottish Parliament. A member of the Scottish Executive who has not taken an oath as required by section 84 cannot be paid a salary or any other form of remuneration (s 83(2))[2].

1 An affirmation can be made in place of the oath (Oaths Act 1978, s 5).
2 See para 3.2 above.

Jury service

7.14 Members of the Scottish Executive and junior Scottish Ministers are exempt from jury service in Scotland and England

and Wales (s 85). Exemption from jury service in Northern Ireland is to be effected by making equivalent amendments to the Juries (Northern Ireland) Order 1996[1].

1 SI 1996/1141.

THE SCOTTISH ADMINISTRATION

7.15 The Scottish Executive will have charge of the Scottish Administration. The Act defines the Scottish Administration as the office-holders in the Scottish Administration and the members of staff of the Scottish Administration (s 126(6)). The office-holders in the Scottish Administration comprise the members of the Scottish Executive, junior Scottish Ministers and various holders of non-ministerial office. The latter include the Registrar General of Births, Marriages and Deaths for Scotland, the Keeper of the Registers of Scotland and the Keeper of the Records of Scotland, who are specified in the Act as forming part of the Scottish Administration. The other non-ministerial office holders such as the Accountant in Bankruptcy and the Chief Social Work Inspector will be specified by Order in Council (s 126(8)).

Structure

7.16 The Act does not prescribe the structure of the Scottish Administration, treating it as a matter for the Scottish Executive itself. Under the Act the functions transferred or conferred on the Scottish Ministers will be capable of being exercised by any of them (s 53(2)). The First Minister will therefore enjoy almost complete freedom in the allocation of ministerial portfolios untrammelled by the vesting of functions in particular Ministers. The main exceptions are the Lord Advocate's 'retained functions', which will not be exercisable by other members of the Executive[1]. One consequence of this will be to prevent the setting up of a Ministry of Justice, unless it is under the direction of the Lord Advocate. It is assumed that the Scottish Administration will be made up of a maximum of nine or ten ministerial departments.

1 For the Lord Advocate's retained functions, see para 7.20 below.

Staff

7.17 The Act empowers the Scottish Ministers to appoint members of staff of the Scottish Administration (s 51(1)). The staff of the Scottish Administration do not become members of a separate Scottish Civil Service, but remain members of the Home Civil Service (s 51(2)). In recent years the responsibility for the management of the civil service has been substantially devolved to departments and agencies in the exercise of the powers conferred by the Civil Service (Management Functions) Act 1992. The Scotland Act empowers the Minister for the Civil Service, i e the Prime Minister, who is responsible for the civil service under the Civil Service Order in Council 1995, to delegate civil service management functions to the Scottish Ministers (s 51(4)). In the appointment and management of staff, the Scottish Ministers and office holders in charge of departments of the Scottish Administration will be subject to the same requirements as ministers and office holders in charge of Great Britain or United Kingdom departments. In particular, they will be subject to the Civil Service Management Code[1], which sets out the 'key principles' which apply to the recruitment and management of staff throughout the service, together with 'a minimum framework of centrally-determined rules', which all departments and agencies are required to apply directly to their staff[2]. The Scottish Parliament itself has no power to legislate for the Civil Service (Sch 5, Part 1, para 8).

1 The Code is issued under the (prerogative) Civil Service Order in Council 1995.
2 *The Civil Service: Continuity and Change* (Cm 2627, 1994) para 2.35.

MINISTERIAL FUNCTIONS

7.18 Statutory functions may be conferred on the Scottish Ministers, the First Minister or the Lord Advocate. Where Acts of Parliament confer functions on 'the Secretary of State', they may be exercised by any Secretary of State unless they are conferred on a named Secretary of State[1]. So, too, functions conferred on the Scottish Ministers may be exercised by any member of the Scottish Executive (s 53(2)). Although the functions of the Scottish Ministers may thus be exercised individually rather than collectively, the Act expressly provides that acts of individual members of the Executive are binding on all of them (s 52(4)). The Executive cannot therefore disavow responsibility for the acts and omissions of its members. The principle that functions conferred on the Scottish Ministers may be exercised by any member of the Executive does to extend to functions conferred on the First Minister alone and the retained functions of the Lord Advocate, which on normal administrative law principles must be exercised by them and no-one else. Nor are their acts attributable to the Executive as whole (s 52(5)). Statutory functions of the Scottish Ministers, the First Minister, and the Lord Advocate are exercisable on behalf of the Crown (s 52(2)).

1 The rule is illustrated in *Agee v Lord Advocate* 1977 SLT (Notes) 54.

General transfer of functions

7.19 It will be open to the Scottish (and United Kingdom) Parliament to confer functions on the Scottish Ministers, the First Minister and the Lord Advocate. In time such functions will account for the bulk of the functions exercised by the Scottish Ministers. At the outset, however, the Scottish Minister's functions will be transferred from United Kingdom Ministers. The Act transfers the exercise of existing ministerial functions 'within devolved competence' to the Scottish Ministers (s 53(1)). The concept of 'devolved competence' is defined by reference to the legislative competence of the Scottish Parliament (s 54). The effect is to transfer functions to the extent that it would be within the legislative competence of the Scottish Parliament to confer such functions on the Scottish Ministers. The functions which will transfer therefore are those functions which are exercisable in or as regards Scotland and which do not relate to the reserved matters listed in Schedule 5. The Act enables provision to be made by subordinate legislation for the separate exercise of functions within devolved competence as a preliminary to their transfer to the Scottish Ministers (s 106). Section 53 of the Act should be read in conjunction with section 117, which provides that for the purposes of the exercise of functions within devolved competence, pre-commencement enactments are to be read as if references to Ministers of the Crown were, or included, references to the Scottish Ministers. This means that where an existing enactment refers to the Secretary of State it will be necessary to check carefully whether this still means the Secretary of State or should be read as referring to the Scottish Ministers since the function in question falls within devolved competence, or has been transferred by executive devolution order[1].

1 See para 7.22 below.

The Lord Advocate's retained functions

7.20 The only functions within devolved competence which are not transferred to the Scottish Ministers are the Lord Advocate's 'retained functions' (s 53(2)). The Lord Advocate's retained functions are those functions which he exercised as a Minister of the Crown immediately before devolution and those which are conferred by statute on him alone (s 52(6)). They consist primarily of his responsibilities for the investigation and prosecution of crimes and offences, the investigation of deaths and his Law Officer functions. Those functions do not become part of the general pool of functions exercisable by members of the Scottish Executive, but continue to be exercisable only by the Lord Advocate.

Shared functions

7.21 As a general rule transferred functions are no longer exercisable within devolved competence by United Kingdom Ministers (s 53(1)). They are exercisable by the Scottish Ministers rather than Ministers of the Crown. Section 56 of the Act, however, makes provision for the concurrent exercise of powers, i e the exercise of powers by United Kingdom as well as Scottish Ministers, under a number of enactments. This will enable the United Kingdom government to continue, for example: to provide grants or loans for transport infrastructure or services; to impose levies on industry for funding scientific research, promotion of exports and improving design; to fund scientific research and related matters; to provide financial assistance to industry; and to promote and fund road safety measures. The list of shared functions concurrently exercisable may be extended by subordinate legislation (s 56(2)). Section 57 provides for a further exception in respect of powers exercisable for the purposes set out in section 2(2) of the European Communities Act 1972, i e for the purposes of implementing Community obligations or of dealing with matters arising out of such obligations[1]. The Act also makes provision for the joint exercise by United Kingdom Ministers and the Scottish Ministers of powers to establish, maintain or abolish bodies which have functions in relation to both devolved and reserved matters (s 56(4)).

1 See paras 7.30–7.32 below.

Executive devolution

7.22 'Executive devolution' is the term used to describe the transfer to the Scottish Ministers of functions in relation to reserved matters, i e matters for which legislative competence is reserved to Westminster. The Act makes provision for the transfer of such functions by executive devolution order to the Scottish Ministers (s 63). The Scottish Parliament will have no power to make laws in relation to the functions transferred, but the functions, including the power to make subordinate legislation, will be exercisable in or as regards Scotland by the Scottish Ministers. Functions may be transferred on the basis that they are exercisable by the Scottish Ministers instead of, or concurrently with, the United Kingdom Ministers in whom they are vested. In the latter case, they may continue to be exercised in or as regards Scotland by United Kingdom Ministers. The draft Transfer of Functions (Scottish Ministers) Order 1999 lists those reserved functions which it is proposed should be exercisable in or as regards Scotland by the Scottish Ministers instead of, or concurrently with, United Kingdom Ministers. They include, for example, functions relating to betting, gaming and lotteries, firearms licensing, extradition, funding Gaelic broadcasting, appointments to tribunals, powers and duties in respect of electricity supply, roads and airports, the running of public sector pension schemes and the approving of places where abortions may be carried out[1]. Functions are transferable by agreement: executive devolution orders require the approval of both the United Kingdom and the Scottish Parliaments[2]. The Act enables provision to be made by subordinate legislation for the separate exercise of functions within devolved competence as a preliminary to their executive devolution to the Scottish Ministers (s 106).

1 Chapter 6 above notes those functions which it is proposed should be executively devolved.
2 Executive devolution orders are subject to affirmative resolution procedure in both the Scottish and United Kingdom Parliaments (Sch 7).

Inter-governmental consultation and agreement

7.23 The exercise of functions conferred on United Kingdom Ministers may be conditional on consultation or agreement with other United Kingdom Ministers. The exercise of a power by the Secretary of State for Social Security, for example, may be conditional on Treasury agreement. The retention of such requirements where functions are devolved would obviously defeat the purpose of devolution. Where therefore the legislation or other instrument governing transferred functions requires United Kingdom Ministers to be consulted or their agreement to be secured as a condition of their valid exercise, such requirements as a general rule cease to apply (ss 55(1), 63(2)). Where functions are transferred by section 53 of the Act, all such requirements cease to apply with the sole exception of the designation of enterprise zones, which, because of the tax privileges conferred by such status, continues to require Treasury consent (s 55(2)). Where functions are transferred by executive devolution order under section 63, existing requirements as to consultation or agreement no longer apply unless express provision is made saving the requirement (s 63(2)). An executive devolution order can make the exercise of functions transferred by the order conditional upon the agreement of or consultation with a United Kingdom Minister or other person (s 63(3)). The draft Transfer of Functions (Scottish Ministers) Order 1999 lists those devolved functions which it is proposed should be exercisable by the Scottish Ministers only with the agreement of, or after consultation with, United Kingdom Ministers.

7.24 Where functions are reserved, i e where they continue to be exercisable in or as regards Scotland by United Kingdom Ministers, their exercise may be made subject to the agreement of or consultation with the Scottish Ministers by executive devolution order made under section 63 of the Act. The Act enables provision to be made, by executive devolution order, for the exercise of reserved functions in or as regards Scotland only with the agreement of, or after consultation with, the Scottish Ministers (s 63(1)(c)). This power will be used to ensure that account is taken of the interests of the Scottish Executive and Scottish Parliament in reserved matters. The draft Transfer of Functions (Scottish Ministers) Order 1999 lists those reserved functions which it is proposed should be exercisable by United Kingdom Ministers in or as regards Scotland only with the agreement of, or after consultation with, the Scottish Ministers.

Agreed re-distribution of functions

7.26 The Act also makes provision for the 'reverse transfer' of functions from the Scottish Ministers to the United Kingdom

Government by Order in Council made with the agreement of the Scottish and Westminster Parliaments. This will enable the resumption of devolved functions following, for example, an extension of the list of reserved matters or an agreement to vary the functions that are exercisable by the Scottish Ministers under executive devolution. Functions may be resumed on the basis that they are exercisable by United Kingdom Ministers instead of, or concurrently with, members of the Scottish Executive. Alternatively, functions may continue to be exercisable by members of the Scottish Executive, but only with the agreement of, or after consultation with United Kingdom Ministers (s 108(1)). The power to resume functions does not extend to the functions exercisable by the Lord Advocate before he ceased to be a Minister of the Crown (s 108(4)).

Agency arrangements

7.26 The Act enables the Scottish Ministers and Ministers of the Crown to make arrangements to exercise certain functions on each other's behalf (s 93(1)). The functions which may be the subject of such arrangements do not include those of making, confirming or approving subordinate legislation (s 93(3)). Where arrangements are made, ministerial responsibility for the exercise of the functions concerned remains unaffected (s 93(2)). It is expected that such arrangements will be used, for example, to permit the Ministry of Agriculture, Fisheries and Food to carry out certain functions in relation to animal health and welfare.

Limits

7.27 The Act also defines the limits to the powers of the Scottish Ministers. The key restriction is that they have no power to make subordinate legislation or take executive action which is outside their 'devolved competence', which is defined in terms of the legislative competence of the Scottish Parliament (ss 53(1), 54). They thus have no power to make subordinate legislation or take executive action:

(1) with extra-territorial effect;
(2) in relation to reserved matters, save insofar as the power to do so has been specifically conferred on them by executive

devolution order under section 63 of the Act. They also have a limited power to modify Scots private or criminal law in its application to reserved matters, but only for the purpose of making the law in question consistent in its application to reserved and devolved matters (s 29(4));

(3) which would be in breach of the restrictions in Schedule 4[1];

(4) which is incompatible with Convention rights, as defined in the Human Rights Act 1998[2], or with 'Community law'[3], a prohibition which is restated by section 57(2) of the Act;

(5) which would remove the Lord Advocate from his position as head of the systems of criminal prosecution and investigation of deaths in Scotland (s 29(2)).

1 See paras 5.7–5.20 above.
2 Human Rights Act 1998, s 1(1).
3 'Community law' is defined by section 126(9) of the Scotland Act 1998.

7.28 It is also implicit in the scheme of the Act that the Scottish Ministers have no power to make subordinate legislation or take executive action which is incompatible with the United Kingdom's 'international obligations'. The Act defines international obligations as those of the United Kingdom other than obligations to observe and implement Community law or Convention rights (s 126(9)). In contrast to a breach of Convention rights or of Community law, a breach of the United Kingdom's international obligations is administratively rather than legally enforceable[1]. Ministers also have no power to make subordinate legislation which is incompatible with the interests of defence or national security.

1 See paras 7.30–7.33 below.

Enforcement of limits

7.29 The Act contemplates that legal proceedings will provide the normal mechanism of enforcing the limits on the Scottish Ministers. Legal proceedings are discussed in chapter 8 below. The Act, however, makes provision for ministerial intervention by the Secretary of State[1] in three types of case:

1 *International obligations*. An alleged breach by the Scottish Executive of the United Kingdom's international obligations cannot be the subject of legal proceedings[2]. Where, however, the Secretary of State has reasonable grounds to believe that action, including legislative action, which a member of the

Scottish Executive proposes to take would be incompatible with the United Kingdom's international obligations, he may by order direct that the proposed action should not be taken (s 58(1)). He may also revoke subordinate legislation made by the Scottish Executive, or which could be revoked by the Scottish Executive, where it contains provisions which he has reasonable grounds to believe are incompatible with the United Kingdom's international obligations (s 58(4)(a)). The Act thus gives what might be termed domestic executive effect as opposed to legal effect to the United Kingdom's international obligations. This is in contrast to Convention rights and Community law which have domestic legal as well as executive effect. Civil servants, it should be noted, including civil servants working for the Scottish Administration, are bound by the Civil Service Code, which forms part of their terms and conditions of service, to comply with the law, including 'international law and treaty obligations'[3]. The Act is therefore imposing an obligation on members of the Scottish Executive which is already incumbent on civil servants.

2 *Reserved matters.* The Secretary of State has power to revoke subordinate legislation made by the Scottish Executive, or which could be revoked by the Scottish Executive, which modifies Scots private or criminal law in relation to reserved matters and which the Secretary of State has reasonable grounds to believe would have an adverse effect on the operation of the law as it applies to reserved matters (s 58(4)(b)).

3 *Defence and national security.* The Secretary of State also has power to revoke subordinate legislation made by the Scottish Executive, or which could be revoked by the Scottish Executive, which he has reasonable grounds to believe is incompatible with the interests of defence or national security (s 58(4)(a)).

An order made in the exercise of these powers must state the reasons for making the order (s 58(5)). This will facilitate judicial review of their exercise.

1 The Secretary of State for the purpose of the exercise of these powers it should be stressed may be but need not be the Secretary of State for Scotland. As with all powers conferred on 'the Secretary of State' these powers may be exercised by any Secretary of State within the United Kingdom Government.

2 In accordance with the rule that international obligations must first be incorporated if they are to have domestic legal effect: *A-G for Canada* v *A-G for Ontario* [1937] AC 326.

3 The Civil Service Code 1996, para 3. The Code is issued under the Civil Service Order in Council 1995.

Implementation of international including EU obligations

7.30 The obligation on the Scottish Executive not to do anything which is incompatible with Convention rights, Community law or the United Kingdom's international obligations more generally is complemented by an obligation to take such action as may be necessary to give effect to the United Kingdom's international, including EU, obligations in relation to devolved matters. The obligation to give effect to Convention rights is covered by the Human Rights Act 1998.

EU obligations

7.31 The Scottish Ministers are responsible for ensuring the implementation in Scotland of EU obligations which concern devolved matters. The functions transferred by section 53 of the Act are regarded as including the functions of observing and implementing obligations under Community law in relation to devolved matters (s 57(1)). For the purpose of implementing EC obligations, the Scottish Ministers have access to the powers conferred by section 2(2) of the European Communities Act 1972. These powers continue to be exercisable by United Kingdom Ministers concurrently with their Scottish counterparts (s 57(1)). This means that it will be possible to implement EC obligations on a United Kingdom-wide basis where it is agreed that this is the most convenient and sensible way in which to proceed. It also means that United Kingdom Ministers will be able to intervene to give effect to Community obligations where the Scottish Executive has failed for whatever reason to do so. Devolution does not absolve the United Kingdom Government of its responsibility for ensuring that Community law is given effect throughout the United Kingdom[1]. It was therefore regarded as essential that it retain the ability to legislate to give effect to Community obligations in Scotland where the Scottish Executive had failed to do so or had done so inadequately. Section 57(1) of the Act achieves that purpose.

1 Case 77/69 *Commission* v *Belgium* [1970] ECR 237.

International obligations

7.32 It also falls to the Scottish Executive (and Parliament) to give effect to the United Kingdom's international obligations in relation to devolved matters. Should it fail to do so, the Secretary of State is empowered to direct members of the Executive to take any action, which may extend to the introduction of legislation, which he or she has reasonable grounds to believe they are capable of taking to give effect to international obligations (s 58(2)). In contrast to a failure to give effect to Convention rights or EC obligations, a failure to give effect to the United Kingdom's international obligations cannot be the subject of domestic legal proceedings.

PROPERTY AND LIABILITIES

7.33 In addition to the transfer of functions, the Act makes provision for the transfer of property and liabilities to the Scottish Ministers and to the Lord Advocate. Sections 59 and 60 of the Act make provision for the transfer to the Scottish Ministers of the property and liabilities of the United Kingdom Government which are held or used or have been incurred for or in connection with devolved functions. They also make provision for the Scottish Ministers to be provided with rights or interests in such property where it is not being transferred. Section 61 and 62 makes analogous provision to sections 59 and 60 in relation to the Lord Advocate. The Act also makes provision for rights acquired or liabilities incurred by the First Minister (s 61(4)). Section 64 makes provision for the transfer of property and liabilities consequential on the executive devolution of functions in relation to reserved matters to the Scottish Ministers.

FINANCIAL PROVISIONS

Introduction

7.34 Part III of the Act provides for the financial arrangements for the Parliament and the Executive, and for accounting and auditing of the funds made available to them. The financial framework for the Scottish Parliament follows closely the existing arrangements for financing the Scottish Office. The White Paper proposed a continuation of the existing 'block and formula' system of funding most of Scotland's public expenditure programmes which has been followed since the late 1970s. It proposed also that the Scottish Parliament should be able to raise limited income by means of a power to vary the basic rate of income tax in Scotland[1].

1 *Scotland's Parliament* (Cm 3658) para 7.1.

The Scottish Consolidated Fund

7.35 The arrangements for financial control set out in the Act are modelled on those which apply at the United Kingdom level. The Act establishes a Scottish Consolidated Fund into which the Parliamentary grant and sums received by office-holders in the Scottish Administration are to be paid (s 64(1)-(3)), and out of which the expenditure of the Scottish Administration is to be met. The Scottish Parliament may authorise office-holders to retain receipts to set against expenditure (s 64(4)). This will allow receipts to be appropriated in aid of sums voted. It will also enable the Scottish Parliament to make provision for the net accounting of receipts in certain circumstances. Payments out of the Fund are strictly controlled. A sum may only be paid out of the Fund if: it has been charged on the Fund by an enactment (s 65(1)(a)); it is payable out of the Fund without the need for further approval by the Scotland Act itself (s 65(1)(b)); or it is paid out in accordance with rules made by or under an Act of the Scottish Parliament (i e in accordance with the Parliament's annual supply procedure) for the purpose of meeting expenditure of the Scottish administration or expenditure payable out of the Fund under any enactment (s 65(1)(c), (2)). Sums charged on or paid out of the Fund must not be applied any purposes other than those for which they were charged or paid out (s 65(3)). This requirement provides the starting point for the audit of expenditure. The Act makes provision for sums which relate to Scottish functions to be paid into or charged on or paid out of the Scottish Consolidated Fund rather than the Consolidated Fund or the National Loans Fund (s 119).

Borrowing and lending

Borrowing

7.36 The Scottish Ministers have only limited borrowing powers. The Act empowers the Scottish Ministers to borrow from the

Secretary of State sums that are required for meeting temporary shortfalls of cash, or for providing a working balance, in the Scottish Consolidated Fund (s 66). Section 67 sets a ceiling on borrowings of £500 million, which the Secretary of State may increase with the Treasury's consent. The financing of borrowings is a charge on the Scottish Consolidated Fund: this means that repayments are not subject to parliamentary approval. Section 66 also provides that members of the Executive may only borrow under that section or under powers conferred by an Act of the United Kingdom Parliament. The Scottish Parliament itself will not be able to confer additional borrowing powers on members of the Executive.

Lending

7.37 The Act prohibits members of the Scottish Executive from making loans to statutory bodies at favourable rates of interest, i e at rates of interest lower than the lowest rate determined by the Treasury in respect of similar loans made out of the National Loans Fund on the day the loan was made (s 68(1)). Public bodies are also prohibited from borrowing money under powers conferred by Acts of the Scottish Parliament in currencies other than sterling without the consent of the Scottish Ministers, given with the approval of the Treasury (s 68(2)).

Financial control, accounts and audit

The Auditor General for Scotland

7.38 The Act establishes the office of Auditor General for Scotland with functions analogous to those of the Comptroller and Auditor General in relation to United Kingdom expenditure. The Auditor General is a servant of the Parliament, not of the Executive. He is appointed by the Queen on the recommendation of the Parliament (s 69(1)). He may not be removed from office without a recommendation from the Parliament. Where a recommendation is opposed, the number of members voting in favour must be not less than two-thirds of the total number of seats for members of the Parliament (s 69(2)). Save in the preparation of accounts, the Auditor General is not subject to the direction or control of the Executive or the Parliament in the exercise of his functions (s 69(3), (4)), nor are persons auditing expenditure on his behalf (s 70(5)).

7.39 The precise details of the Auditor General's responsibilities fall to be determined by the Scottish Parliament, but the Scotland Act requires the Auditor General to be responsible, by or under an Act of the Scottish Parliament, for:

1 issuing credits for the payment of sums out of the Fund;
2 examining parliamentary accounts and certifying and reporting on them;
3 carrying out examinations into the economy, efficiency and effectiveness with which the Scottish Ministers and the Lord Advocate have used their resources in discharging their functions; and
4 carrying out examinations into the economy, efficiency and effectiveness, with which other specified persons to whom sums are paid out of the Fund have used those sums in discharging their functions (s 70(2)).

The Act also requires statutory provision to be made for the preparation of accounts; for access to documents for audit purposes; for the appointment of members of staff of the Scottish Administration as accounting officers, answerable to the Parliament for the expenditure and receipts of each element of the Scottish Administration; and for the publication and laying before Parliament of accounts and reports (s 70(1)). The Scottish Parliament's standing orders must make provision for the consideration by Parliament of reports and accounts laid before it (s 70(3)).

Repayment of existing debt

7.40 The Act makes provision for the repayment to the Scottish Ministers rather than the Secretary of State of any outstanding loans made by the Secretary of State before the passing of the Scotland Act (s 71). It interposes the Scottish Ministers between the Secretary of State and the recipients of loans so that loans fall to be repaid to the Scottish Ministers and by them to the Secretary of State rather than directly to the Secretary of State. Sums repaid to the Secretary of State fall to be paid into the National Loans Fund.

Secretary of State's accounts

7.41 The Act also makes provision for the preparation and audit of accounts of loans to the Scottish Executive. The Secretary of State is required to prepare for each financial year, in such form and manner as the Treasury may direct, an account of sums paid to and received by him from the Scottish Ministers under sections 66, 67 (short-term borrowings and their repayment) and 71 (repayments of existing debt) and to send the account to the Comptroller and Auditor General not later than the end of November in the following financial year. The Comptroller and Auditor General is required to examine, certify and report on the account and to lay a copy of it and his report before each House of Parliament (s 72).

Provision of information to the Treasury

7.42 Section 96 empowers the Treasury to require such information from the Scottish Ministers as it may reasonably specify. This will enable the Treasury to obtain such information as it may require to, for example, monitor expenditure or compile other macro-economic information on a United Kingdom basis. If the information is not within their possession or control, the Scottish Ministers are required to take all reasonable steps to comply with the requirement.

THE TAX-VARYING POWER

7.43 Part IV of the Act empowers the Scottish Parliament to increase or decrease the basic rate of income tax for Scottish taxpayers by up to no more than 3%. The tax-varying power is exercisable by resolution, which under the Scottish Parliament's standing orders may be moved only by a member of the Scottish Executive (s 74(5)). As in the Westminster Parliament, the initiative belongs to the Executive. Where a resolution is passed, the *basic* rate of income tax determined by the United Kingdom Parliament for the tax year as it applies to the income of Scottish taxpayers is varied by the amount specified in the resolution (s 73(2)). The increase or decrease does not apply to income from savings and dividends (s 73(3)). The power itself is not exercisable before the year 2000–01, i e before 6 April 2000, which is the first full tax year of the Parliament's existence (s 74(6)). The sum capable of being raised in the exercise of this power has been variously calculated at between £420 and £450 millions, which while not in itself negligible is only a minute fraction of the total expenditure of the Scottish Administration.

7.44 The Act sets out two basic conditions which tax-varying resolutions must satisfy. First, a tax-varying resolution must relate to no more than a single year of assessment (s 74(2)(a)). An increase or decrease cannot therefore be levied or foregone for the life of a Parliament. It must instead be levied or foregone annually. Second, the tax year to which the resolution applies must begin within the next twelve months (s 74(2)(a). Like the first condition, this condition prevents an administration coming to power and passing a series of resolutions covering the life of the Parliament. If the United Kingdom Parliament has not determined the basic rate for the year in question at the time the resolution is passed, the resolution has effect in relation to the rate as eventually determined, i e the rate is plus or minus the rate eventually determined. If the rate eventually determined by the United Kingdom Parliament is 22p and the Scottish Parliament has resolved to increase the rate by 3p, the basic rate of income tax payable by Scottish taxpayers will be 25p. Normally, the power is exercisable before the start of the tax year to which it relates. There is no power to vary the rate once the year has begun. Where, however, the United Kingdom Parliament determines the rate after, or less than a month before, the beginning of a tax year, i e where it has not determined the basic rate for a year before 6 March in the preceding tax year, the Scottish Parliament may vary the basic rate for that year by means of a resolution passed within one month of the United Kingdom Parliament's determination (s 74(3)).

The definition of a Scottish taxpayer

7.45 The power conferred by the Act is a power to vary the rate of income tax for 'Scottish taxpayers'. The Act provides that an individual is a Scottish taxpayer in a tax year if during that year he or she is resident in the United Kingdom for income tax purposes, and Scotland is the part of the United Kingdom with which he or she has the closest connection (s 75(1)). Scotland is the part of the United Kingdom with which a person resident in the United Kingdom for tax purposes has the closest connection if he or she satisfies one or more of the following three tests:

1 *The principal United Kingdom home in Scotland test.* There are three elements to this test. First, he or she must spend at least part of the year in Scotland. Second, for at least part of that time his or her principal United Kingdom home must be located in Scotland and he or she must make use of it as place of residence. Third, his or her principal United Kingdom home must be located in Scotland for at least as much of the year as it is not located in Scotland (s 75(2)(a), (3)). An individual's principal United Kingdom home is located in Scotland if his or her place of residence is in Scotland or, in the case of an individual with two or more places of residence in the United Kingdom, his or her main place of residence is in Scotland. 'Place' includes a place on board a vessel or other means of transport (s 75(6)). Spending six months of the year on a boat on the West Coast or in a camper van in the North West Highlands could therefore qualify an individual as a Scottish taxpayer.

2 *The number of days spent in Scotland test.* The second test is satisfied by a taxpayer if the number of days he or she spends in Scotland in the tax year equals or exceeds the number of days he or she spends elsewhere in the United Kingdom (s 75(2)(b)). A day is spent in Scotland if he or she is in Scotland at the end of the day. A day is spent elsewhere in the United Kingdom if he or she is elsewhere in the United Kingdom at the end of the day *and* it is not a day spent in Scotland, i e he or she is not in Scotland at the end of that day (s 75(4)). Going to London from Scotland for the day thus counts as a day spent in Scotland.

3 *The elected representative test.* An individual also has his or her closest connection with Scotland during a year if for the whole or part of that year he or she is an MP for a Scottish constituency, an MEP for Scotland or an MSP (s 75(2)(c)).

Accounting arrangements

7.46 Where the basic rate of income tax is increased for Scottish taxpayers, the resources available to the Scottish Ministers are increased by the appropriate amount. The Act requires the Inland Revenue to pay into the Scottish Consolidated Fund an amount equal to the estimated yield from the additional tax to be paid by Scottish taxpayers (s 77(1)).The Inland Revenue is also required to determine the amount and frequency of payments into the Fund and to notify the Scottish Ministers as soon as reasonably practicable after the resolution is passed. Provision may be made for the amounts paid to be adjusted where they are based on inaccurate estimates (s 77(5)). Where income tax is reduced for Scottish taxpayers, the resources available to the Scottish Ministers fall to be adjusted downwards by the appropriate amount. The Act requires payments to be made out of the Scottish Consolidated Fund reflecting the shortfall in the yield of income tax resulting for the reduced rate, and for those payments to be accounted for to the Consolidated Fund. As in the case of the tax increases, the Inland Revenue is required to determine the amount and frequency of payments out of the Fund and to notify the Scottish Ministers as soon as reasonably practicable after the resolution is passed. The amounts paid may be adjusted where they are based on inaccurate estimates (s 78(5)). Payments are treated as part of the gross revenues of the Inland Revenue and paid into the Consolidated Fund accordingly.

Consequential subordinate legislation

7.47 The Act empowers the Treasury to make such modifications of enactments by order as they consider necessary or expedient to take account of the Scottish Parliament's tax-varying power. In particular, an order may exclude the effect of a tax-varying resolution in relation to enactments (s 79(2)), or postpone the effect of such a resolution in relation to the operation of the PAYE system (s 75(3)). Orders may have retrospective effect from the beginning of the tax year in which they were made (s 79(4)). The interaction between the tax and social security systems is addressed by section 110 of the Act which empowers the Secretary of State for Social Security to determine by order who is to be treated as a Scottish taxpayer and the basic rate of tax payable by Scottish taxpayers for the purpose of the payment of social security benefits. This means that the payment of benefits will not be held up by uncertainty over who is or is not a Scottish taxpayer or the basic rate of tax payable by Scottish taxpayers.

Future changes to the structure of United Kingdom income tax

7.48 Section 76 makes provision to take account of future changes to the structure of United Kingdom income tax. It provides that where changes to the income tax structure are proposed which would have a significant effect on the amount of tax which could be raised or foregone by means of the tax-varying power, the Treasury must bring forward appropriate proposals for amending the power (s 76(2)). The power to make proposals is subject to a number of restrictions. First, the proposals must not involve any alteration to the essential nature of the tax-varying power. They must therefore be confined to income tax and they must not extend to income from savings or dividends (s 76(3)(a), (c)). Second the amounts of income tax capable of being raised or foregone under the amended power must so far as possible and after making due allowances for changes in the Retail Prices Index be broadly the same as would be the case under the existing power (s 76(3)(b), (4)). Third, the effects of their exercise on the after-tax income of Scottish taxpayers generally must not be significantly different from the effect of the exercise of the existing powers. They must not therefore involve any significant difference in the after-tax income of Scottish taxpayers (s 76(3)(b), (5)).

CROSS-BORDER PUBLIC AUTHORITIES

7.49 The Act makes special provision for the control and accountability of 'cross-border public authorities'. Cross-border public authorities are authorities such as the Intervention Board for Agricultural Produce or the Criminal Injuries Compensation Board which have functions in relation to both devolved and reserved matters[1]. They are to be distinguished from authorities such as the BBC or the Post Office whose functions are confined to reserved matters and authorities such as Scottish Environment Protection Agency and the Scottish Legal Aid Board whose functions are confined to devolved matters. The former remain within the competence of the Westminster Parliament and United Kingdom Ministers. The latter fall within the legislative competence of the Scottish Parliament and the devolved competence of the Scottish Ministers (Sch 5 Part III, para 1)[2]. The purpose of making special provision for the control and accountability of cross-border public authorities is to enable such authorities to continue to operate on a United Kingdom- or Great Britain-wide basis. An authority may be designated a cross-border public authority if it has, in addition to other functions, functions which are exercisable in or as regards Scotland and do not relate to reserved matters (s 88(6)). Its functions must therefore include but not be confined to devolved matters.

1 *The Scotland Bill: A Guide* (The Scottish Office December 1997) contains a list at Annex E.

2 For a list, see *The Scotland Bill: A Guide* (The Scottish Office December 1997) Annex F.

7.50 Where an authority is designated, functions which would otherwise be exercisable by the Scottish Ministers in relation to the authority are not so exercisable (s 88(1)). Instead United Kingdom Ministers are required to consult the Scottish Ministers before exercising powers of appointment etc in relation to such authorities, or powers whose exercise might affect Scotland otherwise than wholly in relation to reserved matters (s 88(2)). Reports in relation to such bodies which must be laid before the United Kingdom Parliament must also be laid before the Scottish Parliament (s 88(3)). Alternative provision for the control and accountability of cross-border public authorities, tailor-made to the circumstances of individual authorities, may be made in the exercise of the subordinate law-making powers conferred by section 89 of the Act. These powers are exercisable only after consultation with the cross-border public authority concerned[1].

1 An analogous provision allows arrangements to be made to regulate fishing in the Border rivers (s 111).

7.51 The White Paper anticipated that the Scottish Parliament would wish to continue most existing cross-border arrangements in the light of the advantages of sharing knowledge and expertise on a United Kingdom- or Great Britain-wide basis and of the greater efficiency in the use of resources[1]. It will be open to the Scottish Parliament, however, to replace them with separate Scottish arrangements. Where it decides to do so, the Act makes provision for the reorganisation of the authority and the division of its property and liabilities (s 90).

1 *Scotland's Parliament* (Cm 3658) para 2.10.

APPOINTMENT AND REMOVAL OF JUDGES

7.52 The Act provides that the Lord President of the Court of Session and the Lord Justice Clerk should continue to be appointed by Her Majesty on the recommendation of the Prime

Minister, but that the Prime Minister should act on the nomination of the First Minister rather than the Secretary of State for Scotland as at present. The First Minister is required to consult the Lord President and the Lord Justice Clerk before making a nomination (s 95(1)–(3)). Other Court of Session judges, sheriffs and sheriffs principal will be appointed by Her Majesty on the recommendation of the First Minister, rather than the Secretary of State, made after consultation with the Lord President (s 95(4)). If the Scottish Parliament establishes a Judicial Appointments Committee, the First Minister will, depending on how the Act establishing the Committee is framed, be obliged under the Scotland Act to take its recommendations into account in making recommendations or nominations for appointment (s 95(5))[1].

1 593 HL Official Report (5th Series) col 405, 6 October 1998.

7.53 The Act also makes provision for the removal of Court of Session judges and the Chairman of the Scottish Land Court. Traditionally, Court of Session judges have held office *ad vitam aut culpam*, i e for life or until fault is established, but while this would allow a judge who is no longer fit to hold office to be removed, the procedure for the removal of a judge from office has been uncertain. One suggestion has been that their removal would require an Act of Parliament[1]. Under the Bill as originally introduced a judge would have been removable by Her Majesty on the recommendation of the First Minister made with the support of a two-thirds majority of the Scottish Parliament, but this proposal attracted widespread criticism on the grounds that it did not afford the judiciary sufficient guarantees of their independence at a time when, because of their role in policing the boundaries of the Scottish Parliament and Administration's competence, their decisions would attract a much greater degree of attention and inevitably criticism than in the past. The procedure now set out in the Act was introduced in response to this criticism. Under it a judge may be removed from office by Her Majesty on the recommendation of the First Minister made with the approval of the Scottish Parliament (s 95(6)–(7)). Before requesting the Parliament to approve a recommendation for the removal of a judge, however, the First Minister must constitute a tribunal convened by a member of the Judicial Committee of the Privy Council to investigate and report on whether the judge is unfit for office by reason of inability, neglect of duty or misbehaviour (s 95(8)). The tribunal's report must then be laid before the Parliament. Only where the tribunal has concluded that the judge in question is unfit for office by reason of inability, neglect of duty or misbehaviour may the First Minister request the Parliament to approve a recommendation for his removal (s 95(10)). This procedure is broadly similar to that required for the dismissal of a sheriff, but with the addition of the need for parliamentary approval[2].

1 5 *Stair Memorial Encyclopaedia* para 664.
2 Sheriff Courts (Scotland) Act 1971, s 12; see *Stewart v Secretary of State for Scotland* 1998 SLT 385.

7.54 Section 23 exempts judges and tribunal members from the Scottish Parliament's power of summons. Under Schedule 5 the determination of senior judicial salaries and pensions are reserved matters.

SUBORDINATE LEGISLATION

7.55 The Act confers extensive subordinate law-making powers on Her Majesty in Council, Ministers of the Crown (including the Treasury), and (in one case) the Scottish Ministers. Where no provision is made as to the person by whom a subordinate law-making power is exercisable, the power may be exercised by Her Majesty by Order in Council or by a Minister of the Crown by order (s 112(1)). Such powers are referred to in the Act as 'open powers' (s 112(3)). The rationale for their conferral in this form is that it enables the arrangements for making them to be varied according to the importance of the subject matter. The procedures in the Westminster and the Scottish Parliaments to which the exercise of subordinate law-making powers are subject is set out in Schedule 7 to the Act. Some powers are subject to control by both Parliaments, others to control by the United Kingdom Parliament only.

Scope

7.56 The subordinate law-making powers conferred on United Kingdom Ministers by the Act include the power to 'modify' Acts of Parliament (s 113(5))[1]. They have no power, however, to amend the Scotland Act itself, or subordinate legislation made under it, unless power to do so is expressly conferred on them by the Act (s 113(6)). Such powers are conferred on them in relation to cross-border public authorities (s 89), legislation consequential on 'Scottish' legislation (s 104), legislation remedying *ultra vires* acts, i e acts which are outside the powers of the Scottish Parliament or Executive (s 107), the agreed re-distribution of functions (s 108) and the making of transitional provisions (s 129(1)) (s 114(1)). These powers do not extend to Schedules 4 and 5 of the Act for the modification of which special provision is made by section 30(2). United Kingdom Ministers are also empowered to make retrospective provision in the exercise of the powers conferred on them by sections 30, 58(4), 104 and 107 of the Act (s 114(2)).

1 'Modify' includes amend or repeal (s 126(1)).

'Supplementary' subordinate law-making powers

7.57 It was not thought practical to make provision for every modification of existing legislation which may be required as a result of devolution. The Act therefore empowers the United Kingdom Government to make such modifications to pre-commencement enactments, instruments or documents as appear necessary or expedient consequent on the Scotland Act by means of subordinate legislation (s 105). The Act also confers subordinate law-making power on the United Kingdom Government to make such provision as is considered necessary or expedient consequent on any provision made by or under an Act of the Scottish Parliament (s 104(1)) or under an Act of Parliament in the exercise of devolved functions (s 104(2)). This will allow the United Kingdom Government, for example, to make provision for the enforcement of the Acts of the Scottish Parliament throughout the United Kingdom where their effectiveness depends on their being so enforceable.

Exercise of devolved subordinate law-making powers

7.58 Where the exercise of subordinate law-making powers is devolved, the Act makes provision for their exercise to be subject to the same procedures in the Scottish Parliament as they would be in the Westminster Parliament (s 118).

8 Devolution and the courts

8.1 With devolution comes an enhanced role for the courts. As in most systems in which power is shared, the Scotland Act makes provision for resolving division of powers disputes between the Scottish and United Kingdom Parliaments and between the Scottish and United Kingdom Executives in the courts. As the Scotland Act limits the legislative powers of the Parliament, the provisions of Acts of the Scottish Parliament are open to judicial challenge on the grounds that they are outwith its competence[1]. Furthermore, the courts may be asked to determine whether action by a member of the Scottish Executive is outside the area of devolved executive competence. This is in addition to their normal powers of judicial review. Both of these types of questions constitute what are described in the Act as 'devolution issues'. The Law Officers may institute judicial proceedings for the determination of such issues or they may arise in the normal course of litigation between parties in any court or tribunal in the United Kingdom. The Act sets out certain common procedures to be followed when devolution issues arise in these cases in order to minimise the risk of contradictory decisions and to provide a common court of final appeal, the Judicial Committee of the Privy Council. The Act also establishes procedures for 'fast track solutions' to cure legal defects and to prevent the Scottish Parliament or Executive from acting beyond their powers.

1 See also paras 5.32–5.33 above.

DEVOLUTION ISSUES

8.2 The Act establishes special procedures for resolving devolution issues. In the absence of the procedures, these issues could only be determined in the normal course of litigation creating a risk of uncertainty and conflicting decisions. Under Schedule 6 of the Act 'devolution issues' comprise of the following six questions:

(1) whether an Act of the Scottish Parliament or any of its provisions is within the legislative competence of the Parliament;
(2) whether any function (being a function which any person has purported or is proposing to exercise) is a function of the Scottish Ministers, the First Minister or the Lord Advocate;
(3) whether a purported or proposed exercise of a function by a member of the Scottish Executive is, or would be, within devolved competence[1];
(4) whether a purported or proposed exercise of a function by a member of the Scottish Executive is, or would be, incompatible with any Convention rights or European Community law;
(5) whether a failure to act by a member of the Scottish Executive is incompatible with any Convention rights or Community law;
(6) any other question about whether a function is exercisable within devolved competence or in or as regards Scotland and any other question arising by virtue of the Act about reserved matters. This last provision is a catch-all provision which enables any question to be aired by means of the procedure laid down.

1 Section 54(2) provides that it is outside devolved competence: (a) to make any provision by subordinate legislation which would be outside the legislative competence of the Parliament if it were included in an Act of the Scottish Parliament; or (b) to confirm or approve any subordinate legislation containing such provision. Section 54(3) provides that it is outside devolved competence to exercise any other function so far as a provision of an Act of the Scottish Parliament conferring the function (or conferring it so as to be exercisable in that way) would be outside the legislative competence of the Parliament.

8.3 The legitimacy of Acts of the Scottish Parliament may be challenged even if they have not been referred to the Judicial Committee under section 33 at the time of their passing[1]. However, the validity of any proceedings leading to the enactment of an Act of the Scottish Parliament cannot be questioned in legal proceedings (s 28(5)). Unlike many federal systems[2], Acts of the United Kingdom Parliament which touch on devolved matters are not subject to any form of scrutiny. In accordance with the theory of Parliamentary sovereignty, they can not be subject to review.

1 See para 5.32 above.
2 For example, Canada and the United States.

8.4 In order to avoid disputes and reduce the need to amend legislation, section 101(2) provides that provisions of Acts and Bills of the Scottish Parliament and provisions of subordinate legislation are to be read as narrowly as is required to be within competence. If such a reading is possible, the provision is to have effect accordingly. This is the principle of efficacy and it is the normal rule of construction which courts apply in construing legislation from parliaments with limited powers. Under the principle, the courts seek to give effect to legislation rather than to invalidate it. For example, the Scottish Parliament could pass an Act empowering the Scottish Ministers to hold a referendum on any matter. In order to preserve the validity of this Act, section 102(1) requires the courts to read the Act as enabling only the holding of referendums on matters within the competence of the Parliament such as education and not in regard to reserved matters such as independence or the monarchy[1].

1 593 HL Official Report (5th series) col 1953, 28 October 1998.

8.5 Legal challenges to the validity of provisions can arise in a variety of circumstances and may involve disputes between the Scottish Executive and the United Kingdom Government[1], between an individual or company and the Scottish Executive or between two individuals. As a result, a 'devolution issue' could arise before virtually any court or tribunal. A court or tribunal may hold contentions which appear to be frivolous or vexatious as not giving rise to devolution issues (Sch 6 para 2). Provision is made in Schedule 6 to the Act for proceedings to be held in Scotland, England and Wales and Northern Ireland and for cases in each jurisdiction to be referred to the appropriate court for decision. It is expected that the majority of these cases will be held in Scotland.

1 Section 99 sets out the rights and liabilities of the Crown in different capacities.

PROCEEDINGS IN SCOTLAND

8.6 In Scotland, either the Lord Advocate or the Advocate General may initiate proceedings for the determination of a devolution issue[1]. Proceedings raised by the Advocate General may be defended by the Lord Advocate (para 4). These powers are not exclusive and devolution issues may be raised or defended by other persons, for example, as part of a wider challenge to the legality of the actions of a Scottish Minister.

1 See also para 5.32 above.

8.7 When a devolution issue arises, the court or tribunal hearing the case must order the Advocate General and Lord Advocate to be given intimation of it unless they are already party to the proceedings. Once such intimation is given, the Lord Advocate and/or Advocate General may participate in the case in regard to the devolution issue (paras 5–6).

8.8 Some courts and tribunals have the discretion to refer devolution issues to a higher court while others must refer such issues to the higher court. A tribunal from which there is no appeal must refer any devolution issue that comes before it to the Inner House of the Court of Session. A court or tribunal from which there is an appeal may choose to settle the issue itself or refer the matter to the Inner House of the Court of Session (para 8). Devolution issues which arise in civil court proceedings (other than in the House of Lords or in a court of three or more judges of the Court of Session) may be referred to the Inner House of the Court of Session. In effect, this allows devolution issues which arise in the civil proceedings in the Sheriff Court and in the Outer House of the Court of Session to be referred to the Inner House (para 7). Where a devolution issue arises in a criminal case before the district court, Sheriff Court or before a single judge in the High Court, reference may be made to a larger bench of the High Court of Justiciary (para 9).

8.9 A court consisting of three or more judges from the Court of Session or two or more judges from the High Court of Justiciary may refer a devolution issue which comes before it to the Judicial Committee. However, such a reference may not be made where the devolution issue has been referred to the court by another court (under paras 7, 8 or 9). Thus, the Inner House may only refer a devolution issue which comes before it to the Judicial Committee when it is acting as a court of first instance or an appeal court in the ordinary course. Similarly, only when a bench of two or more judges of the High Court is acting as the court of criminal appeal may it make such a reference (paras 10, 11). These provisions ensure that when a court receives such a reference they must take a decision and not simply pass the reference on.

8.10 An appeal lies to the Judicial Committee against a determination of a devolution issue made by the Inner House of the Court of Session on a reference from a court or tribunal under paragraphs 7 or 8. An appeal also lies with the Judicial Committee against the determination of a devolution issue by a bench of two or more judges of the High Court of Judiciary (sitting in ordinary course or on a reference from another court under paragraph 9) or by a court of three or more judges of the Court of Session from which there is no appeal to the House of Lords (eg the Lands Valuation Appeal Court). An appeal may only be made with the leave of the relevant court or if leave is refused, with leave of the Judicial Committee (paras 12–13).

PROCEEDINGS IN ENGLAND AND WALES

8.11 Similar provisions govern proceedings in England and Wales. The Attorney General may initiate proceedings for the determination of a devolution issue and the Lord Advocate may defend such proceedings (para 15). In civil cases, a magistrates' court may refer any devolution issue which arises before it to the High Court and other lower courts and tribunals may refer devolution issues to the Court of Appeal. Tribunals from which there is no appeal must refer devolution issues to the Court of Appeal. In criminal proceedings, courts other than the House of Lords and the Court of Appeal may refer any devolution issue which arises in summary proceedings to the High Court and issues which arise in proceedings on indictment to the Court of Appeal[1]. The Court of Appeal may refer any devolution issue which arises in proceedings before it (other than those made on a reference above) to the Judicial Committee. An appeal against a determination of a devolution issue by the High Court or the Court of Appeal lies to the Judicial Committee but only with leave of the relevant court or, if leave is refused, with leave of the Judicial Committee (paras 14–23).

1 This matches the standard appeal routes in criminal cases.

PROCEEDINGS IN NORTHERN IRELAND

8.12 In Northern Ireland, the Attorney General for Northern Ireland may initiate proceedings. A court, other than the House of Lords or the Court of Appeal in Northern Ireland, may refer a devolution issue which arises in any proceedings (criminal or civil) before it to the Court of Appeal in Northern Ireland. This court may refer any devolution issue which arises in proceedings before it (other than on a reference) to the Judicial Committee. Again, an appeal against a determination of a devolution issue made by the Court of Appeal in Northern Ireland lies to the Judicial Committee. Leave to appeal must be granted by the Court of Appeal or, if such leave is refused, leave must be sought from the Judicial Committee (paras 24–31).

PROCEEDINGS IN THE HOUSE OF LORDS

8.13 Devolution issues which arise in judicial proceedings in the House of Lords must be referred to the Judicial Committee unless the House considers it more appropriate, having regard to all the circumstances, that it should determine the issue (para 32). Thus the House has the discretion to decide the issue itself or to refer it to the Judicial Committee. Section 103(1) provides that any decision of the Judicial Committee in proceedings under the Act shall be stated in open court and shall be binding in all proceedings (other than proceedings before the Committee). Thus, the House of Lords, the highest court of appeal in the United Kingdom, is bound by decisions of the Judicial Committee on devolution issues. While on the face of it significant, the provision is likely to have little effect in practice. Under the Schedule 6 procedure described above, devolution issues will seldom be decided by the House of Lords, which in most cases will refer such issues to the Judicial Committee. During the House of Lords debates on this section, the Government argued that it would be inappropriate for the House of Lords to depart from previous Judicial Committee decision noting that the two courts have common members and the vast experience of the Judicial Committee in dealing with constitutional issues from the Commonwealth[1].

1 593 HL Official Report (5th Series) col 619, 8 October 1998.

THE JUDICIAL COMMITTEE OF THE PRIVY COUNCIL

8.14 The composition of the Judicial Committee for the purpose of proceedings under the Scotland Act is of interest. The Judicial Committee of the Privy Council, in its entirety, currently consists of 109 members of whom 52 are from Commonwealth countries.

Section 103(2) of the Scotland Act limits membership of the Committee for the purpose of proceedings under the Scotland Act to those who hold or have held the office of a Lord Appeal in ordinary or high judicial office as defined in section 25 of the Appellate Jurisdiction Act 1876 (ignoring for this purpose section 5 of the Appellate Jurisdiction Act 1887)[1]. This has the effect of excluding the Commonwealth judges and ensuring that only United Kingdom judges are able to determine 'devolution issues' and make orders under the pre-legislative scrutiny provisions set out in section 33[2]. There is no provision in the Act to ensure a 'geographical balance' in the court to ensure some representation from Scotland. However, in practice it will be the senior Law Lord who will decide on the composition of the Judicial Committee in devolution cases. It is expected that a convention will develop similar to that for Scottish civil appeals to the House of Lords whereby the Judicial Committee in Scottish devolution cases will always include at least one Scottish judge[3].

1 Thus, membership is limited to serving or retired Law Lords and those who hold or have held the posts of Lord Chancellor, judge of the High Court or Court of Appeal in England and Wales, judge of the Court of Session in Scotland and judge of the High Court or Court of Appeal in Northern Ireland. There is no requirement that a panel of the Judicial Committee include a Scottish member.
2 See para 5.32 above.
3 593 HL Official Report (5th series) col 1984, 28 October 1998.

REFERENCES BY THE PRINCIPAL LAW OFFICERS

8.15 All the principal Law Officers (Lord Advocate, Advocate General, Attorney General and Attorney General for Northern Ireland) may require any court or tribunal to refer to the Judicial Committee any devolution issue that has arisen in proceedings to which he or she is a party (para 33).

8.16 All the principal Law Officers may also refer to the Judicial Committee any devolution issue which is not the subject of proceedings. Thus, the principal Law Officers are able to refer an issue to the Judicial Committee even though it is not the subject of a judicial dispute and has not arisen in the legislative process (para 34). Where such a reference is made in relation to the proposed exercise of a function by a Scottish Minister, the referring Law Officer must notify a member of the Scottish Executive that he or she is doing so. Once notified, no member of the Scottish Executive may exercise the function as proposed until the reference has been decided. The Advocate General may institute proceedings relating to any possible failure by a member of the Scottish Executive to comply with this paragraph (para 35).

EFFECT OF DECISIONS

8.17 Normally, where any legal provision or action is held to be invalid, it is treated as null and void and as never having had any legal effect. However, because of the disruption and uncertainty which could be caused if an Act of the Scottish Parliament was held to be invalid some time after it was enacted and had been acted on by government and individuals, the courts are given the power to limit the effect of a finding of invalidity.

8.18 Where a court or tribunal decides that an Act of the Scottish Parliament or a provision of it is outwith the competence of the Scottish Parliament or that a member of the Scottish Executive did not have the power to make subordinate legislation that he or she has purported to make, the court or tribunal may remove, or limit the retrospective effect of its decision or suspend its effect to allow the defect to be corrected (s 102). This is a general provision which applies wherever a court or tribunal makes such a decision and not just under the Schedule 6 procedure[1]. It gives the court or tribunal the power to protect those who had been acting on the assumption that the legislation was valid. A court may, for example, limit any retrospective effect which its decision may have by providing that it should only take effect from the date of its decision. It would also allow the court to preserve the legal effects of anything already done in reliance on the erroneous provision. The power also permits the court or tribunal, by suspending its decision, to allow the Scottish Parliament or Scottish Minister, as the case may be, the opportunity to cure the defect.

1 For instance, under other grounds for judicial review.

8.19 Notice must be given to the Lord Advocate and the appropriate Law Officer[1] if the court or tribunal is considering using this power. Following the receipt of such notice, a Law Officer may participate in the proceedings in so far as they relate to the making of the order. In deciding whether to invoke the power the court or tribunal must consider the extent to which third parties (i e those not party to the proceedings in which the decision is made) would be adversely affected if the power were or were not exercised. The court or tribunal may also take other relevant criteria into account as it sees fit.

1 Section 102(7): If proceedings are in: Scotland – the Advocate General; England and Wales – the Attorney General; Northern Ireland – the Attorney General for Northern Ireland.

8.20 The Act also makes provision in Schedule 6 for expenses and provides that any power to regulate the procedures by which courts and tribunals act includes the power to make provisions for the purposes of Schedule 6 (paras 36–37). This includes matters relating to when a devolution issue is to be raised or referred, the procedure for sisting or staying a case and the manner and timescale in which notice and intimation must be given. The Schedule also provides that any power or duty to refer a devolution issue to a court is to be interpreted as a power, or as the case may be, a duty to refer the issue to the court for a decision.

REMEDIAL PROVISIONS

8.21 The Act sets out several procedures for dealing with instances where either the courts or, more likely, the United Kingdom Government decide that the Scottish Parliament or Executive have overstepped their powers. These powers are designed to provide fast track solutions to cure a legal defect or to prevent the Scottish Parliament or Ministers acting outwith their competence. Some of the powers may be invoked by members of the United Kingdom Executive to correct a defect themselves. Others allow a Secretary of State in certain prescribed circumstances to make an order prohibiting a Bill from being sent for Royal Assent, revoking primary or secondary legislation or directing certain action be taken or not taken by the Scottish Ministers.

Power to prevent a Bill from receiving Royal Assent

8.22 The first of these provisions is found in section 35 and was discussed above[1]. Under section 35 the Secretary of State may make an order prohibiting the Presiding Officer from submitting a

Bill for Royal Assent if he or she has reasonable grounds to believe that the Bill either: (a) contains provisions which would either be incompatible with the United Kingdom's international obligations or the interests of defence or national security; or (b) makes modifications of the law as it applies to reserved matters which would have an adverse effect on the operation of the law as it applies to reserved matters.

1 See para 5.34 above.

Power to prevent action being taken

8.23 Under section 58(1) if the Secretary of State has reasonable grounds to believe that any action proposed to be taken by a member of the Scottish Executive would be incompatible with the United Kingdom's international obligations, he or she may by order, direct that the proposed action should not be taken.

Power to require action to be taken

8.24 The Secretary of State may also order action to be taken by a member of the Scottish Executive (including the introduction of a Bill before Parliament) in order to give effect to the United Kingdom's international obligations (s 58(2)).

8.25 McFadden highlights the difficulties presented by the power given to Ministers of the Crown under this section to issue an order requiring the members of the Scottish Executive to introduce a Bill. What if the members of the Scottish Executive refused to do so or the Scottish Parliament then refused to pass it? What sanction is available to the Secretary of State? Presumably, the Westminster Parliament could pass the necessary law themselves but this could lead to a political crisis between the two Parliaments[1].

1 McFadden *The Scottish Parliament: Provisions for Dispute Resolution* [1998] JR, 221–235 at 231.

Power to revoke legislation

8.26 If any subordinate legislation which has been made by or which could be revoked by a member of the Scottish Executive contains provisions which the Secretary of State has reasonable grounds to believe: (a) would be incompatible with the United Kingdom's international obligations or the interests of defence or national security; or (b) make modifications of the law as it applies to reserved matters which would have an adverse effect on the operation of the law as it applies to reserved matters, then the Secretary of State may revoke the legislation (s 58(4)). The Secretary of State must give reasons for making an order under this section (s 58(5)). During the House of Commons debate on this section, the Secretary of State for Scotland said that it was a 'belt and braces and fail-safe measure, not a general override which the Secretary of State can use at whim'[1]. He maintained that since the clause requires the Secretary of State to lay the order before the United Kingdom Parliament, that Parliament could restrain the Secretary of State if the order was arbitrary. If the United Kingdom Parliament did nothing to restrain the Secretary of State, the reasonableness test built into the clause should ensure that the matter was justiciable. In the past, however, courts in both England and Scotland have been reluctant to question the 'reasonableness' of a decision where it has been approved by Parliament[2].

1 306 HC Official Report col 243, 16 February 1998.

2 *Nottinghamshire County Council v Secretary of State for the Environment* [1986] AC 240 at 250, where Lord Scarman notes 'If a minister exercises a power conferred on him by legislation, the courts can investigate whether he has abused his power. But if, as in this case, effect cannot be given to the Secretary of State's determination without the consent of the House of Commons and the House of Commons has consented, it is not open to the courts to intervene unless the minister and the House must have misconstrued the statute or the minister has ... deceived the House'. See also: *City of Edinburgh District Council v the Secretary of State for Scotland* 1985 SLT 551 and *R v Secretary of State for the Environment, ex parte Hammersmith and Fulham London Borough Council* [1991] 1 AC 521.

Power to make legislation

8.27 A broader remedial power is provided under section 107. This section permits the introduction of subordinate legislation to make such provision as the person making the legislation considers necessary or expedient in consequence of:

1 any provision of an Act of the Scottish Parliament which is not or may not be within the legislative competence of the Parliament; or

2 any purported exercise by a member of the Scottish Executive of his or her functions which is not or may not be, an exercise or proper exercise of those functions.

This power is an 'open' power which is exercisable by Her Majesty by Order in Council or by a Minister of the Crown by order[1]. It allows an Act which is beyond the legislative competence of the Parliament to be amended and remedies any consequential problems, for example, concerning rights purportedly accrued or liabilities purportedly incurred by virtue of the Act. In most cases, the Act is likely to be referred back to the Scottish Parliament. However, this may not always be possible. There will be circumstances where it will be outwith the competence of the Parliament to pass any necessary remedial provision. This provision permits the United Kingdom Government to correct the problem themselves or fill a hole left by the invalid Scottish provision. Such a provision could be given retrospective effect, thus putting parties in the position they thought they were in before the flaw was discovered (s 114(3)). A determination from the courts is not a prerequisite for the use of this power. It could therefore be used to remedy a defect or suspected defect before judicial proceedings were commenced thereby avoiding the need for such proceedings. However, the power contained in section 107 is not intended to be used as a form of legislative override and it is intended that, where there has not been a court decision, this power should only be used with the consent of the Scottish Ministers. Where they are opposed to its use, the matter would fall to be decided by the courts[2].

1 Section 112(1) provides that where no provision is made as to the person by whom a subordinate law-making power is exercisable, the power is exercisable by Her Majesty by Order in Council or by a Minister of the Crown by order – see para 7.55 above.
2 594 HL Official Report (5th series) col 599, 9 November 1998.

CONCLUSION

8.28 Read out of context, these remedial powers appear capable of undermining the devolution settlement altogether. They are in fact intended to provide the basis for discussion and negotiation between the two governments. As Lord Sewel explained:

'These powers of intervention are of course meant to be long stops. Their use would require to be justified and would be liable to be scrutinised by judicial review. . . . But the powers of intervention provide essential balance to ensure that there is a sensible outcome in relation to reserved matters. Their existence should be sufficient to ensure consultation between Whitehall and Edinburgh so that there may be no need for them to be used. But there should be no doubt that this Government will be willing to use the powers of intervention if it became necessary.'

1 592 HL Official Report (5th series) col 1392, 28 July 1998.

9 Conclusion

INTRODUCTION

9.1 The Scotland Act focuses attention on the role of the Scottish Parliament and the Scottish Executive in the future governance of Scotland. The devolved Scottish Administration, however, will not be responsible for the whole of the government of Scotland. After the first Parliament is elected in May 1999, it will count as one of four tiers or layers of government with a bearing on the well-being of people working and living in Scotland. One of those tiers is constituted by local government, which will fall within the competence of the Scottish Parliament. The Government anticipated that the Scottish Executive would not want to change a system which was restructured in only 1996[1]. In particular, it did not expect the Scottish Parliament and its Executive to accumulate a range of new functions at the centre which would be more appropriately and efficiently delivered by other bodies within Scotland[2], but it will be open to a future Scottish Executive to adjust the boundary between the central and local government, and between local government and other public service providers, in the light of the devolution settlement. In addition to local government, there will also be a continuing role for the United Kingdom Government and the European Union.

1 Local Government etc (Scotland) Act 1994.
2 *Scotland's Parliament* (Cm 3658) para 6.2.

THE UNITED KINGDOM DIMENSION

9.2 For the foreseeable future, the United Kingdom Government will continue to play a key part in the government of Scotland. Under the Act, the United Kingdom government will be responsible for financing the devolved government of Scotland, for the conduct of international relations, including relations with the

European Union, and for the government of Scotland in respect of reserved matters.

9.3 Co-operation between the two levels of government will be crucial to the success of the devolution settlement. Devolution will put a premium on effective co-ordination across different levels of government. The Secretary of State for Scotland, most of whose existing responsibilities will be assumed by the Scottish Executive, will be responsible for promoting communication between the two administrations in relation to matters of mutual interest, and for representing Scottish interests in the reserved areas[1], though for how long the post of Secretary of State for Scotland will survive a devolved Scotland remains to be seen. A joint ministerial committee is proposed as a forum for consultation on reserved matters which impinge on devolved responsibilities[2]. Non-statutory concordats designed to promote effective communications and joint workings between the Scottish Executive and United Kingdom Departments are also planned. The retention of a unified civil service (s 50(2)) will help maintain working relations between the two administrations.

1 *Scotland's Parliament* (Cm 3658) para 4.12.
2 592 HL Official Report (5th Series) col 1488, 28 July 1998.

9.4 The Act is predicated on co-operation, but not entirely reliant on it. The United Kingdom Government retains limited but significant powers of intervention under the Act. It will be able to intervene where action by the Scottish Parliament or Scottish Executive is incompatible with the United Kingdom's international obligations or with the interests of defence or national security or would have an adverse effect on the operation of the law governing reserved matters (ss 35, 58(4)). It will be able to require the Scottish Executive to take action to give effect to the United Kingdom's international obligations (s 58(1)), and it will be able to give effect to EC obligations should the Scottish Executive fail to do so.

9.5 These powers are in the nature of remedies of last resort. The interest of the United Kingdom Government lies in making devolution work for which purpose there is scope for adjusting the boundaries between reserved and devolved matters by mutual agreement (s 30(2)), for the agreed redistribution of functions (s 108) and for legislative intervention by the Westminster Parliament to repair any unanticipated shortcomings in the devolution settlement.

THE EUROPEAN DIMENSION

9.6 Beyond the United Kingdom Government there is the European Union, the law of which will restrict the Scottish Parliament and Executive in ways their members may not always find congenial. The negotiation of future EC obligations will fall to the United Kingdom Government. The definition of reserved matters includes the conduct of international relations including relations with the European Communities (Sch 5, Part 1, para 7). The Act makes provision for the Scottish Ministers to participate in the law-making process, but does not guarantee them a role. The implementation of EC obligations in relation to devolved matters on the other hand will fall to the Scottish Executive, with scope for intervention by United Kingdom Ministers should they fail to do so. The smooth implementation of EC obligations and international obligations more generally is likely to be made easier if the Scottish Ministers have been fully involved in the negotiations leading up to the taking of decisions. Again co-operation will be crucial to the success of the process.

CONCLUSION

9.7 The Scotland Act 1998 represents a defining moment in the history of modern Scotland. Whether the election of the first Scottish Parliament in almost three hundred years will cement Scotland's position within the Union, as the Government intends, or marks a staging post on the road to its eventual break up, as its critics fear, remains to be seen. Devolution will generate its own dynamic with results that cannot be confidently predicted. Important though the Act is, it is unlikely to represent the last word on the governance of Scotland.

APPENDIX 1

Voting for the Scottish Parliament

The following tables provide an illustration of how the electoral system for the Scottish Parliament might operate. These tables are based on the voting figures at the 1997 General Election, but there are several major qualifications about their use in this way, quite apart from the changes in the support for parties between May 1997 and the first election for the Scottish Parliament in May 1999. The tables are therefore merely to demonstrate the workings of the system and how the result can differ from a system based on 'first-past-the-post'. The operation of the electoral system is explained at paras 2.4–2.8 above.

The figures here make the assumption that all voters would cast their regional vote for the party of the candidate whom they voted for as constituency MP. With two separate votes to cast, it is possible that voters will divide their support. There are many examples of individual politicians who have gained strong local support transcending party loyalties (and some earning local opposition), and with the opportunity to reflect party preference in the regional vote, issues affecting the individual candidates may become more important. The figures also ignore independent candidates and the minor parties. More people may be encouraged to consider voting for such parties or independents given the opportunity for these to gain a regional seat on the basis of a proportion of the vote well below what would be needed to win a constituency (perhaps about 6–7% of the vote across a region). However, the number of actual votes required is still very substantial and obtaining that level of support across a whole region may be difficult for those without significant party backing.

The figures are also calculated on the basis of the European constituencies in force at the time of the 1997 election, not the revised ones which will in fact be used for the first election to the Scottish Parliament. It is further assumed that the Liberal Democrats would win both Orkney and Shetland which become separate seats for the Scottish Parliament.

These tables are based on information provided by Ian Clark and John Berridge and prepared in connection with their publication in August 1998 of a full analysis of recent electoral results and voting patterns in *Scotland Votes: The General Election 1997 in Scotland*, published by General Election Studies, Department of Political Science, University of Dundee. We are most grateful for their assistance.

OVERALL SUMMARY

	Labour	SNP	Conservative	Lib Dem
Share of vote	46%	22%	18%	13%
Constituency seats	56	6	0	11
Share of constituency seats	77%	8%	0%	15%
Regional seats	6	23	21	6
Total seats	62	29	21	17
Share of total seats	48%	23%	16%	13%

GLASGOW

	Labour	SNP	Conservative	Lib Dem
Party vote	172,997	56,220	24,078	18,182
Constituency seats	9	0	0	0
Stage 1: divide by	9+1= 10	0+1= 1	0+1= 1	0+1= 1
Stage 1 figure	17,300	**56,220**	24,078	18,182
Stage 2: divide by	9+1= 10	1+1= 2	0+1= 1	0+1= 1
Stage 2 figure	17,300	**28,110**	24,078	18,182
Stage 3: divide by	9+1= 10	2+1= 3	0+1= 1	0+1= 1
Stage 3 figure	17,300	18,740	**24,078**	18,182
Stage 4: divide by	9+1= 10	2+1= 3	1+1= 2	0+1= 1
Stage 4 figure	17,300	**18,740**	12,039	18,182
Stage 5: divide by	9+1= 10	3+1= 4	1+1= 2	0+1= 1
Stage 5 figure	17,300	14,055	12,039	**18,182**
Stage 6: divide by	9+1= 10	3+1= 4	1+1= 2	1+1= 2
Stage 6 figure	**17,300**	14,055	12,039	9,091
Stage 7: divide by	10+1= 11	3+1= 4	1+1= 2	1+1= 2
Stage 7 figure	**15,727**	14,055	12,039	9,091
Constituency seats	9	0	0	0
Regional seats	2	3	1	1
Total seats	11	3	1	1

HIGHLANDS AND ISLANDS

	Labour	SNP	Conservative	Lib Dem
Party vote	61,974	61,189	37,206	63,362
Constituency seats	2	1	0	5
Stage 1: divide by	2+1= 3	1+1= 2	0+1= 1	5+1= 6
Stage 1 figure	20,658	30,595	**37,206**	10,560
Stage 2 divide by	2+1= 3	1+1= 2	1+1= 2	5+1= 6
Stage 2 figure	20,658	**30,595**	18,603	10,560
Stage 3 divide by	2+1= 3	2+1= 3	1+1= 2	5+1= 6
Stage 3 figure	**20,658**	20,396	18,603	10,560
Stage 4 divide by	3+1= 4	2+1= 3	1+1= 2	5+1= 6
Stage 4 figure	15,494	**20,396**	18,603	10,560
Stage 5 divide by	3+1= 4	3+1= 4	1+1= 2	5+1= 6
Stage 5 figure	15,494	15,297	**18,603**	10,560
Stage 6 divide by	3+1= 4	3+1= 4	2+1= 3	5+1= 6
Stage 6 figure	**15,494**	15,297	12,402	10,560
Stage 7 divide by	4+1= 5	3+1= 4	2+1= 3	5+1= 6
Stage 7 figure	12,395	**15,297**	12,402	10,560
Constituency seats	2	1	0	5
Regional seats	2	3	2	0
Total seats	4	4	2	5

LOTHIANS

	Labour	SNP	Conservative	Lib Dem
Party vote	175,354	70,353	73,363	56,957
Constituency seats	8	0	0	1
Stage 1: divide by	8+1= 9	0+1= 1	0+1= 1	1+1= 2
Stage 1 figure	19,484	70,353	**73,363**	28,479
Stage 2: divide by	8+1= 9	0+1= 1	1+1= 2	1+1= 2
Stage 2 figure	19,484	**70,353**	36,682	28,479
Stage 3: divide by	8+1= 9	1+1= 2	1+1= 2	1+1= 2
Stage 3 figure	19,484	35,177	**36,682**	28,479
Stage 4: divide by	8+1= 9	1+1= 2	2+1= 3	1+1= 2
Stage 4 figure	19,484	**35,177**	24,454	28,479
Stage 5: divide by	8+1= 9	2+1= 3	2+1= 3	1+1= 2
Stage 5 figure	19,484	23,451	24,454	**28,479**
Stage 6: divide by	8+1= 9	2+1= 3	2+1= 3	2+1= 3
Stage 6 figure	19,484	23,451	**24,454**	18,986
Stage 7: divide by	8+1= 9	2+1= 3	3+1= 4	2+1= 3
Stage 7 figure	19,484	**23,451**	18,341	18,986
Constituency seats	8	0	0	1
Regional seats	0	3	3	1
Total seats	8	3	3	2

SCOTLAND MID AND FIFE

	Labour	SNP	Conservative	Lib Dem
Party vote	187,963	91,402	71,660	46,843
Constituency seats	8	1	0	1
Stage 1: divide by	8+1= 9	1+1= 2	0+1= 1	1+1= 2
Stage 1 figure	20,885	45,701	**71,660**	23,422
Stage 2: divide	by 8+1= 9	1+1= 2	1+1= 2	1+1= 2
Stage 2 figure	20,885	**45,701**	35,830	23,422
Stage 3: divide by	8+1= 9	2+1= 3	1+1= 2	1+1= 2
Stage 3 figure	20,885	30,467	**35,830**	23,422
Stage 4: divide by	8+1= 9	2+1= 3	2+1= 3	1+1= 2
Stage 4 figure	20,885	**30,467**	23,887	23,422
Stage 5: divide by	8+1= 9	3+1= 4	2+1= 3	1+1= 2
Stage 5 figure	20,885	22,851	**23,887**	23,422
Stage 6: divide by	8+1= 9	3+1= 4	3+1= 4	1+1= 2
Stage 6 figure	20,885	22,851	17,915	**23,422**
Stage 7: divide by	8+1= 9	3+1= 4	3+1= 4	2+1= 3
Stage 7 figure	20,885	**22,851**	17,915	15,614
Constituency seats	8	1	0	1
Regional seats	0	3	3	1
Total seats	8	4	3	2

SCOTLAND NORTH-EAST

	Labour	SNP	Conservative	Lib Dem
Party vote	118,162	115,950	98,366	72,880
Constituency seats	5	3	0	2
Stage 1: divide by	5+1= 6	3+1= 4	0+1= 1	2+1= 3
Stage 1 figure	19,694	28,988	**98,366**	24,293
Stage 2: divide by	5+1= 6	3+1= 4	1+1= 2	2+1= 3
Stage 2 figure	19,694	28,988	**49,183**	24,293
Stage 3: divide by	5+1= 6	3+1= 4	2+1= 3	2+1= 3
Stage 3 figure	19,694	28,988	**32,789**	24,293
Stage 4: divide by	5+1= 6	3+1= 4	3+1= 4	2+1= 3
Stage 4 figure	19,694	**28,988**	24,592	24,293
Stage 5: divide by	5+1= 6	4+1= 5	3+1= 4	2+1= 3
Stage 5 figure	19,694	23,190	**24,592**	24,293
Stage 6: divide by	5+1= 6	4+1= 5	4+1= 5	2+1= 3
Stage 6 figure	19,694	23,190	19,673	**24,293**
Stage 7: divide by	5+1= 6	4+1= 5	4+1= 5	3+1= 4
Stage 7 figure	19,694	**23,190**	19,673	18,220
Constituency seats	5	3	0	2
Regional seats	0	2	4	1
Total seats	5	5	4	3

SCOTLAND SOUTH

	Labour	SNP	Conservative	Lib Dem
Party vote	166,354	73,110	86,769	51,312
Constituency seats	6	1	0	2
Stage 1: divide by	6+1= 7	1+1= 2	0+1= 1	2+1= 3
Stage 1 figure	23,765	36,555	**86,769**	17,104
Stage 2: divide by	6+1= 7	1+1= 2	1+1= 2	2+1= 3
Stage 2 figure	23,765	36,555	**43,385**	17,104
Stage 3: divide by	6+1= 7	1+1= 2	2+1= 3	2+1= 3
Stage 3 figure	23,765	**36,555**	28,923	17,104
Stage 4: divide by	6+1= 7	2+1= 3	2+1= 3	2+1= 3
Stage 4 figure	23,765	24,370	**28,923**	17,104
Stage 5: divide by	6+1= 7	2+1= 3	3+1= 4	2+1= 3
Stage 5 figure	23,765	**24,370**	21,692	17,104
Stage 6: divide by	6+1= 7	3+1= 4	3+1= 4	2+1= 3
Stage 6 figure	**23,765**	18,278	21,692	17,104
Stage 7: divide by	7+1= 8	3+1= 4	3+1= 4	2+1= 3
Stage 7 figure	20,794	18,278	**21,692**	17,104
Constituency seats	6	1	0	2
Regional seats	1	2	4	0
Total seats	7	3	4	2

STRATHCLYDE EAST

	Labour	SNP	Conservative	Lib Dem
Party vote	210,981	79,766	34,419	21,668
Constituency seats	9	0	0	0
Stage 1: divide by	9+1= 10	0+1= 1	0+1= 1	0+1= 1
Stage 1 figure	21,098	**79,766**	34,419	21,668
Stage 2: divide by	9+1= 10	1+1= 2	0+1= 1	0+1= 1
Stage 2 figure	21,098	**39,883**	34,419	21,668
Stage 3: divide by	9+1= 10	2+1= 3	0+1= 1	0+1= 1
Stage 3 figure	21,098	26,589	**34,419**	21,668
Stage 4: divide by	9+1= 10	2+1= 3	1+1= 2	0+1= 1
Stage 4 figure	21,098	**26,589**	17,210	21,668
Stage 5: divide by	9+1= 10	3+1= 4	1+1= 2	0+1= 1
Stage 5 figure	21,098	19,942	17,210	**21,668**
Stage 6: divide by	9+1= 10	3+1= 4	1+1= 2	1+1= 2
Stage 6 figure	**21,098**	19,942	17,210	10,834
Stage 7: divide by	10+1= 11	3+1= 4	1+1= 2	1+1= 2
Stage 7 figure	19,180	**19,942**	17,210	10,834
Constituency seats	9	0	0	0
Regional seats	1	4	1	1
Total seats	10	4	1	1

STRATHCLYDE WEST

	Labour	SNP	Conservative	Lib Dem
Party vote	189,565	73,570	67,198	34,155
Constituency seats	9	0	0	0
Stage 1: divide by	9+1= 10	0+1= 1	0+1= 1	0+1= 1
Stage 1 figure	18,957	**73,570**	67,198	34,155
Stage 2: divide by	9+1= 10	1+1= 2	0+1= 1	0+1= 1
Stage 2 figure	18,957	36,785	**67,198**	34,155
Stage 3: divide by	9+1= 10	1+1= 2	1+1= 2	0+1= 1
Stage 3 figure	18,957	**36,785**	33,599	34,155
Stage 4: divide by	9+1= 10	2+1= 3	1+1= 2	0+1= 1
Stage 4 figure	18,957	24,523	33,599	**34,155**
Stage 5: divide by	9+1= 10	2+1= 3	1+1= 2	1+1= 2
Stage 5 figure	18,957	24,523	**33,599**	17,078
Stage 6: divide by	9+1= 10	2+1= 3	2+1= 3	1+1= 2
Stage 6 figure	18,957	**24,523**	22,399	17,078
Stage 7: divide by	9+1= 10	3+1= 4	2+1= 3	1+1= 2
Stage 7 figure	18,957	18,393	**22,399**	17,078
Constituency seats	9	0	0	0
Regional seats	0	3	3	1
Total seats	9	3	3	1

APPENDIX 2

Regions for elections to the Scottish Parliament

The eight regions for elections to the Scottish Parliament are defined in the European Parliamentary Constituencies (Scotland) Order 1996 (SI 1996/1926). The regions contain the following parliamentary constituencies:

Central Scotland	Airdrie and Shotts Coatbridge and Chryston Cumbernauld and Kilsyth East Kilbride Falkirk East Falkirk West Hamilton North and Bellshill Hamilton South Kilmarnock and Loudoun Motherwell and Wishaw
Glasgow	Glasgow Anniesland Glasgow Baillieston Glasgow Cathcart Glasgow Govan Glasgow Kelvin Glasgow Maryhill Glasgow Pollok Glasgow Rutherglen Glasgow Shettleston Glasgow Springburn
Highlands and Islands	Argyll and Bute Caithness, Sutherland and Easter Ross Inverness East, Nairn and Lochaber Moray Orkney and Shetland Ross, Skye and Inverness West Western Isles

Lothians	Edinburgh Central Edinburgh East and Musselburgh Edinburgh North and Leith Edinburgh Pentlands Edinburgh South Edinburgh West Linlithgow Livingston Midlothian
Mid Scotland and Fife	Central Fife Dunfermline East Dunfermline West Kirkcaldy North East Fife North Tayside Ochil Perth Stirling
North East Scotland	Aberdeen Central Aberdeen North Aberdeen South Angus Banff and Buchan Dundee East Dundee West Gordon West Aberdeenshire and Kincardine
South of Scotland	Ayr Carrick, Cumnock and Doon Valley Clydesdale Cunninghame South Dumfries East Lothian Galloway and Upper Nithsdale Roxburgh and Berwickshire Tweeddale, Ettrick and Lauderdale

West of Scotland	Clydebank and Milngavie
	Cunninghame North
	Dumbarton
	Eastwood
	Greenock and Inverclyde
	Paisley North
	Paisley South
	Strathkelvin and Bearsden
	West Renfrewshire

APPENDIX 3

Scotland Act 1998

1998 CHAPTER 46

ARRANGEMENT OF SECTIONS

PART I
THE SCOTTISH PARLIAMENT

The Scottish Parliament

Section

Presiding Officer and administration

19 Presiding Officer
20 Clerk of the Parliament
21 Scottish Parliamentary Corporate Body

Proceedings etc

22 Standing orders
23 Power to call for witnesses and documents
24 Witnesses and documents: notice
25 Witnesses and documents: offences
26 Witnesses and documents: general
27 Participation of the Scottish Law Officers

Legislation

28 Acts of the Scottish Parliament
29 Legislative competence
30 Legislative competence: supplementary
31 Scrutiny of Bills before introduction
32 Submission of Bills for Royal Assent
33 Scrutiny of Bills by the Judicial Committee
34 ECJ references
35 Power to intervene in certain cases
36 Stages of Bills

Other provisions

37 Acts of Union
38 Letters Patent and proclamations
39 Members' interests

Legal issues

40 Proceedings by or against the Parliament etc
41 Defamatory statements
42 Contempt of court
43 Corrupt practices

PART II THE SCOTTISH ADMINISTRATION

Ministers and their staff

44 The Scottish Executive
45 The First Minister
46 Choice of the First Minister
47 Ministers
48 The Scottish Law Officers
49 Junior Scottish Ministers

PART V MISCELLANEOUS AND GENERAL

Remuneration of members of the Parliament and Executive

81 Remuneration of members of the Parliament and Executive
82 Limits on salaries of members of the Parliament
83 Remuneration: supplementary

Other provision about members of the Parliament etc

84 Oaths
85 Exemption from jury service

Arrangements at Westminster

86 Scottish representation at Westminster
87 The Advocate General for Scotland

Cross-border public authorities

88 Cross-border public authorities: initial status
89 Power to adapt etc cross-border public authorities
90 Power to transfer property of cross-border public authorities

Miscellaneous

91 Maladministration
92 Queen's Printer for Scotland
93 Agency arrangements
94 Private legislation
95 Appointment and removal of judges
96 Provision of information to the Treasury
97 Assistance for opposition parties

Juridical

98 Devolution issues
99 Rights and liabilities of the Crown in different capacities
100 Human rights
101 Interpretation of Acts of the Scottish Parliament etc
102 Powers of courts or tribunals to vary retrospective decisions
103 The Judicial Committee

Supplementary powers

104 Power to make provision consequential on legislation of, or scrutinised by, the Parliament
105 Power to make provision consequential on this Act
106 Power to adapt functions
107 Legislative power to remedy ultra vires acts
108 Agreed redistribution of functions exercisable by the Scottish Ministers etc
109 Agreed redistribution of property and liabilities

An Act to provide for the establishment of a Scottish Parliament and Administration and other changes in the government of Scotland; to provide for changes in the constitution and functions of certain public authorities; to provide for the variation of the basic rate of income tax in relation to income of Scottish taxpayers in accordance with a resolution of the Scottish Parliament; to amend the law about parliamentary constituencies in Scotland; and for connected purposes.

[19th November 1998]

BE IT ENACTED by the Queen's most Excellent Majesty, by and with the advice and consent of the Lords Spiritual and Temporal, and Commons, in this present Parliament assembled, and by the authority of the same, as follows—

PART I THE SCOTTISH PARLIAMENT

The Scottish Parliament

1 The Scottish Parliament

(1) There shall be a Scottish Parliament.

(2) One member of the Parliament shall be returned for each constituency (under the simple majority system) at an election held in the constituency.

(3) Members of the Parliament for each region shall be returned at a general election under the additional member system of proportional representation provided for in this Part and vacancies among such members shall be filled in accordance with this Part.

(4) The validity of any proceedings of the Parliament is not affected by any vacancy in its membership.

(5) Schedule 1 (which makes provision for the constituencies and regions for the purposes of this Act and the number of regional members) shall have effect.

General elections

2 Ordinary general elections

(1) The day on which the poll at the first ordinary general election for membership of the Parliament shall be held, and the day, time and place for the meeting of the Parliament following that poll, shall be appointed by order made by the Secretary of State.

(2) The poll at subsequent ordinary general elections shall be held on the first Thursday in May in the fourth calendar year following that in which the previous ordinary general election was held, unless the day of the poll is determined by a proclamation under subsection (5).

(3) If the poll is to be held on the first Thursday in May, the Parliament—
(a) is dissolved by virtue of this section at the beginning of the minimum period which ends with that day, and
(b) shall meet within the period of seven days beginning immediately after the day of the poll.

(4) In subsection (3), "the minimum period" means the period determined in accordance with an order under section 12(1).

(5) If the Presiding Officer proposes a day for the holding of the poll which is not more than one month earlier, nor more than one month later, than the first Thursday in May, Her Majesty may by proclamation under the Scottish Seal—
(a) dissolve the Parliament,
(b) require the poll at the election to be held on the day proposed, and
(c) require the Parliament to meet within the period of seven days beginning immediately after the day of the poll.

(6) In this Act "the Scottish Seal" means Her Majesty's Seal appointed by the Treaty of Union to be kept and used in Scotland in place of the Great Seal of Scotland.

3 Extraordinary general elections

(1) The Presiding Officer shall propose a day for the holding of a poll if—
(a) the Parliament resolves that it should be dissolved and, if the resolution is passed on a division, the number of members voting in favour of it is not less than two-thirds of the total number of seats for members of the Parliament, or
(b) any period during which the Parliament is required under section 46 to nominate one of its members for appointment as First Minister ends without such a nomination being made.

(2) If the Presiding Officer makes such a proposal, Her Majesty may by proclamation under the Scottish Seal—
(a) dissolve the Parliament and require an extraordinary general election to be held,
(b) require the poll at the election to be held on the day proposed, and

(c) require the Parliament to meet within the period of seven days beginning immediately after the day of the poll.

(3) If a poll is held under this section within the period of six months ending with the day on which the poll at the next ordinary general election would be held (disregarding section 2(5)), that ordinary general election shall not be held.

(4) Subsection (3) does not affect the year in which the subsequent ordinary general election is to be held.

4 Calculating time for meeting of the Parliament

In calculating any period of days for the purposes of section 2(3)(b) or (5)(c) or section 3(2)(c), Saturday, Sunday, Christmas Eve, Christmas Day, Good Friday, a bank holiday in Scotland or a day appointed for public thanksgiving or mourning shall be disregarded.

5 Candidates

(1) At a general election, the candidates may stand for return as constituency members or regional members.

(2) A person may not be a candidate to be a constituency member for more than one constituency.

(3) The candidates to be regional members shall be those included in a list submitted under subsection (4) or individual candidates.

(4) Any registered political party may submit to the regional returning officer a list of candidates to be regional members for a particular region (referred to in this Act, in relation to the region, as the party's "regional list").

(5) A registered political party's regional list has effect in relation to the general election and any vacancy occurring among the regional members after that election and before the next general election.

(6) Not more than twelve persons may be included in the list (but the list may include only one person).

(7) A registered political party's regional list must not include a person—
(a) who is included in any other list submitted under subsection (4) for the region or any list submitted under that subsection for another region,
(b) who is an individual candidate to be a regional member for the region or another region,
(c) who is a candidate to be a constituency member for a constituency not included in the region, or
(d) who is a candidate to be a constituency member for a constituency included in the region but is not a candidate of that party.

(8) A person may not be an individual candidate to be a regional member for a particular region if he is—
(a) included in a list submitted under subsection (4) for the region or another region,
(b) an individual candidate to be a regional member for another region,
(c) a candidate to be a constituency member for a constituency not included in the region, or
(d) a candidate of any registered political party to be a constituency member for a constituency included in the region.

(9) In this Act, "registered political party" means a party registered under the Registration of Political Parties Act 1998.

6 Poll for regional members

(1) This section and sections 7 and 8 are about the return of regional members at a general election.

(2) In each of the constituencies for the Parliament, a poll shall be held at which each person entitled to vote as elector may give a vote (referred to in this Act as a "regional vote") for—
(a) a registered political party which has submitted a regional list, or
(b) an individual candidate to be a regional member for the region.

(3) The right conferred on a person by subsection (2) is in addition to any right the person may have to vote in any poll for the return of a constituency member.

7 Calculation of regional figures

(1) The persons who are to be returned as constituency members for constituencies included in the region must be determined before the persons who are to be returned as the regional members for the region.

(2) For each registered political party which has submitted a regional list, the regional figure for the purposes of section 8 is—
(a) the total number of regional votes given for the party in all the constituencies included in the region,
divided by
(b) the aggregate of one plus the number of candidates of the party returned as constituency members for any of those constituencies.

(3) Each time a seat is allocated to the party under section 8, that figure shall be recalculated by increasing (or further increasing) the aggregate in subsection (2)(b) by one.

(4) For each individual candidate to be a regional member for the region, the regional figure for the purposes of section 8 is the total number of regional votes given for him in all the constituencies included in the region.

8 Allocation of seats to regional members

(1) The first regional member seat shall be allocated to the registered political party or individual candidate with the highest regional figure.

(2) The second and subsequent regional member seats shall be allocated to the registered political party or individual candidate with the highest regional figure, after any recalculation required by section 7(3) has been carried out.

(3) An individual candidate already returned as a constituency or regional member shall be disregarded.

(4) Seats for the region which are allocated to a registered political party shall be filled by the persons in the party's regional list in the order in which they appear in the list.

(5) For the purposes of this section and section 10, a person in a registered political party's regional list who is returned as a member of the Parliament shall be treated as ceasing to be in the list (even if his return is void).

(6) Once a party's regional list has been exhausted (by the return of persons included in it as constituency members or by the previous application of subsection (1) or (2)) the party shall be disregarded.

(7) If (on the application of subsection (1) or any application of subsection (2)) the highest regional figure is the regional figure of two or more parties or individual candidates, the subsection shall apply to each of them.

Vacancies

9 Constituency vacancies

(1) Where the seat of a constituency member is vacant, an election shall be held to fill the vacancy (subject to subsection (4)).

(2) The date of the poll shall be fixed by the Presiding Officer.

(3) The date shall fall within the period of three months—
(a) beginning with the occurrence of the vacancy, or
(b) if the vacancy does not come to the notice of the Presiding Officer within the period of one month beginning with its occurrence, beginning when it does come to his notice.

(4) The election shall not be held if the latest date for holding the poll would fall within the period of three months ending with the day on which the poll at the next ordinary general election would be held (disregarding section 2(5)).

(5) For the purposes of this section, the date on which a vacancy is to be treated as occurring shall be determined under standing orders.

(6) A person may not be a candidate at such an election if he is a member of the Parliament or a candidate in another election to fill a vacancy.

10 Regional vacancies

(1) This section applies where the seat of a regional member is vacant.

(2) If the regional member was returned as an individual candidate, or the vacancy is not filled in accordance with the following provisions, the seat shall remain vacant until the next general election.

(3) If the regional member was returned (under section 8 or this section) from a registered political party's regional list, the regional returning officer shall notify the Presiding Officer of the name of the person who is to fill the vacancy.

(4) He must be a person who—
(a) is included in that list, and
(b) is willing to serve as a regional member for the region.

(5) Where more than one person satisfies the conditions in subsection (4), the regional returning officer shall notify the name of whichever of them was higher, or highest, in the list.

(6) Where a person's name has been notified under subsection (3), this Act shall apply as if he had been declared to be returned as a regional member for the region on the day on which notification of his name was received by the Presiding Officer.

(7) For the purposes of this section, the date on which a vacancy is to be treated as occurring shall be determined under standing orders.

Franchise and conduct of elections

11 Electors

(1) The persons entitled to vote as electors at an election for membership of the Parliament held in any constituency are those who on the day of the poll—
(a) would be entitled to vote as electors at a local government election in an electoral area falling wholly or partly within the constituency, and
(b) are registered in the register of local government electors at an address within the constituency.

(2) A person is not entitled to vote as elector in any constituency—
(a) more than once at a poll for the return of a constituency member, or
(b) more than once at a poll for the return of regional members,

or to vote as elector in more than one constituency at a general election.

12 Power to make provision about elections

(1) The Secretary of State may by order make provision as to—
(a) the conduct of elections for membership of the Parliament,
(b) the questioning of such an election and the consequences of irregularities, and
(c) the return of members of the Parliament otherwise than at an election.

(2) The provision that may be made under subsection (1)(a) includes, in particular, provision—
(a) about the registration of electors,
(b) for disregarding alterations in a register of electors,
(c) about the limitation of the election expenses of candidates and registered political parties,
(d) for the combination of polls at elections for membership of the Parliament with polls at other elections,
(e) for modifying the application of section 7(1) where the poll at an election for the return of a constituency member is abandoned (or notice of it is countermanded), and
(f) for modifying section 8(7) to ensure the allocation of the correct number of seats for the region.

(3) The provision that may be made under subsection (1)(c) includes, in particular, provision modifying section 10(4) and (5).

(4) An order under subsection (1) may—
(a) apply, with or without modifications or exceptions, any provision made by or under the Representation of the People Acts or the European Parliamentary Elections Act 1978 or by any other enactment relating to parliamentary elections, European Parliamentary elections or local government elections,
(b) modify any form contained in, or in regulations or rules made under, the Representation of the People Acts so far as may be necessary to enable it to be used both for the original purpose and in relation to elections for membership of the Parliament, and
(c) so far as may be necessary in consequence of any provision made by this Act or an order under subsection (1), modify any provision made by any enactment relating to the registration of parliamentary electors or local government electors.

(5) The return of a member of the Parliament at an election may be questioned only under Part III of the Representation of the People Act 1983 as applied by an order under subsection (1).

(6) For the purposes of this Act, the regional returning officer for any region is the person designated as such in accordance with an order made by the Secretary of State under this subsection.

Duration of membership

13 Term of office of members

The term of office of a member of the Parliament begins on the day on which the member is declared to be returned and ends with the dissolution of the Parliament.

14 Resignation of members

A member of the Parliament may at any time resign his seat by giving notice in writing to the Presiding Officer.

Disqualification

15 Disqualification from membership of the Parliament

(1) A person is disqualified from being a member of the Parliament (subject to section 16) if—
(a) he is disqualified from being a member of the House of Commons under paragraphs (a) to (e) of section 1(1) of the House of Commons Disqualification Act 1975 (judges, civil servants, members of the armed forces, members of police forces and members of foreign legislatures),
(b) he is disqualified otherwise than under that Act (either generally or in relation to a particular parliamentary constituency) from being a member of the House of Commons or from sitting and voting in it,
(c) he is a Lord of Appeal in Ordinary, or
(d) he is an office-holder of a description specified in an Order in Council made by Her Majesty under this subsection.

(2) An office-holder of a description specified in an Order in Council made by Her Majesty under this subsection is disqualified from being a member of the Parliament for any constituency or region of a description specified in the Order in relation to the office-holder.

(3) In this section "office-holder" includes employee or other post-holder.

16 Exceptions and relief from disqualification

(1) A person is not disqualified from being a member of the Parliament merely because—
(a) he is a peer (whether of the United Kingdom, Great Britain, England or Scotland), or
(b) he has been ordained or is a minister of any religious denomination.

(2) A citizen of the European Union who is resident in the United Kingdom is not disqualified from being a member of the Parliament merely because of section 3 of the Act of Settlement (disqualification of persons born outside the United Kingdom other than Commonwealth and citizens of the Republic of Ireland).

(3) Subsection (4) applies where a person was, or is alleged to have been, disqualified from being a member of the Parliament (either generally or in relation to a particular constituency or region) on any ground other than one falling within section 15(1)(b).

(4) The Parliament may resolve to disregard any disqualification incurred by that person on the ground in question if it considers that—
(a) the ground has been removed, and
(b) it is proper to disregard any disqualification so incurred.

(5) A resolution under this section shall not—
(a) affect any proceedings under Part III of the Representation of the People Act 1983 as applied by an order under section 12, or

(b) enable the Parliament to disregard any disqualification which has been established in such proceedings or in proceedings under section 18.

17 Effect of disqualification

(1) If a person who is disqualified from being a member of the Parliament or from being a member for a particular constituency or region is returned as a member of the Parliament or (as the case may be) as a member for the constituency or region, his return shall be void and his seat vacant.

(2) If a member of the Parliament becomes disqualified from being a member of the Parliament or from being a member for the particular constituency or region for which he is sitting, he shall cease to be a member of the Parliament (so that his seat is vacant).

(3) Subsections (1) and (2) have effect subject to any resolution of the Parliament under section 16.

(4) Subsection (2) also has effect subject to section 141 of the Mental Health Act 1983 (mental illness) and section 427 of the Insolvency Act 1986 (sequestration etc); and where, in consequence of either of those sections, the seat of a disqualified member of the Parliament is not vacant he shall not cease to be a member of the Parliament until his seat becomes vacant but—

(a) he shall not participate in any proceedings of the Parliament, and
(b) any of his other rights and privileges as a member of the Parliament may be withdrawn by a resolution of the Parliament.

(5) The validity of any proceedings of the Parliament is not affected by the disqualification of any person from being a member of the Parliament or from being a member for the constituency or region for which he purports to sit.

18 Judicial proceedings as to disqualification

(1) Any person who claims that a person purporting to be a member of the Parliament is disqualified or has been disqualified at any time since being returned may apply to the Court of Session for a declarator to that effect.

(2) An application in respect of any person may be made whether the grounds on which it is made are alleged to have subsisted when the person was returned or to have arisen subsequently.

(3) No declarator shall be made—

(a) on grounds which subsisted when the person was returned, if an election petition is pending or has been tried in which the disqualification on those grounds of the person concerned is or was in issue, or
(b) on any ground, if a resolution under section 16 requires that any disqualification incurred on that ground by the person concerned is to be disregarded.

(4) The person in respect of whom an application is made shall be the defender.

(5) The applicant shall give such caution for the expenses of the proceedings as the Court of Session may direct; but any such caution shall not exceed £5,000 or such other sum as the Scottish Ministers may by order specify.

(6) The decision of the court on an application under this section shall be final.

(7) In this section "disqualified" means disqualified from being a member of the Parliament or from being a member for the constituency or region for which the person concerned purports to sit.

Presiding Officer and administration

19 Presiding Officer

(1) The Parliament shall, at its first meeting following a general election, elect from among its members a Presiding Officer and two deputies.

(2) A person elected Presiding Officer or deputy shall hold office until the conclusion of the next election for Presiding Officer under subsection (1) unless he previously resigns, ceases to be a member of the Parliament otherwise than by virtue of a dissolution or is removed from office by resolution of the Parliament.

(3) If the Presiding Officer or a deputy ceases to hold office before the Parliament is dissolved, the Parliament shall elect another from among its members to fill his place.

(4) The Presiding Officer's functions may be exercised by a deputy if the office of Presiding Officer is vacant or the Presiding Officer is for any reason unable to act.

(5) The Presiding Officer may (subject to standing orders) authorise any deputy to exercise functions on his behalf.

(6) Standing orders may include provision as to the participation (including voting) of the Presiding Officer and deputies in the proceedings of the Parliament.

(7) The validity of any act of the Presiding Officer or a deputy is not affected by any defect in his election.

20 Clerk of the Parliament

(1) There shall be a Clerk of the Parliament.

(2) The Clerk shall be appointed by the Scottish Parliamentary Corporate Body (established under section 21).

(3) The Clerk's functions may be exercised by any Assistant Clerk if the office of Clerk is vacant or the Clerk is for any reason unable to act.

(4) The Clerk may authorise any Assistant Clerk or other member of the staff of the Parliament to exercise functions on his behalf.

21 Scottish Parliamentary Corporate Body

(1) There shall be a body corporate to be known as "The Scottish Parliamentary Corporate Body" (referred to in this Act as the Parliamentary corporation) to perform the functions conferred on the corporation by virtue of this Act or any other enactment.

(2) The members of the corporation shall be—
(a) the Presiding Officer, and
(b) four members of the Parliament appointed in accordance with standing orders.

(3) The corporation shall provide the Parliament, or ensure that the Parliament is provided, with the property, staff and services required for the Parliament's purposes.

(4) The Parliament may give special or general directions to the corporation for the purpose of or in connection with the exercise of the corporation's functions.

(5) Any property or liabilities acquired or incurred in relation to matters within the general responsibility of the corporation to which (apart from this subsection) the Parliament would be entitled or subject shall be treated for all purposes as property or (as the case may be) liabilities of the corporation.

(6) Any expenses of the corporation shall be payable out of the Scottish Consolidated Fund.

(7) Any sums received by the corporation shall be paid into that Fund, subject to any provision made by or under an Act of the Scottish Parliament for the disposal of or accounting for such sums.

(8) Schedule 2 (which makes further provision about the corporation) shall have effect.

Proceedings etc

22 Standing orders

(1) The proceedings of the Parliament shall be regulated by standing orders.

(2) Schedule 3 (which makes provision as to how certain matters are to be dealt with by standing orders) shall have effect.

23 Power to call for witnesses and documents

(1) The Parliament may require any person—
(a) to attend its proceedings for the purpose of giving evidence, or
(b) to produce documents in his custody or under his control,

concerning any subject for which any member of the Scottish Executive has general responsibility.

(2) Subject to subsection (3), the Parliament may impose such a requirement on a person outside Scotland only in connection with the discharge by him of—

(a) functions of the Scottish Administration, or
(b) functions of a Scottish public authority or cross-border public authority, or Border rivers functions (within the meaning of section 111(4)), which concern a subject for which any member of the Scottish Executive has general responsibility.

(3) In relation to the exercise of functions of a Minister of the Crown, the Parliament may not impose such a requirement on—

(a) him (whether or not he continues to be a Minister of the Crown), or
(b) a person who is or has been in Crown employment, within the meaning of section 191(3) of the Employment Rights Act 1996,

unless the exercise concerns a subject for which any member of the Scottish Executive has general responsibility.

(4) But the Parliament may not impose such a requirement in pursuance of subsection (3) in connection with the exercise of functions which are exercisable—

(a) by the Scottish Ministers as well as by a Minister of the Crown, or
(b) by a Minister of the Crown only with the agreement of, or after consultation with, the Scottish Ministers.

(5) Subsection (4)(b) does not prevent the Parliament imposing such a requirement in connection with the exercise of functions which do not relate to reserved matters.

(6) Where all the functions of a body relate to reserved matters, the Parliament may not impose such a requirement on any person in connection with the discharge by him of those functions.

(7) The Parliament may not impose such a requirement on—

(a) a judge of any court, or
(b) a member of any tribunal in connection with the discharge by him of his functions as such.

(8) Such a requirement may be imposed by a committee or sub-committee of the Parliament only if the committee or sub-committee is expressly authorised to do so (whether by standing orders or otherwise).

(9) A person is not obliged under this section to answer any question or produce any document which he would be entitled to refuse to answer or produce in proceedings in a court in Scotland.

(10) A procurator fiscal is not obliged under this section to answer any question or produce any document concerning the operation of the system of criminal prosecution in any particular case if the Lord Advocate—

(a) considers that answering the question or producing the document might prejudice criminal proceedings in that case or would otherwise be contrary to the public interest, and
(b) has authorised the procurator fiscal to decline to answer the question or produce the document on that ground.

24 Witnesses and documents: notice

(1) A requirement under section 23 shall be imposed by the Clerk giving the person in question notice in writing specifying—
(a) the time and place at which the person is to attend and the particular subjects concerning which he is required to give evidence, or
(b) the documents, or types of documents, which he is to produce, the date by which he is to produce them and the particular subjects concerning which they are required.

(2) Such notice shall be given—
(a) in the case of an individual, by sending it, by registered post or the recorded delivery service, addressed to him at his usual or last known address or, where he has given an address for service, at that address,
(b) in any other case, by sending it, by registered post or the recorded delivery service, addressed to the person at the person's registered or principal office.

25 Witnesses and documents: offences

(1) Any person to whom a notice under section 24(1) has been given who—
(a) refuses or fails to attend proceedings as required by the notice,
(b) refuses or fails, when attending proceedings as required by the notice, to answer any question concerning the subjects specified in the notice,
(c) deliberately alters, suppresses, conceals or destroys any document which he is required to produce by the notice, or
(d) refuses or fails to produce any such document,

is guilty of an offence.

(2) Subsection (1) is subject to sections 23(9) and (10) and 27(3).

(3) It is a defence for a person charged with an offence under subsection (1)(a), (b) or (d) to prove that he had a reasonable excuse for the refusal or failure.

(4) A person guilty of an offence under this section is liable on summary conviction to a fine not exceeding level 5 on the standard scale or to imprisonment for a period not exceeding three months.

(5) Where an offence under this section which has been committed by a body corporate is proved to have been committed with the consent or connivance of, or to be attributable to any neglect on the part of—

(a) a director, manager, secretary or other similar officer of the body corporate, or
(b) any person who was purporting to act in any such capacity,

he, as well as the body corporate, is guilty of that offence and liable to be proceeded against accordingly.

26 Witnesses and documents: general

(1) The Presiding Officer or such other person as may be authorised by standing orders may—
(a) administer an oath to any person giving evidence in proceedings of the Parliament, and
(b) require him to take the oath.

(2) Any person who refuses to take an oath when required to do so under subsection (1)(b) is guilty of an offence.

(3) Subsection (4) of section 25 applies to an offence under subsection (2) as it applies to an offence under that section.

(4) Standing orders may provide for the payment of allowances and expenses to persons—
(a) attending proceedings of the Parliament to give evidence, or
(b) producing documents which they have been required or requested to produce,

whether or not in pursuance of a notice under section 24(1).

(5) For the purposes of sections 23 to 25 and this section, a person shall be taken to comply with a requirement to produce a document if he produces a copy of, or an extract of the relevant part of, the document.

27 Participation of the Scottish Law Officers

(1) If the Lord Advocate or the Solicitor General for Scotland is not a member of the Parliament—
(a) he may participate in the proceedings of the Parliament to the extent permitted by standing orders, but may not vote, and
(b) standing orders may in other respects provide that they are to apply to him as if he were such a member.

(2) Subsection (1) is without prejudice to section 39.

(3) The Lord Advocate or the Solicitor General for Scotland may, in any proceedings of the Parliament, decline to answer any question or produce any document relating to the operation of the system of criminal prosecution in any particular case if he considers that answering the question or producing the document—
(a) might prejudice criminal proceedings in that case, or
(b) would otherwise be contrary to the public interest.

Legislation

28 Acts of the Scottish Parliament

(1) Subject to section 29, the Parliament may make laws, to be known as Acts of the Scottish Parliament.

(2) Proposed Acts of the Scottish Parliament shall be known as Bills; and a Bill shall become an Act of the Scottish Parliament when it has been passed by the Parliament and has received Royal Assent.

(3) A Bill receives Royal Assent at the beginning of the day on which Letters Patent under the Scottish Seal signed with Her Majesty's own hand signifying Her Assent are recorded in the Register of the Great Seal.

(4) The date of Royal Assent shall be written on the Act of the Scottish Parliament by the Clerk, and shall form part of the Act.

(5) The validity of an Act of the Scottish Parliament is not affected by any invalidity in the proceedings of the Parliament leading to its enactment.

(6) Every Act of the Scottish Parliament shall be judicially noticed.

(7) This section does not affect the power of the Parliament of the United Kingdom to make laws for Scotland.

29 Legislative competence

(1) An Act of the Scottish Parliament is not law so far as any provision of the Act is outside the legislative competence of the Parliament.

(2) A provision is outside that competence so far as any of the following paragraphs apply—
(a) it would form part of the law of a country or territory other than Scotland, or confer or remove functions exercisable otherwise than in or as regards Scotland,
(b) it relates to reserved matters,
(c) it is in breach of the restrictions in Schedule 4,
(d) it is incompatible with any of the Convention rights or with Community law,
(e) it would remove the Lord Advocate from his position as head of the systems of criminal prosecution and investigation of deaths in Scotland.

(3) For the purposes of this section, the question whether a provision of an Act of the Scottish Parliament relates to a reserved matter is to be determined, subject to subsection (4), by reference to the purpose of the provision, having regard (among other things) to its effect in all the circumstances.

(4) A provision which—
(a) would otherwise not relate to reserved matters, but
(b) makes modifications of Scots private law, or Scots criminal law, as it applies to reserved matters,

is to be treated as relating to reserved matters unless the purpose of the provision is to make the law in question apply consistently to reserved matters and otherwise.

30 Legislative competence: supplementary

(1) Schedule 5 (which defines reserved matters) shall have effect.

(2) Her Majesty may by Order in Council make any modifications of Schedule 4 or 5 which She considers necessary or expedient.

(3) Her Majesty may by Order in Council specify functions which are to be treated, for such purposes of this Act as may be specified, as being, or as not being, functions which are exercisable in or as regards Scotland.

(4) An Order in Council under this section may also make such modifications of—
(a) any enactment or prerogative instrument (including any enactment comprised in or made under this Act), or
(b) any other instrument or document,

as Her Majesty considers necessary or expedient in connection with other provision made by the Order.

31 Scrutiny of Bills before introduction

(1) A member of the Scottish Executive in charge of a Bill shall, on or before introduction of the Bill in the Parliament, state that in his view the provisions of the Bill would be within the legislative competence of the Parliament.

(2) The Presiding Officer shall, on or before the introduction of a Bill in the Parliament, decide whether or not in his view the provisions of the Bill would be within the legislative competence of the Parliament and state his decision.

(3) The form of any statement, and the manner in which it is to be made, shall be determined under standing orders, and standing orders may provide for any statement to be published.

32 Submission of Bills for Royal Assent

(1) It is for the Presiding Officer to submit Bills for Royal Assent.

(2) The Presiding Officer shall not submit a Bill for Royal Assent at any time when—
(a) the Advocate General, the Lord Advocate or the Attorney General is entitled to make a reference in relation to the Bill under section 33,
(b) any such reference has been made but has not been decided or otherwise disposed of by the Judicial Committee, or
(c) an order may be made in relation to the Bill under section 35.

(3) The Presiding Officer shall not submit a Bill in its unamended form for Royal Assent if—
(a) the Judicial Committee have decided that the Bill or any provision of it would not be within the legislative competence of the Parliament, or
(b) a reference made in relation to the Bill under section 33 has been withdrawn following a request for withdrawal of the reference under section 34(2)(b).

(4) In this Act—
"Advocate General" means the Advocate General for Scotland,
"Judicial Committee" means the Judicial Committee of the Privy Council.

33 Scrutiny of Bills by the Judicial Committee

(1) The Advocate General, the Lord Advocate or the Attorney General may refer the question of whether a Bill or any provision of a Bill would be within the legislative competence of the Parliament to the Judicial Committee for decision.

(2) Subject to subsection (3), he may make a reference in relation to a Bill at any time during—
(a) the period of four weeks beginning with the passing of the Bill, and
(b) any period of four weeks beginning with any subsequent approval of the Bill in accordance with standing orders made by virtue of section 36(5).

(3) He shall not make a reference in relation to a Bill if he has notified the Presiding Officer that he does not intend to make a reference in relation to the Bill, unless the Bill has been approved as mentioned in subsection (2)(b) since the notification.

34 ECJ references

(1) This section applies where—
(a) a reference has been made in relation to a Bill under section 33,
(b) a reference for a preliminary ruling has been made by the Judicial Committee in connection with that reference, and
(c) neither of those references has been decided or otherwise disposed of.

(2) If the Parliament resolves that it wishes to reconsider the Bill—
(a) the Presiding Officer shall notify the Advocate General, the Lord Advocate and the Attorney General of that fact, and
(b) the person who made the reference in relation to the Bill under section 33 shall request the withdrawal of the reference.

(3) In this section "a reference for a preliminary ruling" means a reference of a question to the European Court under Article 177 of the Treaty establishing the European Community, Article 41 of the Treaty establishing the European Coal and Steel Community or Article 150 of the Treaty establishing the European Atomic Energy Community.

35 Power to intervene in certain cases

(1) If a Bill contains provisions—
(a) which the Secretary of State has reasonable grounds to believe would be incompatible with any international obligations or the interests of defence or national security, or
(b) which make modifications of the law as it applies to reserved matters and which the Secretary of State has reasonable grounds to believe would have an adverse effect on the operation of the law as it applies to reserved matters,

he may make an order prohibiting the Presiding Officer from submitting the Bill for Royal Assent.

(2) The order must identify the Bill and the provisions in question and state the reasons for making the order.

(3) The order may be made at any time during—
(a) the period of four weeks beginning with the passing of the Bill,
(b) any period of four weeks beginning with any subsequent approval of the Bill in accordance with standing orders made by virtue of section 36(5),
(c) if a reference is made in relation to the Bill under section 33, the period of four weeks beginning with the reference being decided or otherwise disposed of by the Judicial Committee.

(4) The Secretary of State shall not make an order in relation to a Bill if he has notified the Presiding Officer that he does not intend to do so, unless the Bill has been approved as mentioned in subsection (3)(b) since the notification.

(5) An order in force under this section at a time when such approval is given shall cease to have effect.

36 Stages of Bills

(1) Standing orders shall include provision—
(a) for general debate on a Bill with an opportunity for members to vote on its general principles,
(b) for the consideration of, and an opportunity for members to vote on, the details of a Bill, and
(c) for a final stage at which a Bill can be passed or rejected.

(2) Subsection (1) does not prevent standing orders making provision to enable the Parliament to expedite proceedings in relation to a particular Bill.

(3) Standing orders may make provision different from that required by subsection (1) for the procedure applicable to Bills of any of the following kinds—
(a) Bills which restate the law,
(b) Bills which repeal spent enactments,
(c) private Bills.

(4) Standing orders shall provide for an opportunity for the reconsideration of a Bill after its passing if (and only if)—
(a) the Judicial Committee decide that the Bill or any provision of it would not be within the legislative competence of the Parliament,
(b) a reference made in relation to the Bill under section 33 is withdrawn following a request for withdrawal of the reference under section 34(2)(b), or
(c) an order is made in relation to the Bill under section 35.

(5) Standing orders shall, in particular, ensure that any Bill amended on reconsideration is subject to a final stage at which it can be approved or rejected.

(6) References in subsection (4), sections 28(2) and 38(1)(a) and paragraph 7 of Schedule 3 to the passing of a Bill shall, in the case of a Bill which has been amended on reconsideration, be read as references to the approval of the Bill.

Other provisions

37 Acts of Union

The Union with Scotland Act 1706 and the Union with England Act 1707 have effect subject to this Act.

38 Letters Patent and proclamations

(1) The Keeper of the Registers of Scotland shall record in the Register of the Great Seal—
(a) all Letters Patent signed with Her Majesty's own hand signifying Her Assent to a Bill passed by the Parliament, and
(b) all royal proclamations under sections 2(5) and 3(2),

which have passed under the Scottish Seal.

(2) On recording such Letters Patent he shall intimate the date of recording to the Clerk.

(3) Her Majesty may by Order in Council make provision as to—
(a) the form and manner of preparation, and
(b) the publication,

of such Letters Patent and proclamations.

(4) If the First Minister so directs, impressions with the same device as the Scottish Seal shall be taken in such manner, of such size and on such material as is specified in the direction.

(5) Each such impression—
(a) shall be known as a Wafer Scottish Seal, and
(b) shall be kept in accordance with directions of the First Minister.

(6) If a Wafer Scottish Seal has been applied to Letters Patent or a proclamation mentioned in subsection (1), the document has the same validity as if it had passed under the Scottish Seal.

39 Members' interests

(1) Provision shall be made for a register of interests of members of the Parliament and for the register to be published and made available for public inspection.

(2) Provision shall be made—
(a) requiring members of the Parliament to register in that register financial interests (including benefits in kind), as defined for the purposes of this paragraph,
(b) requiring that any member of the Parliament who has a financial interest (including benefits in kind), as defined for the purposes of this paragraph, in any matter declares that interest before taking part in any proceedings of the Parliament relating to that matter.

(3) Provision made in pursuance of subsection (2) shall include any provision which the Parliament considers appropriate for preventing or restricting the participation in proceedings of the Parliament of a member with an interest defined for the purposes of subsection (2)(a) or (b) in a matter to which the proceedings relate.

(4) Provision shall be made prohibiting a member of the Parliament from—
(a) advocating or initiating any cause or matter on behalf of any person, by any means specified in the provision, in consideration of any payment or benefit in kind of a description so specified, or
(b) urging, in consideration of any such payment or benefit in kind, any other member of the Parliament to advocate or initiate any cause or matter on behalf of any person by any such means.

(5) Provision made in pursuance of subsections (2) to (4) shall include any provision which the Parliament considers appropriate for excluding from proceedings of the Parliament any member who fails to comply with, or contravenes, any provision made in pursuance of those subsections.

(6) Any member of the Parliament who—
(a) takes part in any proceedings of the Parliament without having complied with, or in contravention of, any provision made in pursuance of subsection (2) or (3), or
(b) contravenes any provision made in pursuance of subsection (4),

is guilty of an offence.

(7) A person guilty of an offence under subsection (6) is liable on summary conviction to a fine not exceeding level 5 on the standard scale.

(8) In this section—
(a) "provision" means provision made by or under an Act of the Scottish Parliament,

(b) references to members of the Parliament include references to the Lord Advocate and the Solicitor General for Scotland, whether or not they are such members.

Legal issues

40 Proceedings by or against the Parliament etc

(1) Proceedings by or against the Parliament shall be instituted by or (as the case may be) against the Parliamentary corporation on behalf of the Parliament.

(2) Proceedings by or against—
(a) the Presiding Officer or a deputy, or
(b) any member of the staff of the Parliament,

shall be instituted by or (as the case may be) against the corporation on his behalf.

(3) In any proceedings against the Parliament, the court shall not make an order for suspension, interdict, reduction or specific performance (or other like order) but may instead make a declarator.

(4) In any proceedings against—
(a) any member of the Parliament,
(b) the Presiding Officer or a deputy,
(c) any member of the staff of the Parliament, or
(d) the Parliamentary corporation,

the court shall not make an order for suspension, interdict, reduction or specific performance (or other like order) if the effect of doing so would be to give any relief against the Parliament which could not have been given in proceedings against the Parliament.

(5) References in this section to an order include an interim order.

41 Defamatory statements

(1) For the purposes of the law of defamation—
(a) any statement made in proceedings of the Parliament, and
(b) the publication under the authority of the Parliament of any statement,

shall be absolutely privileged.

(2) In subsection (1), "statement" has the same meaning as in the Defamation Act 1996.

42 Contempt of court

(1) The strict liability rule shall not apply in relation to any publication—
(a) made in proceedings of the Parliament in relation to a Bill or subordinate legislation, or
(b) to the extent that it consists of a fair and accurate report of such proceedings made in good faith.

(2) In subsection (1), "the strict liability rule" and "publication" have the same meanings as in the Contempt of Court Act 1981.

43 Corrupt practices

The Parliament shall be a public body for the purposes of the Prevention of Corruption Acts 1889 to 1916.

PART II THE SCOTTISH ADMINISTRATION

Ministers and their staff

44 The Scottish Executive

(1) There shall be a Scottish Executive, whose members shall be—
(a) the First Minister,
(b) such Ministers as the First Minister may appoint under section 47, and
(c) the Lord Advocate and the Solicitor General for Scotland.

(2) The members of the Scottish Executive are referred to collectively as the Scottish Ministers.

(3) A person who holds a Ministerial office may not be appointed a member of the Scottish Executive; and if a member of the Scottish Executive is appointed to a Ministerial office he shall cease to hold office as a member of the Scottish Executive.

(4) In subsection (3), references to a member of the Scottish Executive include a junior Scottish Minister and "Ministerial office" has the same meaning as in section 2 of the House of Commons Disqualification Act 1975.

45 The First Minister

(1) The First Minister shall be appointed by Her Majesty from among the members of the Parliament and shall hold office at Her Majesty's pleasure.

(2) The First Minister may at any time tender his resignation to Her Majesty and shall do so if the Parliament resolves that the Scottish Executive no longer enjoys the confidence of the Parliament.

(3) The First Minister shall cease to hold office if a person is appointed in his place.

(4) If the office of First Minister is vacant or he is for any reason unable to act, the functions exercisable by him shall be exercisable by a person designated by the Presiding Officer.

(5) A person shall be so designated only if—
(a) he is a member of the Parliament, or
(b) if the Parliament has been dissolved, he is a person who ceased to be a member by virtue of the dissolution.

(6) Functions exercisable by a person by virtue of subsection (5)(a) shall continue to be exercisable by him even if the Parliament is dissolved.

(7) The First Minister shall be the Keeper of the Scottish Seal.

46 Choice of the First Minister

(1) If one of the following events occurs, the Parliament shall within the period allowed nominate one of its members for appointment as First Minister.

(2) The events are—
(a) the holding of a poll at a general election,
(b) the First Minister tendering his resignation to Her Majesty,
(c) the office of First Minister becoming vacant (otherwise than in consequence of his so tendering his resignation),
(d) the First Minister ceasing to be a member of the Parliament otherwise than by virtue of a dissolution.

(3) The period allowed is the period of 28 days which begins with the day on which the event in question occurs; but—
(a) if another of those events occurs within the period allowed, that period shall be extended (subject to paragraph (b)) so that it ends with the period of 28 days beginning with the day on which that other event occurred, and
(b) the period shall end if the Parliament passes a resolution under section 3(1)(a) or when Her Majesty appoints a person as First Minister.

(4) The Presiding Officer shall recommend to Her Majesty the appointment of any member of the Parliament who is nominated by the Parliament under this section.

47 Ministers

(1) The First Minister may, with the approval of Her Majesty, appoint Ministers from among the members of the Parliament.

(2) The First Minister shall not seek Her Majesty's approval for any appointment under this section without the agreement of the Parliament.

(3) A Minister appointed under this section—
(a) shall hold office at Her Majesty's pleasure,
(b) may be removed from office by the First Minister,
(c) may at any time resign and shall do so if the Parliament resolves that the Scottish Executive no longer enjoys the confidence of the Parliament,
(d) if he resigns, shall cease to hold office immediately, and
(e) shall cease to hold office if he ceases to be a member of the Parliament otherwise than by virtue of a dissolution.

48 The Scottish Law Officers

(1) It is for the First Minister to recommend to Her Majesty the appointment or removal of a person as Lord Advocate or Solicitor General for Scotland; but he shall not do so without the agreement of the Parliament.

(2) The Lord Advocate and the Solicitor General for Scotland may at any time resign and shall do so if the Parliament resolves that the Scottish Executive no longer enjoys the confidence of the Parliament.

(3) Where the Lord Advocate resigns in consequence of such a resolution, he shall be deemed to continue in office until the warrant of appointment of the person succeeding to the office of Lord Advocate is granted, but only for the purpose of exercising his retained functions.

(4) Subsection (3) is without prejudice to section 287 of the Criminal Procedure (Scotland) Act 1995 (demission of office by Lord Advocate).

(5) Any decision of the Lord Advocate in his capacity as head of the systems of criminal prosecution and investigation of deaths in Scotland shall continue to be taken by him independently of any other person.

(6) In Schedule 2 to the House of Commons Disqualification Act 1975 (Ministerial offices) and Part III of Schedule 1 to the Ministerial and other Salaries Act 1975 (salaries of the Law Officers), the entries for the Lord Advocate and the Solicitor General for Scotland are omitted.

49 Junior Scottish Ministers

(1) The First Minister may, with the approval of Her Majesty, appoint persons from among the members of the Parliament to assist the Scottish Ministers in the exercise of their functions.

(2) They shall be known as junior Scottish Ministers.

(3) The First Minister shall not seek Her Majesty's approval for any appointment under this section without the agreement of the Parliament.

(4) A junior Scottish Minister—
(a) shall hold office at Her Majesty's pleasure,
(b) may be removed from office by the First Minister,
(c) may at any time resign and shall do so if the Parliament resolves that the Scottish Executive no longer enjoys the confidence of the Parliament,
(d) if he resigns, shall cease to hold office immediately, and
(e) shall cease to hold office if he ceases to be a member of the Parliament otherwise than by virtue of a dissolution.

50 Validity of acts of Scottish Ministers etc

The validity of any act of a member of the Scottish Executive or junior Scottish Minister is not affected by any defect in his nomination by the Parliament or (as the case may be) in the Parliament's agreement to his appointment.

51 The Civil Service

(1) The Scottish Ministers may appoint persons to be members of the staff of the Scottish Administration.

(2) Service as—
(a) the holder of any office in the Scottish Administration which is not a ministerial office, or
(b) a member of the staff of the Scottish Administration,

shall be service in the Home Civil Service.

(3) Subsection (1) and the other enactments conferring power to appoint such persons shall have effect subject to any provision made in relation to the Home Civil Service by or under any Order in Council.

(4) Any Civil Service management function shall be exercisable by the Minister for the Civil Service in relation to the persons mentioned in subsection (2) as it is exercisable in relation to other members of the Home Civil Service; and, accordingly, section 1 of the Civil Service (Management Functions) Act 1992 (delegation of functions by Ministers) shall apply to any such function as extended by this section.

(5) Any salary or allowances payable to or in respect of the persons mentioned in subsection (2) (including contributions to any pension scheme) shall be payable out of the Scottish Consolidated Fund.

(6) Section 1(2) and (3) of the Superannuation Act 1972 (delegation of functions relating to civil service superannuation schemes etc) shall have effect as if references to a Minister of the Crown (other than the Minister for the Civil Service) included the Scottish Ministers.

(7) The Scottish Ministers shall make payments to the Minister for the Civil Service, at such times as he may determine, of such amounts as he may determine in respect of—
(a) the provision of pensions, allowances or gratuities by virtue of section 1 of the Superannuation Act 1972 to or in respect of persons who are or have been in such service as is mentioned in subsection (2), and
(b) any expenses to be incurred in administering those pensions, allowances or gratuities.

(8) Amounts required for payments under subsection (7) shall be charged on the Scottish Consolidated Fund.

(9) In this section—
"Civil Service management function" means any function to which section 1 of the Civil Service (Management Functions) Act 1992 applies and which is vested in the Minister for the Civil Service,
"the Home Civil Service" means Her Majesty's Home Civil Service.

Ministerial functions

52 Exercise of functions

(1) Statutory functions may be conferred on the Scottish Ministers by that name.

(2) Statutory functions of the Scottish Ministers, the First Minister or the Lord Advocate shall be exercisable on behalf of Her Majesty.

(3) Statutory functions of the Scottish Ministers shall be exercisable by any member of the Scottish Executive.

(4) Any act or omission of, or in relation to, any member of the Scottish Executive shall be treated as an act or omission of, or in relation to, each of them; and any property acquired, or liability incurred, by any member of the Scottish Executive shall be treated accordingly.

(5) Subsection (4) does not apply in relation to the exercise of—
(a) functions conferred on the First Minister alone, or
(b) retained functions of the Lord Advocate.

(6) In this Act, "retained functions" in relation to the Lord Advocate means—
(a) any functions exercisable by him immediately before he ceases to be a Minister of the Crown, and
(b) other statutory functions conferred on him alone after he ceases to be a Minister of the Crown.

(7) In this section, "statutory functions" means functions conferred by virtue of any enactment.

53 General transfer of functions

(1) The functions mentioned in subsection (2) shall, so far as they are exercisable within devolved competence, be exercisable by the Scottish Ministers instead of by a Minister of the Crown.

(2) Those functions are—
(a) those of Her Majesty's prerogative and other executive functions which are exercisable on behalf of Her Majesty by a Minister of the Crown,
(b) other functions conferred on a Minister of the Crown by a prerogative instrument, and
(c) functions conferred on a Minister of the Crown by any pre-commencement enactment,

but do not include any retained functions of the Lord Advocate.

(3) In this Act, "pre-commencement enactment" means—
(a) an Act passed before or in the same session as this Act and any other enactment made before the passing of this Act,
(b) an enactment made, before the commencement of this section, under such an Act or such other enactment,
(c) subordinate legislation under section 106, to the extent that the legislation states that it is to be treated as a pre-commencement enactment.

(4) This section and section 54 are modified by Part III of Schedule 4.

54 Devolved competence

(1) References in this Act to the exercise of a function being within or outside devolved competence are to be read in accordance with this section.

(2) It is outside devolved competence—
(a) to make any provision by subordinate legislation which would be outside the legislative competence of the Parliament if it were included in an Act of the Scottish Parliament, or
(b) to confirm or approve any subordinate legislation containing such provision.

(3) In the case of any function other than a function of making, confirming or approving subordinate legislation, it is outside devolved competence to exercise the function (or exercise it in any way) so far as a provision of an Act of the Scottish Parliament conferring the function (or, as the case may be, conferring it so as to be exercisable in that way) would be outside the legislative competence of the Parliament.

55 Functions exercisable with agreement

(1) A statutory provision, or any provision not contained in an enactment, which provides for a Minister of the Crown to exercise a function with the agreement of, or after consultation with, any other Minister of the Crown shall cease to have effect in relation to the exercise of the function by a member of the Scottish Executive by virtue of section 53.

(2) In subsection (1) "statutory provision" means any provision in a pre-commencement enactment other than paragraph 5 or 15 of Schedule 32 to the Local Government, Planning and Land Act 1980 (designation of enterprise zones).

56 Shared powers

(1) Despite the transfer by virtue of section 53 of any function under—
(a) section 17(1) of the Ministry of Transport Act 1919 (power to make advances for certain purposes),
(b) any Order in Council under section 1 of the United Nations Act 1946 (measures to give effect to Security Council decisions),
(c) section 9 of the Industrial Organisation and Development Act 1947 (levies for scientific research, promotion of exports, etc),
(d) section 5 of the Science and Technology Act 1965 (funding of scientific research),
(e) section 1 of the Mineral Exploration and Investment Grants Act 1972 (contributions in respect of mineral exploration),
(f) sections 10 to 12 of the Industry Act 1972 (credits and grants for construction of ships and offshore installations),
(g) sections 2, 11(3) and 12(4) of the Employment and Training Act 1973 (power to make arrangements for employment and training etc and to make certain payments),
(h) sections 7 to 9 and 11 to 13 of the Industrial Development Act 1982 (financial and other assistance for industry), and
(i) sections 39 and 40 of the Road Traffic Act 1988 (road safety information and training),

the function shall be exercisable by a Minister of the Crown as well as by the Scottish Ministers.

(2) Despite the transfer of any other function by virtue of section 53, the function shall, if subordinate legislation so provides, be exercisable (or be exercisable so far as the legislation provides) by a Minister of the Crown as well as by the Scottish Ministers.

(3) Subordinate legislation under subsection (2) may not be made so as to come into force at any time after the function in question has become exercisable by the Scottish Ministers.

(4) Any power referred to in section 53(2)(a) to establish, maintain or abolish a body, office or office-holder having functions which include both—
(a) functions which are exercisable in or as regards Scotland and do not relate to reserved matters, and
(b) other functions,

shall, despite that section, be exercisable jointly by the Minister of the Crown and the Scottish Ministers.

(5) In subsection (4), "office-holder" includes employee or other post-holder.

57 Community law and Convention rights

(1) Despite the transfer to the Scottish Ministers by virtue of section 53 of functions in relation to observing and implementing obligations under Community law, any function of a Minister of the Crown in relation to any matter shall continue to be exercisable by him as regards Scotland for the purposes specified in section 2(2) of the European Communities Act 1972.

(2) A member of the Scottish Executive has no power to make any subordinate legislation, or to do any other act, so far as the legislation or act is incompatible with any of the Convention rights or with Community law.

(3) Subsection (2) does not apply to an act of the Lord Advocate—
(a) in prosecuting any offence, or
(b) in his capacity as head of the systems of criminal prosecution and investigation of deaths in Scotland,

which, because of subsection (2) of section 6 of the Human Rights Act 1998, is not unlawful under subsection (1) of that section.

58 Power to prevent or require action

(1) If the Secretary of State has reasonable grounds to believe that any action proposed to be taken by a member of the Scottish Executive would be incompatible with any international obligations, he may by order direct that the proposed action shall not be taken.

(2) If the Secretary of State has reasonable grounds to believe that any action capable of being taken by a member of the Scottish Executive is required for the purpose of giving effect to any such obligations, he may by order direct that the action shall be taken.

(3) In subsections (1) and (2), "action" includes making, confirming or approving subordinate legislation and, in subsection (2), includes introducing a Bill in the Parliament.

(4) If any subordinate legislation made or which could be revoked by a member of the Scottish Executive contains provisions—
(a) which the Secretary of State has reasonable grounds to believe to be incompatible with any international obligations or the interests of defence or national security, or
(b) which make modifications of the law as it applies to reserved matters and which the Secretary of State has reasonable grounds to believe to have an adverse effect on the operation of the law as it applies to reserved matters,

the Secretary of State may by order revoke the legislation.

(5) An order under this section must state the reasons for making the order.

Property and liabilities

59 Property and liabilities of the Scottish Ministers

(1) Property may be held by the Scottish Ministers by that name.

(2) Property acquired by or transferred to the Scottish Ministers shall belong to, and liabilities incurred by the Scottish Ministers shall be liabilities of, the Scottish Ministers for the time being.

(3) In relation to property to be acquired by or transferred to, or belonging to, the Scottish Ministers or liabilities incurred by the Scottish Ministers, references to the Scottish Ministers—
(a) in any title recorded in the Register of Sasines or registered in the Land Register of Scotland, or
(b) in any other document,

shall be read in accordance with subsection (2).

(4) A document shall be validly executed by the Scottish Ministers if it is executed by any member of the Scottish Executive.

60 Transfers to the Scottish Ministers

(1) Subordinate legislation may provide—
(a) for the transfer to the Scottish Ministers of any property belonging to a Minister of the Crown or government department, or
(b) for the Scottish Ministers to have such rights or interests in relation to any property belonging to a Minister of the Crown or government department as the person making the legislation considers appropriate (whether in connection with a transfer or otherwise).

(2) Subordinate legislation may provide for the transfer to the Scottish Ministers of any liabilities to which a Minister of the Crown or government department is subject.

(3) Subordinate legislation under this section may only be made in connection with any transfer or sharing of functions of a Minister of the Crown by virtue of section 53, 63 or 89 or in any other circumstances in which the person making the legislation considers it appropriate to do so for the purposes of this Act.

61 Property and liabilities of the Lord Advocate and the First Minister

(1) Property may be held by the Lord Advocate by that name.

(2) Property acquired by or transferred to the Lord Advocate shall belong to, and liabilities incurred by the Lord Advocate shall be liabilities of, the Lord Advocate for the time being.

(3) In relation to property to be acquired by or transferred to, or belonging to, the Lord Advocate or liabilities incurred by the Lord Advocate, references to the Lord Advocate—
(a) in any title recorded in the Register of Sasines or registered in the Land Register of Scotland, or
(b) in any other document,

shall be read in accordance with subsection (2).

(4) Any rights and liabilities acquired or incurred by the First Minister shall be rights or (as the case may be) liabilities of the First Minister for the time being.

62 Transfers to the Lord Advocate

(1) Subordinate legislation may provide—
(a) for the transfer to the Lord Advocate of any property belonging to a Minister of the Crown or government department, or
(b) for the Lord Advocate to have such rights or interests in relation to any property belonging to a Minister of the Crown or government department as the person making the legislation considers appropriate (whether in connection with a transfer or otherwise).

(2) Subordinate legislation may provide for the transfer to the Lord Advocate of any liabilities to which a Minister of the Crown or government department is subject.

(3) Subordinate legislation under this section may only be made in connection with the Lord Advocate becoming a member of the Scottish Executive or having any retained functions or in any other circumstances in which the person making the legislation considers it appropriate to do so for the purposes of this Act.

Transfer of additional functions

63 Power to transfer functions

(1) Her Majesty may by Order in Council provide for any functions, so far as they are exercisable by a Minister of the Crown in or as regards Scotland, to be exercisable—
(a) by the Scottish Ministers instead of by the Minister of the Crown,
(b) by the Scottish Ministers concurrently with the Minister of the Crown, or
(c) by the Minister of the Crown only with the agreement of, or after consultation with, the Scottish Ministers.

(2) Where an Order is made under subsection (1)(a) or (b) in relation to a function of a Minister of the Crown which is exercisable only with the agreement of, or after consultation with, another Minister of the Crown, the function shall, unless the Order provides otherwise, be exercisable by the Scottish Ministers free from any such requirement.

(3) An Order under this section may, in particular, provide for any function exercisable by the Scottish Ministers by virtue of an Order under subsection (1)(a) or (b) to be exercisable subject to a requirement for the function to be exercised with the agreement of, or after consultation with, a Minister of the Crown or other person.

PART III FINANCIAL PROVISIONS

64 Scottish Consolidated Fund

(1) There shall be a Scottish Consolidated Fund.

(2) The Secretary of State shall from time to time make payments into the Fund out of money provided by Parliament of such amounts as he may determine.

(3) Sums received by an office-holder in the Scottish Administration shall be paid into the Fund.

(4) Subsection (3) is subject to any provision made by or under an Act of the Scottish Parliament for the disposal of or accounting for such sums.

(5) The Treasury may, after consulting with the Scottish Ministers, by order designate receipts of any description specified in the order which are payable into the Fund (or would be but for any provision made by or under an Act of the Scottish Parliament).

(6) The Scottish Ministers shall make payments to the Secretary of State, at such times and by such methods as the Treasury may from time to time determine, of sums equal to the total amount outstanding in respect of designated receipts.

(7) Amounts required for the payment of sums under subsection (6) shall be charged on the Fund.

(8) The Fund shall be held with the Paymaster General.

65 Payments out of the Fund

(1) A sum may only be paid out of the Scottish Consolidated Fund if—
(a) it has been charged on the Fund by any enactment,
(b) it is payable out of the Fund without further approval by virtue of this Act, or
(c) it is paid out for or in connection with any of the purposes mentioned in subsection (2) in accordance with rules made by or under an Act of the Scottish Parliament.

(2) Those purposes are—
(a) meeting expenditure of the Scottish Administration,
(b) meeting expenditure payable out of the Fund under any enactment.

(3) A sum paid out of the Fund shall not be applied for any purpose other than that for which it was charged or (as the case may be) paid out.

66 Borrowing by the Scottish Ministers etc

(1) The Scottish Ministers may borrow from the Secretary of State any sums required by them for the purpose of—
(a) meeting a temporary excess of sums paid out of the Scottish Consolidated Fund over sums paid into that Fund, or
(b) providing a working balance in the Fund.

(2) Amounts required for the repayment of, or the payment of interest on, sums borrowed under this section shall be charged on the Fund.

(3) Sums borrowed under this section shall be repaid to the Secretary of State at such times and by such methods, and interest on them shall be paid to him at such rates and at such times, as the Treasury may from time to time determine.

(4) A member of the Scottish Executive may borrow money only under this section or under any power conferred by any other Act of Parliament.

67 Lending by the Secretary of State

(1) The Treasury may issue to the Secretary of State out of the National Loans Fund such sums as are required by him for making loans under section 66.

(2) The aggregate at any time outstanding in respect of the principal of sums borrowed under that section shall not exceed £500 million.

(3) The Secretary of State may by order made with the consent of the Treasury substitute for the amount (or substituted amount) specified in subsection (2) such increased amount as may be specified in the order.

(4) Sums received by the Secretary of State under section 66(3) shall be paid into the National Loans Fund.

68 Borrowing by statutory bodies

(1) If a member of the Scottish Executive lends money to a body established under any enactment, the rate of interest on the loan shall not be less than the lowest rate determined by the Treasury under section 5 of the National Loans Act 1968 in respect of similar loans made out of the National Loans Fund on the day the loan is made.

(2) A body established under any enactment shall not, in pursuance of a power conferred by virtue of an Act of the Scottish Parliament, borrow money in a currency other than sterling except with the consent of the Scottish Ministers given with the approval of the Treasury.

69 The Auditor General for Scotland

(1) There shall be an Auditor General for Scotland who shall be an individual appointed by Her Majesty on the nomination of the Parliament.

(2) A recommendation shall not be made to Her Majesty for the removal from office of the Auditor General for Scotland unless the Parliament so resolves and, if the resolution is passed on a division, the number of members voting in favour is not less than two-thirds of the total number of seats for members of the Parliament.

(3) The validity of any act of the Auditor General for Scotland is not affected by any defect in his nomination by the Parliament.

(4) The Auditor General for Scotland shall not, in the exercise of any of his functions, be subject to the direction or control of any member of the Scottish Executive or of the Parliament.

(5) Subsection (4) does not apply in relation to any function conferred on him of preparing accounts.

70 Financial control, accounts and audit

(1) Scottish legislation shall provide—

(a) for proper accounts to be prepared by the Scottish Ministers, by the Lord Advocate and by other persons to whom sums are paid out of the Scottish Consolidated Fund, of their expenditure and receipts,

(b) for the Scottish Ministers to prepare an account of payments into and out of the Fund,

(c) for the Auditor General for Scotland to exercise, or ensure the exercise by other persons of, the functions mentioned in subsection (2),

(d) for access by persons exercising those functions to such documents as they may reasonably require,

(e) for members of the staff of the Scottish Administration designated for the purpose to be answerable to the Parliament in respect of the expenditure and receipts of each part of the Scottish Administration, and

(f) for the publication of parliamentary accounts and of reports on such accounts and for the laying of such accounts and reports before the Parliament.

(2) The functions referred to in subsection (1)(c) are—
(a) issuing credits for the payment of sums out of the Fund,
(b) examining parliamentary accounts (which includes determining whether sums paid out of the Fund have been paid out and applied in accordance with section 65), and certifying and reporting on them,
(c) carrying out examinations into the economy, efficiency and effectiveness with which the Scottish Ministers and the Lord Advocate have used their resources in discharging their functions, and
(d) carrying out examinations into the economy, efficiency and effectiveness with which other persons determined under Scottish legislation to whom sums are paid out of the Fund have used those sums in discharging their functions.

(3) Standing orders shall provide for the consideration by the Parliament of accounts and reports laid before it in pursuance of subsection (1)(f).

(4) Scottish legislation may make further provision for the purpose of ensuring that persons who receive sums derived from the Fund are accountable including, in particular, provision for any person to whom subsection (1)(a) does not apply to be accountable for his expenditure and receipts in respect of functions for which he receives sums derived from the Fund.

(5) Persons (other than the Auditor General for Scotland) charged with the exercise of any function mentioned in subsection (2) or other like function conferred by Scottish legislation shall not, in the exercise of that or any ancillary function, be subject to the direction or control of any member of the Scottish Executive or of the Parliament.

(6) Scottish legislation may not require any cross-border public authority to prepare accounts if any other legislation requires—
(a) the authority to prepare accounts of its expenditure and receipts, and
(b) the accounts to be examined, certified and reported on by the Auditor General for Scotland, the Comptroller and Auditor General or a person appointed by either of them.

(7) Subsection (2)(b) does not apply to accounts prepared by the Auditor General for Scotland.

(8) This section does not require Scottish legislation to impose any requirement which is imposed by any other legislation.

(9) In this section—
"parliamentary accounts" means—
(a) any accounts prepared in pursuance of subsection (1)(a) or (b), and
(b) any accounts referred to in subsection (6) which are required to be examined, certified and reported on by the Auditor General for Scotland or any person appointed by him,

"Scottish legislation" means provision made by or under an Act of the Scottish Parliament and "other legislation" means provision made by any other enactment.

71 Existing debt

(1) Subsections (2) to (4) apply where—
(a) power to lend money under a provision of a pre-commencement enactment was exercised by the Secretary of State,
(b) the sums required by him for the exercise of the power were issued by the Treasury out of the National Loans Fund, and
(c) the power is exercisable by the Scottish Ministers by virtue of section 53, or would have been so exercisable but for the repeal of the pre-commencement enactment.

(2) Any amount payable by way of repayment of or interest on the loan shall be paid to the Scottish Ministers and into the Scottish Consolidated Fund (instead of to the Secretary of State and into the National Loans Fund).

(3) Amounts equal to those which are to be received by the Scottish Ministers in repayment of principal shall be treated as being amounts of advances made on the commencement of this section to the Scottish Ministers by the Secretary of State.

(4) Such advances shall be repaid to the Secretary of State at such times and by such methods, and interest on them shall be paid to him at such rates and at such times, as the Treasury may from time to time determine.

(5) Subsection (6) applies to any amount outstanding immediately before the commencement of this subsection in respect of the principal of the sum treated by virtue of section 2(3) of the Government Trading Funds Act 1973 as issued to the Registers of Scotland Executive Agency Trading Fund on the day on which the order establishing that fund came into force ("the issue date").

(6) The Secretary of State may, with the agreement of the Treasury, by order provide—
(a) for the amount to be treated as an advance made by him to the Scottish Ministers on the issue date, and
(b) for the advance to be repaid to him at such times and by such methods, and for interest on the advance to be paid to him at such rates and at such times, as were determined by the Treasury under section 2B(3) of that Act in respect of the sum referred to in subsection (5).

(7) Sums required to be paid under subsection (4) or (6) shall be charged on the Scottish Consolidated Fund.

(8) Sums received under subsection (4) or (6) shall be paid into the National Loans Fund.

72 Accounts of loans to the Scottish Ministers

The Secretary of State shall, for each financial year—

(a) prepare, in such form and manner as the Treasury may direct, an account of sums paid and received by him under sections 66, 67 and 71, and

(b) send the account to the Comptroller and Auditor General not later than the end of November in the following financial year,

and the Comptroller and Auditor General shall examine, certify and report on the account and shall lay copies of it and of his report before each House of Parliament.

PART IV THE TAX-VARYING POWER

73 Power to fix basic rate for Scottish taxpayers

(1) Subject to section 74, this section applies for any year of assessment for which income tax is charged if—

(a) the Parliament has passed a resolution providing for the percentage determined to be the basic rate for that year to be increased or reduced for Scottish taxpayers in accordance with the resolution,

(b) the increase or reduction provided for is confined to an increase or reduction by a number not exceeding three which is specified in the resolution and is either a whole number or half of a whole number, and

(c) the resolution has not been cancelled by a subsequent resolution of the Parliament.

(2) Where this section applies for any year of assessment the Income Tax Acts (excluding this Part) shall have effect in relation to the income of Scottish taxpayers as if any rate determined by the Parliament of the United Kingdom to be the basic rate for that year were increased or reduced in accordance with the resolution of the Scottish Parliament.

(3) In subsection (2) the reference to the income of Scottish taxpayers does not include a reference to any income of Scottish taxpayers which, had it been income for the year 1998–99, would have been income to which section 1A of the Income and Corporation Taxes Act 1988 (income from savings and distributions) applied for that year.

(4) In this section—

(a) a reference, in relation to any year of assessment, to income tax being charged for that year includes a reference to the passing of a PCTA resolution that provides for the charging of that tax for that year, and

(b) a reference, in relation to a year of assessment, to the determination by the Parliament of the United Kingdom of a rate to be the basic rate for that year includes a reference to the passing of a PCTA resolution specifying a percentage to be the basic rate for that year.

(5) In this section "a PCTA resolution" means a resolution of the House of Commons containing such a declaration as is mentioned in section 1(2)(b) of the Provisional Collection of Taxes Act 1968.

74 Supplemental provision with respect to resolutions

(1) This section applies to any resolution of the Parliament ("a tax-varying resolution") which—
(a) provides, in accordance with section 73, for an increase or reduction for Scottish taxpayers of the basic rate for any year of assessment, or
(b) cancels a previous resolution of the Parliament providing for such an increase or reduction.

(2) Subject to subsection (3), a tax-varying resolution—
(a) must be expressed so as to relate to no more than a single year of assessment beginning after, but no more than twelve months after, the passing of the resolution, but
(b) shall have effect in relation to a determination by the Parliament of the United Kingdom of the rate to be the basic rate for that year irrespective of whether that determination had been made at the time of the passing of the resolution.

(3) Subsection (2) shall not prevent a tax-varying resolution relating to any year of assessment from being passed and having effect where—
(a) a determination by the Parliament of the United Kingdom of the rate to be the basic rate for that year is made after, or less than a month before, the beginning of that year,
(b) that determination is not confined to the passing of the enactment by which a determination of the same rate by a PCTA resolution is ratified, and
(c) the tax-varying resolution is passed within the period of one month beginning with the day of the making by the Parliament of the United Kingdom of its determination.

(4) Where, in a case to which subsection (3) applies, a tax-varying resolution is passed after the beginning of the year of assessment to which it relates—
(a) the resolution shall have effect as from the beginning of that year, and
(b) all such payments, repayments, deductions and other adjustments shall be made as are required to restore the position to what it would have been if the resolution had been passed before the beginning of that year.

(5) Standing orders shall ensure that only a member of the Scottish Executive may move a motion for a tax-varying resolution.

(6) A tax-varying resolution shall not be passed so as to have effect in relation to any year of assessment before the year 2000–01.

(7) Subsections (4) and (5) of section 73 apply for the purposes of this section as they apply for the purposes of that section.

75 Scottish taxpayers

(1) For the purposes of this Part a person is a Scottish taxpayer in relation to any year of assessment if—

(a) he is an individual who, for income tax purposes, is treated as resident in the United Kingdom in that year, and

(b) Scotland is the part of the United Kingdom with which he has the closest connection during that year.

(2) For the purposes of this section an individual who is treated for income tax purposes as resident in the United Kingdom in any year of assessment has his closest connection with Scotland during that year if, but only if, one or more of the following paragraphs applies in his case—

(a) he is an individual to whom subsection (3) applies for that year,

(b) the number of days which he spends in Scotland in that year is equal to or exceeds the number of days in that year which he spends elsewhere in the United Kingdom,

(c) he is an individual who, for the whole or any part of that year, is a member of Parliament for a constituency in Scotland, a member of the European Parliament for Scotland or a member of the Scottish Parliament.

(3) This subsection applies to an individual for a year of assessment if—

(a) he spends at least a part of that year in Scotland,

(b) for at least a part of the time that he spends in Scotland in that year, his principal UK home is located in Scotland and he makes use of it as a place of residence, and

(c) the times in that year when Scotland is where his principal UK home is located comprise (in aggregate) at least as much of that year as the times (if any) in that year when the location of his principal UK home is not in Scotland.

(4) For the purposes of this section—

(a) an individual spends a day in Scotland if, but only if, he is in Scotland at the end of that day, and

(b) an individual spends a day elsewhere in the United Kingdom if, but only if, he is in the United Kingdom at the end of that day and it is not a day that he spends in Scotland.

(5) For the purposes of this section an individual's principal UK home at any time is located in Scotland if at that time—

(a) he is an individual with a place of residence in Scotland, and

(b) in the case of an individual with two or more places of residence in the United Kingdom, Scotland is the location of such one of those places as at that time is his main place of residence in the United Kingdom.

(6) In this section "place" includes a place on board a vessel or other means of transport.

76 Changes to income tax structure

(1) This section applies where—
(a) there has been a proposal for the modification of any provision made by or under the Income Tax Acts,
(b) that proposal is one made and published by the Treasury or the Board, or (without having been so made and published) appears to the Treasury to be a proposal to which effect is likely to be given by Act of Parliament, and
(c) it appears to the Treasury that the proposed modification would have a significant effect on the practical extent for any year of assessment of the Parliament's tax-varying powers.

(2) It shall be the duty of the Treasury, as soon as reasonably practicable after the publication of the proposal, or (as the case may be) as soon as reasonably practicable after it first appears to the Treasury that the proposal is likely to be enacted, to lay before the House of Commons—
(a) a statement of whether, in the Treasury's opinion, an amendment of the Parliament's tax-varying powers is required as a consequence of the proposal, and
(b) if in their opinion an amendment of those powers is required, the Treasury's proposals for amending those powers.

(3) Any proposals for amending the Parliament's tax-varying powers that are laid before the House of Commons by the Treasury under this section—
(a) must be confined to income tax,
(b) must appear to the Treasury to satisfy the conditions set out in subsections (4) and (5), and
(c) must not contain any proposal for the Parliament's tax-varying powers to be exercisable in relation to the taxation of income from savings or distributions.

(4) The first condition mentioned in subsection (3)(b) is that the proposals would secure—
(a) so far as possible, and
(b) after making due allowance for annual changes in the retail prices index,

that the practical extent of the Parliament's tax-varying powers would remain broadly the same from year to year as it would be if (apart from any resolution of the Parliament) the law relating to income tax were the same from year to year as it was in relation to the year 1997–98.

(5) The second condition so mentioned is that the proposals would not enable the Parliament's tax-varying powers to be exercised for any year of assessment so as to have an effect on the levels of the after-tax income of Scottish taxpayers generally that would be significantly different from the effect their exercise could have had in any previous year of assessment.

(6) References in this section to the practical extent of the Parliament's tax-varying powers are references to the amounts of income tax for any

year of assessment which appear to be or (as the case may be) to have been the maximum amounts capable of being raised and foregone in that year in pursuance of a resolution of the Parliament.

(7) In this section "income from savings or distributions" means income which, had it been income for the year 1998–99, would have been income to which section 1A of the Income and Corporation Taxes Act 1988 applied for that year.

77 Accounting for additional Scottish tax

(1) Where the basic rate for any year of assessment is increased for Scottish taxpayers by a resolution of the Parliament, it shall be the duty of the Board to pay amounts into the Scottish Consolidated Fund in accordance with this section.

(2) The amounts of the payments to be made by the Board under this section, and the times at which they are to be made, shall be determined by the Board and notified to the Scottish Ministers as soon as reasonably practicable after the passing of the resolution providing for the increase to which they relate.

(3) Any determination made by the Board under subsection (2) for any year of assessment shall be such as appears to the Board to be necessary for securing that, in the course of that year, amounts are paid into the Scottish Consolidated Fund which are equal in total to the amount estimated by the Board to represent the proportion of the income tax receipts for that year that is properly attributable to a resolution of the Parliament.

(4) For the purposes of this section the Board shall make and maintain arrangements as to—

(a) the manner of estimating the proportion of the income tax receipts for a year of assessment that is properly attributable to a resolution of the Parliament,

(b) the circumstances and manner in which an estimate of that proportion or of those receipts may be revised before or in the course of the year of assessment to which it relates,

(c) the manner of determining the amount of each payment to be made in respect of any such estimate, and

(d) the times at which, and manner in which, those amounts are to be paid by the Board into the Scottish Consolidated Fund.

(5) Arrangements under subsection (4) may include provision for the making of adjustments to the amounts paid by the Board where any estimate made for the purposes of this section in respect of any year of assessment (whether the current year or a previous year) turns out to have been inaccurate.

(6) Before making or modifying any arrangements under subsection (4) or (5), the Board shall consult with the Scottish Ministers.

(7) In this section "income tax receipts", in relation to any year of assessment, means so much as is referable to income tax charged for that year of any sums which, disregarding both—
(a) subsection (8), and
(b) any regulations or direction made or given by the Treasury,

are sums that have to be paid into the Consolidated Fund under section 10 of the Exchequer and Audit Departments Act 1866 (gross revenues of Board's department to be paid into that Fund after the making of specified deductions).

(8) Sums required by the Board for making payments under this section shall be paid out of the gross revenues of the Board's department; and, accordingly, those sums shall be treated as included in the amounts to be deducted from those revenues before they are paid into the Consolidated Fund under section 10 of the Exchequer and Audit Departments Act 1866.

78 Effect of tax reduction for Scottish taxpayers

(1) Where the basic rate for any year of assessment is reduced for Scottish taxpayers by a resolution of the Parliament, payments to the Board in accordance with this section shall be charged on the Scottish Consolidated Fund.

(2) The amounts of the payments to be made out of the Scottish Consolidated Fund under this section, and the times at which they are to be made, shall be determined by the Board and notified to the Scottish Ministers as soon as reasonably practicable after the passing of the resolution providing for the reduction to which they relate.

(3) Any determination made by the Board under subsection (2) for any year of assessment shall be such as appears to the Board to be necessary for securing that in the course of that year amounts are paid to the Board which are equal in total to the amount estimated by the Board to represent the shortfall in income tax receipts for that year that is properly attributable to a resolution of the Parliament.

(4) For the purposes of this section the Board shall make and maintain arrangements as to—
(a) the manner of estimating the shortfall in income tax receipts for any year of assessment that is properly attributable to a resolution of the Parliament,
(b) the circumstances and manner in which an estimate of that shortfall may be revised before or in the course of the year of assessment to which it relates,
(c) the manner of determining the amount of each payment to be made in respect of any such estimate, and
(d) the times at which, and manner in which, those amounts are to be paid to the Board.

(5) Arrangements under subsection (4) may include provision for the making of adjustments to the amounts paid to the Board where any estimate made for the purposes of this section in respect of any year of assessment (whether the current year or a previous year) turns out to have been inaccurate.

(6) Before making or modifying any arrangements under subsection (4) or (5), the Board shall consult with the Scottish Ministers.

(7) In this section "income tax receipts" has the same meaning as in section 77.

(8) The sums paid to the Board under this section shall be treated for the purposes of section 10 of the Exchequer and Audit Departments Act 1866 (payment, after the making of the specified deductions, of gross revenues into the Consolidated Fund) as comprised in their department's gross revenues.

79 Supplemental powers to modify enactments

(1) The Treasury may by order make such modifications of any enactment as they consider necessary or expedient in consequence of—
(a) the fact that the Parliament has, or is to have, the power to pass a tax-varying resolution, or
(b) the fact (where it is the case) that the Parliament has passed such a resolution.

(2) The Treasury may by order make provision—
(a) excluding the operation of section 73(2) in relation to any enactment, and
(b) making any such other modifications of any enactment as they consider necessary or expedient in connection with, or for the purposes of, any such exclusion.

(3) Without prejudice to the generality of the powers conferred by the preceding provisions of this section, an order under this section may provide that, where any tax-varying resolution relating to any year of assessment is passed, that resolution does not require any change in the amounts repayable or deductible under section 203 of the Income and Corporation Taxes Act 1988 (PAYE) between—
(a) the beginning of that year, and
(b) such day falling after the passing of the resolution as may be specified in the order.

(4) An order under this section may, to the extent that the Treasury consider it to be appropriate, take effect retrospectively from the beginning of the year of assessment in which it is made.

(5) In this section "tax-varying resolution" has the same meaning as in section 74.

80 Reimbursement of expenses

The Scottish Ministers may reimburse any Minister of the Crown or government department for administrative expenses incurred by virtue of this Part at any time after the passing of this Act by the Minister or department.

PART V MISCELLANEOUS AND GENERAL

Remuneration of members of the Parliament and Executive

81 Remuneration of members of the Parliament and Executive

(1) The Parliament shall make provision for the payment of salaries to members of the Parliament and members of the Scottish Executive.

(2) The Parliament may make provision for the payment of allowances to members of the Parliament or members of the Scottish Executive.

(3) The Parliament may make provision for the payment of pensions, gratuities or allowances to, or in respect of, any person who—
(a) has ceased to be a member of the Parliament or the Scottish Executive, or
(b) has ceased to hold such office, employment or other post in connection with the Parliament or the Scottish Executive as the Parliament may determine but continues to be a member of the Parliament or the Scottish Executive.

(4) Such provision may, in particular, include provision for—
(a) contributions or payments towards provision for such pensions, gratuities or allowances,
(b) the establishment and administration (whether by the Parliamentary corporation or otherwise) of one or more pension schemes.

(5) In this section "provision" includes provision—
(a) by an Act of the Scottish Parliament, or
(b) by a resolution of the Parliament conferring functions on the Parliamentary corporation;

and references to a member of the Scottish Executive include a junior Scottish Minister.

82 Limits on salaries of members of the Parliament

(1) The Parliament shall ensure that the amount of salary payable to a member of the Parliament in accordance with section 81 is reduced if any salary is payable to him—
(a) pursuant to a resolution (or combination of resolutions) of either House of Parliament relating to the remuneration of members of that House, or
(b) under section 1 of the European Parliament (Pay and Pensions) Act 1979 (remuneration of United Kingdom MEPs).

(2) The Parliament shall ensure that the amount of salary is reduced—
(a) to a particular proportion of what it would otherwise be or to a particular amount, or
(b) by the amount of any salary payable to the member as mentioned in subsection (1)(a) or (b), by a particular proportion of that amount or by some other particular amount.

83 Remuneration: supplementary

(1) The Parliament shall ensure that information concerning sums paid as salaries, allowances, pensions or gratuities of the kind mentioned in section 81 is published for each financial year.

(2) No payment of salary or allowances of the kind mentioned in section 81(1) or (2) shall be made to a person who is required by section 84 to take an oath unless he has done so.

(3) Subsection (2) does not affect any entitlement to payments in respect of the period before the person concerned took the oath once he has done so.

(4) For the purposes of sections 81 and 82, a person who is a member of the Parliament immediately before the Parliament is dissolved shall be treated—
(a) if he continues to hold office by virtue of section 19(2) or paragraph 1 of Schedule 2, as if he were such a member until the end of the day on which he ceases to hold such office, and
(b) if he does not fall within paragraph (a) but is nominated as a candidate at the subsequent general election, as if he were such a member until the end of the day on which the election is held.

(5) Different provision may be made under section 81 or 82 for different cases.

Other provision about members of the Parliament etc

84 Oaths

(1) A person who is returned as a member of the Parliament shall take the oath of allegiance (whether or not he has taken the oath after being returned on a previous occasion or otherwise than as a member of the Parliament).

(2) He shall do so at a meeting of the Parliament and shall not take part in any other proceedings of the Parliament until he has done so.

(3) If he has not done so within the period of two months beginning with the day on which he was returned, or such longer period as the Parliament may have allowed before the end of that period, he shall cease to be a member of the Parliament (so that his seat is vacant).

(4) Each member of the Scottish Executive shall on appointment—
(a) take the official oath in the form provided by the Promissory Oaths Act 1868, and
(b) take the oath of allegiance.

(5) Each junior Scottish Minister shall on appointment take the oath of allegiance.

(6) Subsections (4) and (5) do not require a member of the Parliament to take the oath of allegiance again if he has already done so in compliance with his duty as a member.

(7) In this section, references to taking the oath of allegiance are to taking it in the form provided by the Promissory Oaths Act 1868.

85 Exemption from jury service

(1) In Part III of Schedule 1 to the Juries Act 1974 (persons excusable as of right from jury service), after the entries under the heading "Parliament" there is inserted—

"Scottish Parliament and Scottish Executive

Members of the Scottish Parliament.
Members of the Scottish Executive.
Junior Scottish Ministers."

(2) In Part III of Schedule 1 to the Law Reform (Miscellaneous Provisions) (Scotland) Act 1980 (persons excusable as of right from jury service), after the entries in Group A there is inserted—

"Group AB

Scottish Parliament and Scottish Executive

(a) members of the Scottish Parliament;
(b) members of the Scottish Executive; and
(c) junior Scottish Ministers."

Arrangements at Westminster

86 Scottish representation at Westminster

(1) Schedule 2 to the Parliamentary Constituencies Act 1986 (rules for redistribution of seats) is amended as follows.

(2) Rule 1(2) (Scotland to have not less than 71 constituencies) is omitted.

(3) After rule 3 there is inserted—

"3A A constituency which includes the Orkney Islands or the Shetland Islands shall not include the whole or any part of a local government area other than the Orkney Islands and the Shetland Islands.";

and in rule 4, for "3" there is substituted "3A".

(4) In applying rule 5 (electoral quotas for each part of the United Kingdom) to Scotland for the purposes of the first report of the Boundary

Commission for Scotland to be submitted under section 3(1) of that Act after the commencement of this subsection, "electoral quota" means the number which, on the enumeration date in relation to that report, is the electoral quota for England.

(5) In paragraph 7 (Commissions do not have to give full effect to all rules), after "rules" there is inserted "(except rule 3A)".

87 The Advocate General for Scotland

(1) In Schedule 2 to the House of Commons Disqualification Act 1975 (Ministerial offices) and Part III of Schedule 1 to the Ministerial and other Salaries Act 1975 (salaries of the Law Officers), after the entry for the Solicitor General there is inserted—
"Advocate General for Scotland".

(2) The validity of anything done in relation to the Advocate General is not affected by a vacancy in that office.

(3) If that office is vacant or the Advocate General is for any reason unable to act, his functions shall be exercisable by such other Minister of the Crown as the Prime Minister may determine in writing.

Cross-border public authorities

88 Cross-border public authorities: initial status

(1) Sections 53 and 118 to 121 shall not apply in relation to any function which is specifically exercisable in relation to a cross-border public authority; and section 118 shall not apply in relation to any function of such an authority.

(2) A Minister of the Crown shall consult the Scottish Ministers before he exercises, in relation to a cross-border public authority, any specific function—

(a) which relates to any appointment or removal of the cross-border public authority concerned or of any members or office-holders of the cross-border public authority concerned, or
(b) whose exercise might affect Scotland otherwise than wholly in relation to reserved matters.

(3) Any cross-border public authority or other person which is required by a pre-commencement enactment or a prerogative instrument to lay any report relating to a cross-border public authority before Parliament or either House of Parliament shall also lay the report before the Scottish Parliament.

(4) Subsections (1) to (3) are subject to any Order in Council made under section 89.

(5) In this Act "cross-border public authority" means any body, government department, office or office-holder specified in an Order in Council made by Her Majesty under this section.

(6) Such an Order may only specify a body, government department, office or office-holder which (at the time when the Order is made) has, in addition to other functions, functions which are exercisable in or as regards Scotland and do not relate to reserved matters.

(7) In this section—
"office-holder" includes employee or other post-holder,
"report" includes accounts and any statement.

89 Power to adapt etc cross-border public authorities

(1) Her Majesty may by Order in Council make such provision in relation to a cross-border public authority as She considers necessary or expedient in consequence of this Act.

(2) Such provision may, in particular, include provision—
(a) modifying any function of a cross-border public authority or of a Minister of the Crown in relation to such an authority,
(b) conferring any function on a cross-border public authority or on a Minister of the Crown or the Scottish Ministers in relation to such an authority,
(c) modifying the constitution of a cross-border public authority,
(d) modifying the application of section 56(4) or 88(1), (2) or (3),
(e) for any function to be exercisable by the Scottish Ministers instead of by a Minister of the Crown, or by the one concurrently with the other, or by both jointly or by either with the agreement of or after consultation with the other,
(f) apportioning any assets or liabilities,
(g) imposing, or enabling the imposition of, any limits or other restrictions in addition to or in substitution for existing limits or restrictions,
(h) providing for sums to be charged on or payable out of, or paid into, the Scottish Consolidated Fund (instead of or in addition to payments into or out of the Consolidated Fund or the National Loans Fund or out of money provided by Parliament),
(i) requiring payments, with or without interest, to a Minister of the Crown or into the Consolidated Fund or National Loans Fund.

(3) No recommendation shall be made to Her Majesty in Council to make an Order under this section unless the cross-border public authority concerned has been consulted.

90 Power to transfer property of cross-border public authorities

(1) This section applies if an Act of the Scottish Parliament provides for any functions of a cross-border public authority to be no longer exercisable in or as regards Scotland.

(2) Her Majesty may by Order in Council provide—
(a) for the transfer of any property to which this section applies, or

(b) for any person to have such rights or interests in relation to any property to which this section applies as Her Majesty considers appropriate (whether in connection with a transfer or otherwise).

(3) This section applies to property belonging to the cross-border public authority concerned which appears to Her Majesty—
(a) to be held or used wholly or partly for or in connection with the exercise of any of the functions concerned, or
(b) not to be within paragraph (a) but, when last held or used for or in connection with the exercise of any function, to have been so held or used for in connection with the exercise of any of the functions concerned.

(4) Her Majesty may by Order in Council provide for the transfer of any liabilities—
(a) to which the cross-border public authority concerned is subject, and
(b) which appear to Her Majesty to have been incurred wholly or partly for or in connection with the exercise of any of the functions concerned.

(5) No recommendation shall be made to Her Majesty in Council to make an Order under this section unless the cross-border public authority concerned has been consulted.

Miscellaneous

91 Maladministration

(1) The Parliament shall make provision for the investigation of relevant complaints made to its members in respect of any action taken by or on behalf of—
(a) a member of the Scottish Executive in the exercise of functions conferred on the Scottish Ministers, or
(b) any other office-holder in the Scottish Administration.

(2) For the purposes of subsection (1), a complaint is a relevant complaint if it is a complaint of a kind which could be investigated under the Parliamentary Commissioner Act 1967 if it were made to a member of the House of Commons in respect of a government department or other authority to which that Act applies.

(3) The Parliament may make provision for the investigation of complaints in respect of—
(a) any action taken by or on behalf of an office-holder in the Scottish Administration,
(b) any action taken by or on behalf of the Parliamentary corporation,
(c) any action taken by or on behalf of a Scottish public authority with mixed functions or no reserved functions, or
(d) any action concerning Scotland and not relating to reserved matters which is taken by or on behalf of a cross-border public authority.

(4) In making provision of the kind required by subsection (1), the Parliament shall have regard (among other things) to the Act of 1967.

(5) Sections 53 and 117 to 121 shall not apply in relation to functions conferred by or under the Act of 1967.

(6) In this section—
"action" includes failure to act (and related expressions shall be read accordingly),
"provision" means provision by an Act of the Scottish Parliament;

and the references to the Act of 1967 are to that Act as it has effect on the commencement of this section.

92 Queen's Printer for Scotland

(1) There shall be a Queen's Printer for Scotland who shall—
(a) exercise the Queen's Printer functions in relation to Acts of the Scottish Parliament and subordinate legislation to which this section applies, and
(b) exercise any other functions conferred on her by this Act or any other enactment.

(2) In subsection (1), "the Queen's Printer functions" means the printing functions in relation to Acts of Parliament and subordinate legislation of the Queen's Printer of Acts of Parliament.

(3) The Queen's Printer for Scotland shall also on behalf of Her Majesty exercise Her rights and privileges in connection with—
(a) Crown copyright in Acts of the Scottish Parliament,
(b) Crown copyright in subordinate legislation to which this section applies,
(c) Crown copyright in any existing or future works (other than subordinate legislation) made in the exercise of a function which is exercisable by any office-holder in, or member of the staff of, the Scottish Administration (or would be so exercisable if the function had not ceased to exist),
(d) other copyright assigned to Her Majesty in works made in connection with the exercise of functions by any such office-holder or member.

(4) This section applies to subordinate legislation made, confirmed or approved—
(a) by a member of the Scottish Executive,
(b) by a Scottish public authority with mixed functions or no reserved functions, or
(c) within devolved competence by a person other than a Minister of the Crown or such a member or authority.

(5) The Queen's Printer of Acts of Parliament shall hold the office of Queen's Printer for Scotland.

(6) References in this Act to a Scottish public authority include the Queen's Printer for Scotland.

93 Agency arrangements

(1) A Minister of the Crown may make arrangements for any of his specified functions to be exercised on his behalf by the Scottish Ministers; and the Scottish Ministers may make arrangements for any of their specified functions to be exercised on their behalf by a Minister of the Crown.

(2) An arrangement under this section does not affect a person's responsibility for the exercise of his functions.

(3) In this section—
"functions" does not include a function of making, confirming or approving subordinate legislation,
"Minister of the Crown" includes government department,
"specified" means specified in an Order in Council made by Her Majesty under this subsection;

and this section applies to the Lord Advocate as it applies to the Scottish Ministers.

94 Private legislation

(1) This section applies where a pre-commencement enactment makes provision which has the effect of—
(a) requiring any order to be confirmed by Act of Parliament, or
(b) requiring any order (within the meaning of the Statutory Orders (Special Procedure) Act 1945) to be subject to special parliamentary procedure,

and power to make, confirm or approve the order in question is exercisable by the Scottish Ministers by virtue of section 53.

(2) The provision shall have effect, so far as it relates to the exercise of the power to make, confirm or approve the order by virtue of section 53, as if it required the order—
(a) to be confirmed by an Act of the Scottish Parliament, or
(b) (as the case may be) to be subject to such special procedure as may be provided by or under such an Act.

95 Appointment and removal of judges

(1) It shall continue to be for the Prime Minister to recommend to Her Majesty the appointment of a person as Lord President of the Court of Session or Lord Justice Clerk.

(2) The Prime Minister shall not recommend to Her Majesty the appointment of any person who has not been nominated by the First Minister for such appointment.

(3) Before nominating persons for such appointment the First Minister shall consult the Lord President and the Lord Justice Clerk (unless, in either case, the office is vacant).

(4) It is for the First Minister, after consulting the Lord President, to recommend to Her Majesty the appointment of a person as—
(a) a judge of the Court of Session (other than the Lord President or the Lord Justice Clerk), or
(b) a sheriff principal or a sheriff.

(5) The First Minister shall comply with any requirement in relation to—
(a) a nomination under subsection (2), or
(b) a recommendation under subsection (4),

imposed by virtue of any enactment.

(6) A judge of the Court of Session and the Chairman of the Scottish Land Court may be removed from office only by Her Majesty; and any recommendation to Her Majesty for such removal shall be made by the First Minister.

(7) The First Minister shall make such a recommendation if (and only if) the Parliament, on a motion made by the First Minister, resolves that such a recommendation should be made.

(8) Provision shall be made for a tribunal constituted by the First Minister to investigate and report on whether a judge of the Court of Session or the Chairman of the Scottish Land Court is unfit for office by reason of inability, neglect of duty or misbehaviour and for the report to be laid before the Parliament.

(9) Such provision shall include provision—
(a) for the constitution of the tribunal by the First Minister when requested by the Lord President to do so and in such other circumstances as the First Minister thinks fit, and
(b) for the appointment to chair the tribunal of a member of the Judicial Committee who holds or has held any of the offices referred to in section 103(2),

and may include provision for suspension from office.

(10) The First Minister may make a motion under subsection (7) only if—
(a) he has received from a tribunal constituted in pursuance of subsection (8) a written report concluding that the person in question is unfit for office by reason of inability, neglect of duty or misbehaviour and giving reasons for that conclusion,
(b) where the person in question is the Lord President or the Lord Justice Clerk, he has consulted the Prime Minister, and
(c) he has complied with any other requirement imposed by virtue of any enactment.

(11) In subsections (8) to (10)—
"provision" means provision by or under an Act of the Scottish Parliament,
"tribunal" means a tribunal of at least three persons.

96 Provision of information to the Treasury

(1) The Treasury may require the Scottish Ministers to provide, within such period as the Treasury may reasonably specify, such information, in such form and prepared in such manner, as the Treasury may reasonably specify.

(2) If the information is not in their possession or under their control, their duty under subsection (1) is to take all reasonable steps to comply with the requirement.

97 Assistance for opposition parties

(1) Her Majesty may by Order in Council provide for the Parliamentary corporation to make payments to registered political parties for the purpose of assisting members of the Parliament who are connected with such parties to perform their Parliamentary duties.

(2) The corporation shall not make any payment to a party in pursuance of such an Order if any of the members of the Parliament who are connected with the party are also members of the Scottish Executive or junior Scottish Ministers.

(3) But such an Order may, in any circumstances specified in the Order, require the fact that any members who are connected with a party are also members of the Scottish Executive or junior Scottish Ministers to be disregarded.

(4) Such an Order may determine the circumstances in which a member of the Parliament and a registered political party are to be regarded for the purposes of this section as connected.

Juridical

98 Devolution issues

Schedule 6 (which makes provision in relation to devolution issues) shall have effect.

99 Rights and liabilities of the Crown in different capacities

(1) Rights and liabilities may arise between the Crown in right of Her Majesty's Government in the United Kingdom and the Crown in right of the Scottish Administration by virtue of a contract, by operation of law or by virtue of an enactment as they may arise between subjects.

(2) Property and liabilities may be transferred between the Crown in one of those capacities and the Crown in the other capacity as they may be transferred between subjects; and they may together create, vary or extinguish any property or liability as subjects may.

(3) Proceedings in respect of—
(a) any property or liabilities to which the Crown in one of those capacities is entitled or subject under subsection (1) or (2), or

(b) the exercise of, or failure to exercise, any function exercisable by an office-holder of the Crown in one of those capacities,

may be instituted by the Crown in either capacity; and the Crown in the other capacity may be a separate party in the proceedings.

(4) This section applies to a unilateral obligation as it applies to a contract.

(5) In this section—
"office-holder", in relation to the Crown in right of Her Majesty's Government in the United Kingdom, means any Minister of the Crown or other office-holder under the Crown in that capacity and, in relation to the Crown in right of the Scottish Administration, means any office-holder in the Scottish Administration,
"subject" means a person not acting on behalf of the Crown.

100 Human rights

(1) This Act does not enable a person—
(a) to bring any proceedings in a court or tribunal on the ground that an act is incompatible with the Convention rights, or
(b) to rely on any of the Convention rights in any such proceedings,

unless he would be a victim for the purposes of Article 34 of the Convention (within the meaning of the Human Rights Act 1998) if proceedings in respect of the act were brought in the European Court of Human Rights.

(2) Subsection (1) does not apply to the Lord Advocate, the Advocate General, the Attorney General or the Attorney General for Northern Ireland.

(3) This Act does not enable a court or tribunal to award any damages in respect of an act which is incompatible with any of the Convention rights which it could not award if section 8(3) and (4) of the Human Rights Act 1998 applied.

(4) In this section "act" means—
(a) making any legislation,
(b) any other act or failure to act, if it is the act or failure of a member of the Scottish Executive.

101 Interpretation of Acts of the Scottish Parliament etc

(1) This section applies to—
(a) any provision of an Act of the Scottish Parliament, or of a Bill for such an Act, and
(b) any provision of subordinate legislation made, confirmed or approved, or purporting to be made, confirmed or approved, by a member of the Scottish Executive,

which could be read in such a way as to be outside competence.

(2) Such a provision is to be read as narrowly as is required for it to be within competence, if such a reading is possible, and is to have effect accordingly.

(3) In this section "competence"—
(a) in relation to an Act of the Scottish Parliament, or a Bill for such an Act, means the legislative competence of the Parliament, and
(b) in relation to subordinate legislation, means the powers conferred by virtue of this Act.

102 Powers of courts or tribunals to vary retrospective decisions

(1) This section applies where any court or tribunal decides that—
(a) an Act of the Scottish Parliament or any provision of such an Act is not within the legislative competence of the Parliament, or
(b) a member of the Scottish Executive does not have the power to make, confirm or approve a provision of subordinate legislation that he has purported to make, confirm or approve.

(2) The court or tribunal may make an order—
(a) removing or limiting any retrospective effect of the decision, or
(b) suspending the effect of the decision for any period and on any conditions to allow the defect to be corrected.

(3) In deciding whether to make an order under this section, the court or tribunal shall (among other things) have regard to the extent to which persons who are not parties to the proceedings would otherwise be adversely affected.

(4) Where a court or tribunal is considering whether to make an order under this section, it shall order intimation of that fact to be given to—
(a) the Lord Advocate, and
(b) the appropriate law officer, where the decision mentioned in subsection (1) relates to a devolution issue (within the meaning of Schedule 6),

unless the person to whom the intimation would be given is a party to the proceedings.

(5) A person to whom intimation is given under subsection (4) may take part as a party in the proceedings so far as they relate to the making of the order.

(6) Paragraphs 36 and 37 of Schedule 6 apply with necessary modifications for the purposes of subsections (4) and (5) as they apply for the purposes of that Schedule.

(7) In this section—
"intimation" includes notice,
"the appropriate law officer" means—
(a) in relation to proceedings in Scotland, the Advocate General,
(b) in relation to proceedings in England and Wales, the Attorney General,
(c) in relation to proceedings in Northern Ireland, the Attorney General for Northern Ireland.

103 The Judicial Committee

(1) Any decision of the Judicial Committee in proceedings under this Act shall be stated in open court and shall be binding in all legal proceedings (other than proceedings before the Committee).

(2) No member of the Judicial Committee shall sit and act as a member of the Committee in proceedings under this Act unless he holds or has held—
(a) the office of a Lord of Appeal in Ordinary, or
(b) high judicial office as defined in section 25 of the Appellate Jurisdiction Act 1876 (ignoring for this purpose section 5 of the Appellate Jurisdiction Act 1887).

(3) Her Majesty may by Order in Council—
(a) confer on the Judicial Committee in relation to proceedings under this Act such powers as Her Majesty considers necessary or expedient,
(b) apply the Judicial Committee Act 1833 in relation to proceedings under this Act with exceptions or modifications,
(c) make rules for regulating the procedure in relation to proceedings under this Act before the Judicial Committee.

(4) In this section "proceedings under this Act" means proceedings on a question referred to the Judicial Committee under section 33 or proceedings under Schedule 6.

Supplementary powers

104 Power to make provision consequential on legislation of, or scrutinised by, the Parliament

(1) Subordinate legislation may make such provision as the person making the legislation considers necessary or expedient in consequence of any provision made by or under any Act of the Scottish Parliament or made by legislation mentioned in subsection (2).

(2) The legislation is subordinate legislation under an Act of Parliament made by—
(a) a member of the Scottish Executive,
(b) a Scottish public authority with mixed functions or no reserved functions, or
(c) any other person (not being a Minister of the Crown) if the function of making the legislation is exercisable within devolved competence.

105 Power to make provision consequential on this Act

Subordinate legislation may make such modifications in any pre-commencement enactment or prerogative instrument or any other instrument or document as appear to the person making the legislation necessary or expedient in consequence of this Act.

106 Power to adapt functions

(1) Subordinate legislation may make such provision (including, in particular, provision modifying a function exercisable by a Minister of the Crown) as the person making the legislation considers appropriate for the purpose of enabling or otherwise facilitating the transfer of a function to the Scottish Ministers by virtue of section 53 or 63.

(2) Subordinate legislation under subsection (1) may, in particular, provide for any function which—
(a) is not exercisable separately in or as regards Scotland to be so exercisable, or
(b) is not otherwise exercisable separately within devolved competence to be so exercisable.

(3) The reference in subsection (1) to the transfer of a function to the Scottish Ministers shall be read as including the sharing of a function with the Scottish Ministers or its other adaptation.

(4) No recommendation shall be made to Her Majesty in Council to make, and no Minister of the Crown shall make, subordinate legislation under this section which modifies a function of observing or implementing an obligation mentioned in subsection (5) unless the Scottish Ministers have been consulted about the modification.

(5) The obligation is an international obligation, or an obligation under Community law, to achieve a result defined by reference to a quantity (whether expressed as an amount, proportion or ratio or otherwise), where the quantity relates to the United Kingdom (or to an area including the United Kingdom or to an area consisting of a part of the United Kingdom which includes the whole or part of Scotland).

(6) If subordinate legislation under this section modifies a function of observing or implementing such an international obligation so that the function to be transferred to the Scottish Ministers relates only to achieving so much of the result to be achieved under the obligation as is specified in the legislation, references in section 58 to the international obligation are to be read as references to the requirement to achieve that much of the result.

(7) If subordinate legislation under this section modifies a function of observing or implementing such an obligation under Community law so that the function to be transferred to the Scottish Ministers relates only to achieving so much of the result to be achieved under the obligation as is specified in the legislation, references in sections 29(2)(d) and 57(2) and paragraph 1 of Schedule 6 to Community law are to be read as including references to the requirement to achieve that much of the result.

107 Legislative power to remedy ultra vires acts

Subordinate legislation may make such provision as the person making the legislation considers necessary or expedient in consequence of—

(a) an Act of the Scottish Parliament or any provision of an Act of the Scottish Parliament which is not, or may not be, within the legislative competence of the Parliament, or
(b) any purported exercise by a member of the Scottish Executive of his functions which is not, or may not be, an exercise or a proper exercise of those functions.

108 Agreed redistribution of functions exercisable by the Scottish Ministers etc

(1) Her Majesty may by Order in Council provide for any functions exercisable by a member of the Scottish Executive to be exercisable—
(a) by a Minister of the Crown instead of by the member of the Scottish Executive,
(b) by a Minister of the Crown concurrently with the member of the Scottish Executive, or
(c) by the member of the Scottish Executive only with the agreement of, or after consultation with, a Minister of the Crown.

(2) Where an Order is made under subsection (1)(a) or (b) in relation to a function of the Scottish Ministers, the First Minister or the Lord Advocate which is exercisable only with the agreement of, or after consultation with, any other of those persons, the function shall, unless the Order provides otherwise, be exercisable by the Minister of the Crown free from any such requirement.

(3) An Order under this section may, in particular, provide for any function exercisable by a Minister of the Crown by virtue of an Order under subsection (1)(a) or (b) to be exercisable subject to a requirement for the function to be exercised with the agreement of, or after consultation with, another person.

(4) This section does not apply to any retained functions of the Lord Advocate which fall within section 52(6)(a).

109 Agreed redistribution of property and liabilities

(1) Her Majesty may by Order in Council provide—
(a) for the transfer to a Minister of the Crown or government department of any property belonging to the Scottish Ministers or the Lord Advocate, or
(b) for a Minister of the Crown or government department to have such rights or interests in relation to any property belonging to the Scottish Ministers or the Lord Advocate as Her Majesty considers appropriate (whether in connection with a transfer or otherwise).

(2) Her Majesty may by Order in Council provide for the transfer to a Minister of the Crown or government department of any liabilities to which the Scottish Ministers or the Lord Advocate are subject.

(3) An Order in Council under this section may only be made in connection with any transfer or sharing of functions of a member of the Scottish

Executive by virtue of section 108 or in any other circumstances in which Her Majesty considers it appropriate to do so for the purposes of this Act.

110 Scottish taxpayers for social security purposes

(1) The Secretary of State may by order provide for individuals of any description specified in the order to be treated for the purposes of any of the matters that are reserved matters by virtue of Head F of Part II of Schedule 5 as if they were, or were not, Scottish taxpayers.

(2) The Secretary of State may by order provide in relation to any year of assessment that, for those purposes, the basic rate in relation to the income of Scottish taxpayers shall be treated as being such rate as is specified in the order (instead of the rate increased or reduced for that year by virtue of any resolution of the Parliament in pursuance of section 73 passed after the beginning of the year).

(3) An order under this section may apply in respect of any individuals whether Scotland is the part of the United Kingdom with which they have the closest connection or not.

(4) In this section "Scottish taxpayer" has the same meaning as in Part IV.

111 Regulation of Tweed and Esk fisheries

(1) Her Majesty may by Order in Council make provision for or in connection with the conservation, management and exploitation of salmon, trout, eels and freshwater fish in the Border rivers.

(2) An Order under subsection (1) may—
(a) exclude the application of section 53 in relation to any Border rivers function,
(b) confer power to make subordinate legislation.

(3) In particular, provision may be made by such an Order—
(a) conferring any function on a Minister of the Crown, the Scottish Ministers or a public body in relation to the Border rivers,
(b) for any Border rivers function exercisable by any person to be exercisable instead by a person (or another person) mentioned in paragraph (a),
(c) for any Border rivers function exercisable by any person to be exercisable concurrently or jointly with, or with the agreement of or after consultation with, a person (or another person) mentioned in paragraph (a).

(4) In this section—
"the Border rivers" means the Rivers Tweed and Esk,
"Border rivers function" means a function conferred by any enactment, so far as exercisable in relation to the Border rivers,
"conservation", in relation to salmon, trout, eels and freshwater fish, includes the protection of their environment,

"eels", "freshwater fish", "salmon" and "trout" have the same meanings as in the Salmon and Freshwater Fisheries Act 1975,

"the River Tweed" has the same meaning as in section 39 of the Salmon and Freshwater Fisheries Act 1975,

"the River Esk" means the river of that name which, for part of its length, constitutes the border between England and Scotland including—

(a) its tributary streams (which for this purpose include the River Sark and its tributary streams), and

(b) such waters on the landward side of its estuary limits as are determined by an Order under subsection (1), together with its banks;

and references to the Border rivers include any part of the Border rivers.

(5) An Order under subsection (1) may modify the definitions in subsection (4) of the River Tweed and the River Esk.

PART VI SUPPLEMENTARY

Subordinate legislation

112 Subordinate legislation: general

(1) Any power to make subordinate legislation conferred by this Act shall, if no other provision is made as to the person by whom the power is exercisable, be exercisable by Her Majesty by Order in Council or by a Minister of the Crown by order.

(2) But the power to make subordinate legislation under section 129(1) providing—

(a) for the appropriation of sums forming part of the Scottish Consolidated Fund, or

(b) for sums received by any person to be appropriated in aid of sums appropriated as mentioned in paragraph (a),

shall be exercisable only by Her Majesty by Order in Council.

(3) References in this Act to an open power are to a power to which subsection (1) applies (and include a power to make subordinate legislation under section 129(1) whether or not the legislation makes provision as mentioned in subsection (2)).

(4) An Order in Council under an open power may revoke, amend or re-enact an order, as well as an Order in Council, under the power; and an order under an open power may revoke, amend or re-enact an Order in Council, as well as an order, under the power.

(5) Any power to make subordinate legislation conferred by this Act shall, in relation to its exercise by a Minister of the Crown or a member of the Scottish Executive, be exercisable by statutory instrument.

113 Subordinate legislation: scope of powers

(1) References in this section to a power are to an open power and to any other power to make subordinate legislation conferred by this Act which is exercisable by Her Majesty in Council or by a Minister of the Crown, and include a power as extended by this section.

(2) A power may be exercised so as to make different provision for different purposes.

(3) A power (as well as being exercisable in relation to all cases to which it extends) may be exercised in relation to—
(a) those cases subject to specified exceptions, or
(b) any particular case or class of case.

(4) A power includes power to make—
(a) any supplementary, incidental or consequential provision, and
(b) any transitory, transitional or saving provision,

which the person making the legislation considers necessary or expedient.

(5) A power may be exercised by modifying—
(a) any enactment or prerogative instrument,
(b) any other instrument or document,

if the subordinate legislation (or a statutory instrument containing it) would be subject to any of the types of procedure referred to in Schedule 7.

(6) But a power to modify enactments does not (unless otherwise stated) extend to making modifications of this Act or subordinate legislation under it.

(7) A power may be exercised so as to make provision for the delegation of functions.

(8) A power includes power to make provision for sums to be payable out of the Scottish Consolidated Fund or charged on the Fund.

(9) A power includes power to make provision for the payment of sums out of money provided by Parliament or for sums to be charged on and paid out of the Consolidated Fund.

(10) A power may not be exercised so as to create any criminal offence punishable—
(a) on summary conviction, with imprisonment for a period exceeding three months or with a fine exceeding the amount specified as level 5 on the standard scale,
(b) on conviction on indictment, with a period of imprisonment exceeding two years.

(11) The fact that a power is conferred does not prejudice the extent of any other power.

114 Subordinate legislation: particular provisions

(1) A power to make subordinate legislation conferred by any of the following provisions of this Act may be exercised by modifying any enactment comprised in or made under this Act (except Schedules 4 and 5): sections 89, 104, 107, 108 and 129(1).

(2) The reference in subsection (1) to a power to make subordinate legislation includes a power as extended by section 113.

(3) A power to make subordinate legislation conferred by any of the following provisions of this Act may be exercised so as to make provision having retrospective effect: sections 30, 58(4), 104 and 107.

115 Subordinate legislation: procedure

(1) Schedule 7 (which determines the procedure which is to apply to subordinate legislation under this Act in relation to each House of Parliament and the Scottish Parliament) shall have effect.

(2) In spite of the fact that that Schedule provides for subordinate legislation under a particular provision of this Act (or the statutory instrument containing it) to be subject to any type of procedure in relation to the Parliament, the provision conferring the power to make that legislation may be brought into force at any time after the passing of this Act.

(3) Accordingly, any subordinate legislation (or the statutory instrument containing it) made in the exercise of the power in the period beginning with that time and ending immediately before the principal appointed day is to be subject to such other type of procedure (if any) as may be specified in subordinate legislation made under section 129(1).

116 Transfer of property: supplementary

(1) This section applies in relation to subordinate legislation under section 60, 62, 90 or 109 or paragraph 2 of Schedule 2.

(2) Any such subordinate legislation may, in particular—
(a) provide for the creation of rights or interests, or the imposition of liabilities or conditions, in relation to property transferred, or rights or interests acquired, by virtue of such legislation,
(b) provide for any property, liabilities or conditions to be determined under such legislation,
(c) make provision (other than provision imposing a charge to tax) as to the tax treatment of anything done by virtue of such legislation.

(3) No order shall be made by a Minister of the Crown by virtue of subsection (2)(c), and no recommendation shall be made to Her Majesty in Council to make an Order in Council by virtue of subsection (2)(c), without the agreement of the Treasury.

(4) Subordinate legislation to which this section applies shall have effect in relation to any property or liabilities to which it applies despite any

provision (of whatever nature) which would otherwise prevent, penalise or restrict the transfer of the property or liabilities.

(5) A right of pre-emption, right of irritancy, right of return or other similar right shall not operate or become exercisable as a result of any transfer of property by virtue of any subordinate legislation to which this section applies.

(6) Any such right shall have effect in the case of any such transfer as if the transferee were the same person in law as the transferor and as if no transfer of the property had taken place.

(7) Such compensation as is just shall be paid to any person in respect of any such right which would, apart from subsection (5), have operated in favour of, or become exercisable by, that person but which, in consequence of the operation of that subsection, cannot subsequently operate in his favour or (as the case may be) become exercisable by him.

(8) Any compensation payable by virtue of subsection (7) shall be paid by the transferor or by the transferee or by both.

(9) Subordinate legislation under this subsection may provide for the determination of any disputes as to whether and, if so, how much, compensation is payable by virtue of subsection (7) and as to the person to whom or by whom it shall be paid.

(10) Subsections (4) to (9) apply in relation to the creation of rights or interests, or the doing of anything else, in relation to property as they apply in relation to a transfer of property; and references to the transferor and transferee shall be read accordingly.

(11) A certificate issued by the Secretary of State that any property or liability has, or has not, been transferred by virtue of subordinate legislation under section 60 or 62 or paragraph 2 of Schedule 2 shall be conclusive evidence of the transfer or (as the case may be) the fact that there has not been a transfer.

(12) A certificate issued by the Secretary of State and the Scottish Ministers that any property or liability has, or has not, been transferred by virtue of an Order in Council under section 90 or 109 shall be conclusive evidence of the transfer or (as the case may be) the fact that there has not been a transfer.

(13) In this section "right of return" means any right under a provision for the return or reversion of property in specified circumstances.

General modification of enactments

117 Ministers of the Crown

So far as may be necessary for the purpose or in consequence of the exercise of a function by a member of the Scottish Executive within devolved competence, any pre-commencement enactment or prerogative instrument, and any other instrument or document, shall be read as if references to a Minister of the Crown (however described) were or included references to the Scottish Ministers.

118 Subordinate instruments

(1) Subsection (2) applies in relation to the exercise by a member of the Scottish Executive within devolved competence of a function to make, confirm or approve subordinate legislation.

(2) If a pre-commencement enactment makes provision—
(a) for any instrument or the draft of any instrument made in the exercise of such a function to be laid before Parliament or either House of Parliament,
(b) for the annulment or approval of any such instrument or draft by or in pursuance of a resolution of either or both Houses of Parliament, or
(c) prohibiting the making of such an instrument without that approval,

the provision shall have effect, so far as it relates to the exercise of the function by a member of the Scottish Executive within devolved competence, as if any reference in it to Parliament or either House of Parliament were a reference to the Scottish Parliament.

(3) Where—
(a) a function of making, confirming or approving subordinate legislation conferred by a pre-commencement enactment is exercisable by a Scottish public authority with mixed functions or no reserved functions, and
(b) a pre-commencement enactment makes such provision in relation to the exercise of the function as is mentioned in subsection (2),

the provision shall have effect, so far as it relates to the exercise of the function by that authority, as if any reference in it to Parliament or either House of Parliament were a reference to the Scottish Parliament.

(4) Where—
(a) a function of making, confirming or approving subordinate legislation conferred by a pre-commencement enactment is exercisable within devolved competence by a person other than a Minister of the Crown, a member of the Scottish Executive or a Scottish public authority with mixed functions or no reserved functions, and
(b) a pre-commencement enactment makes such provision in relation to the exercise of the function as is mentioned in subsection (2),

the provision shall have effect, so far as it relates to the exercise of the function by that person within devolved competence, as if any reference in it to Parliament or either House of Parliament were a reference to the Scottish Parliament.

(5) If a pre-commencement enactment applies the Statutory Instruments Act 1946 as if a function of the kind mentioned in subsection (3) or (4) were exercisable by a Minister of the Crown, that Act shall apply, so far as

the function is exercisable as mentioned in paragraph (a) of subsection (3) or (as the case may be) (4), as if the function were exercisable by the Scottish Ministers.

119 Consolidated Fund etc

(1) In this section "Scottish functions" means—
(a) functions of the Scottish Ministers, the First Minister or the Lord Advocate which are exercisable within devolved competence,
(b) functions of any Scottish public authority with mixed functions or no reserved functions.

(2) Subject to subsections (3) and (5), a provision of a precommencement enactment which—
(a) requires or authorises the payment of any sum out of the Consolidated Fund or money provided by Parliament, or
(b) requires or authorises the payment of any sum into the Consolidated Fund,

shall cease to have effect in relation to any Scottish functions.

(3) A provision of a pre-commencement enactment which—
(a) charges any sum on the Consolidated Fund,
(b) requires the payment of any sum out of the Consolidated Fund without further appropriation, or
(c) requires or authorises the payment of any sum into the Consolidated Fund by a person other than a Minister of the Crown,

shall have effect in relation to any Scottish functions as if it provided for the sum to be charged on the Scottish Consolidated Fund or required it to be paid out of that Fund without further approval or required or authorised it to be paid into that Fund (as the case may be).

(4) Subsections (2) and (3) do not apply to the words from the beginning of section 2(3) of the European Communities Act 1972 (general implementation of Treaties) to "such Community obligation".

(5) A provision of a pre-commencement enactment which authorises any sums to be applied as money provided by Parliament instead of being paid into the Consolidated Fund shall have effect in relation to any Scottish functions as if it authorised those sums to be applied as if they had been paid out of the Scottish Consolidated Fund in accordance with rules under section 65(1)(c) instead of being paid into that Fund.

(6) Where a power to lend money under a pre-commencement enactment is exercisable by the Scottish Ministers, subsection (7) applies to any sums which, for the purpose or as the result of the exercise of the power, would be required (apart from that subsection)—
(a) to be issued by the Treasury out of the National Loans Fund, or
(b) to be paid into that Fund.

(7) Those sums shall instead—
(a) be paid out of the Scottish Consolidated Fund without further approval, or
(b) be paid into that Fund,

(as the case may be).

120 Accounts and audit

A provision of a pre-commencement enactment which—
(a) requires any account to be examined, certified and reported on by, or to be open to the inspection of, the Comptroller and Auditor General, or
(b) requires him to have access to any other document for carrying out any such examination,

shall have effect in relation to any Scottish functions (within the meaning of section 119) as if the references to the Comptroller and Auditor General were to the Auditor General for Scotland.

121 Requirements to lay reports etc before Parliament

(1) This section applies where—
(a) a pre-commencement enactment makes provision for any report to be laid before Parliament or either House of Parliament, and
(b) the report concerns Scottish functions.

(2) If the report only concerns Scottish functions, it shall be laid instead before the Scottish Parliament.

(3) In any other case, it shall be laid before the Scottish Parliament as well as before Parliament or (as the case may be) either House of Parliament.

(4) In this section—
"report" includes accounts and any statement,
"Scottish functions" has the same meaning as in section 119.

122 Crown land

(1) In any provision about the application of any pre-commencement enactment to Crown land—
(a) references to a Minister of the Crown or government department shall be read as including the Scottish Ministers and the Lord Advocate, and
(b) references to a Minister of the Crown or government department having the management of the land shall be read as including any member of the Scottish Executive having the management of the land.

(2) In this section, "Crown land" has the meaning given by section 242 of the Town and Country Planning (Scotland) Act 1997.

123 Stamp duty

In section 55 of the Finance Act 1987 (Crown exemption from stamp duty) references to a Minister of the Crown shall be read as including the Scottish Ministers, the Lord Advocate and the Parliamentary corporation.

124 Modification of sections 94 and 117 to 122

(1) Subordinate legislation may provide for any provision of sections 94 and 117 to 122 not to apply, or to apply with modifications, in such cases as the person making the legislation considers appropriate.

(2) Subordinate legislation made by Her Majesty in Council or a Minister of the Crown under this Act may, in connection with any other provision made by the legislation, also provide for any provision of sections 94 and 117 to 122 not to apply, or to apply with modifications.

125 Amendments and repeals

(1) Schedule 8 (which makes modifications of enactments) shall have effect.

(2) The enactments mentioned in Schedule 9 are repealed to the extent specified in that Schedule.

Final provisions

126 Interpretation

(1) In this Act—

"body" includes unincorporated association,

"constituencies" and "regions", in relation to the Parliament, mean the constituencies and regions provided for by Schedule 1,

"constituency member" means a member of the Parliament for a constituency,

"the Convention rights" has the same meaning as in the Human Rights Act 1998,

"document" means anything in which information is recorded in any form (and references to producing a document are to be read accordingly),

"enactment" includes an Act of the Scottish Parliament, Northern Ireland legislation (within the meaning of the Northern Ireland Act 1998) and an enactment comprised in subordinate legislation, and includes an enactment comprised in, or in subordinate legislation under, an Act of Parliament, whenever passed or made,

"financial year" means a year ending with 31st March,

"functions" includes powers and duties, and "confer", in relation to functions, includes impose,

"government department" means any department of the Government of the United Kingdom,

"the Human Rights Convention" means—

(a) the Convention for the Protection of Human Rights and Fundamental Freedoms, agreed by the Council of Europe at Rome on 4th November 1950, and
(b) the Protocols to the Convention,

as they have effect for the time being in relation to the United Kingdom,
"Minister of the Crown" includes the Treasury,
"modify" includes amend or repeal,
"occupational pension scheme", "personal pension scheme" and "public service pension scheme" have the meanings given by section 1 of the Pension Schemes Act 1993, but as if the reference to employed earners in the definition of personal pension scheme were to any earners,
"the Parliament" means the Scottish Parliament,
"parliamentary", in relation to constituencies, elections and electors, is to be taken to refer to the Parliament of the United Kingdom,
"prerogative instrument" means an Order in Council, warrant, charter or other instrument made under the prerogative,
"the principal appointed day" means the day appointed by an order under section 130 which is designated by the order as the principal appointed day,
"proceedings", in relation to the Parliament, includes proceedings of any committee or sub-committee,
"property" includes rights and interests of any description,
"regional member" means a member of the Parliament for a region,
"Scotland" includes so much of the internal waters and territorial sea of the United Kingdom as are adjacent to Scotland,
"Scottish public authority" means any public body (except the Parliamentary corporation), public office or holder of such an office whose functions (in each case) are exercisable only in or as regards Scotland,
"the Scottish zone" means the sea within British fishery limits (that is, the limits set by or under section 1 of the Fishery Limits Act 1976) which is adjacent to Scotland,
"standing orders" means standing orders of the Parliament,
"subordinate legislation" has the same meaning as in the Interpretation Act 1978 and also includes an instrument made under an Act of the Scottish Parliament,
"tribunal" means any tribunal in which legal proceedings may be brought.

(2) Her Majesty may by Order in Council determine, or make provision for determining, for the purposes of this Act any boundary between waters which are to be treated as internal waters or territorial sea of the United Kingdom, or sea within British fishery limits, adjacent to Scotland and those which are not.

(3) For the purposes of this Act—
(a) the question whether any function of a body, government department, office or office-holder relates to reserved matters is to be determined by reference to the purpose for which the function is

exercisable, having regard (among other things) to the likely effects in all the circumstances of any exercise of the function, but
(b) bodies to which paragraph 3 of Part III of Schedule 5 applies are to be treated as if all their functions were functions which relate to reserved matters.

(4) References in this Act to Scots private law are to the following areas of the civil law of Scotland—
(a) the general principles of private law (including private international law),
(b) the law of persons (including natural persons, legal persons and unincorporated bodies),
(c) the law of obligations (including obligations arising from contract, unilateral promise, delict, unjustified enrichment and negotiorum gestio),
(d) the law of property (including heritable and moveable property, trusts and succession), and
(e) the law of actions (including jurisdiction, remedies, evidence, procedure, diligence, recognition and enforcement of court orders, limitation of actions and arbitration),

and include references to judicial review of administrative action.

(5) References in this Act to Scots criminal law include criminal offences, jurisdiction, evidence, procedure and penalties and the treatment of offenders.

(6) References in this Act and in any other enactment to the Scottish Administration are to the office-holders in the Scottish Administration and the members of the staff of the Scottish Administration.

(7) For the purposes of this Act—
(a) references to office-holders in the Scottish Administration are to—
   (i) members of the Scottish Executive and junior Scottish Ministers, and
   (ii) the holders of offices in the Scottish Administration which are not ministerial offices, and
(b) references to members of the staff of the Scottish Administration are to the staff of the persons referred to in paragraph (a).

(8) For the purposes of this Act, the offices in the Scottish Administration which are not ministerial offices are—
(a) the Registrar General of Births, Deaths and Marriages for Scotland, the Keeper of the Registers of Scotland and the Keeper of the Records of Scotland, and
(b) any other office of a description specified in an Order in Council made by Her Majesty under this subsection.

(9) In this Act—
(a) all those rights, powers, liabilities, obligations and restrictions from time to time created or arising by or under the Community Treaties, and

(b) all those remedies and procedures from time to time provided for by or under the Community Treaties,

are referred to as "Community law".

(10) In this Act, "international obligations" means any international obligations of the United Kingdom other than obligations to observe and implement Community law or the Convention rights.

(11) In this Act, "by virtue of" includes "by" and "under".

127 Index of defined expressions

In this Act, the expressions listed in the left-hand column have the meaning given by, or are to be interpreted in accordance with, the provisions listed in the right-hand column.

Expression	*Provision of this Act*
Act of the Scottish Parliament	Section 28(1)
Advocate General	Section 32(4)
Auditor General for Scotland	Section 69
Body	Section 126(1)
By virtue of	Section 126(11)
Clerk, and Assistant Clerk	Section 20 and paragraph 3 of Schedule 2
Community law	Section 126(9)
Constituencies and constituency member	Section 126(1)
The Convention rights	Section 126(1)
Cross-border public authority	Section 88(5)
Devolved competence (in relation to the exercise of functions)	Section 54
Document	Section 126(1)
Enactment	Sections 113(6) and 126(1)
Financial year	Section 126(1)
Functions	Section 126(1)
Government department	Section 126(1)
The Human Rights Convention	Section 126(1)
International obligations	Section 126(10)
Judicial Committee	Section 32(4)
Legislative competence	Section 29
Member of the Scottish Executive	Section 44(1)
Members of the staff of the Scottish Administration	Section 126(7)
Minister of the Crown	Section 126(1)
Modify	Section 126(1)
Occupational pension scheme, personal pension scheme and public service pension scheme	Section 126(1)
Office-holders in the Scottish Administration	Section 126(7)

Expression	*Provision of this Act*
Offices in the Scottish Administration which are not ministerial offices	Section 126(8)
Open power	Section 112(3)
The Parliament	Section 126(1)
"parliamentary" (in relation to constituencies, elections and electors)	Section 126(1)
The Parliamentary corporation	Section 21(1)
Pre-commencement enactment	Section 53(3)
Prerogative instrument	Section 126(1)
Presiding Officer	Section 19
Principal appointed day	Section 126(1)
Proceedings	Section 126(1)
Property	Section 126(1)
Regional list (in relation to a party)	Section 5(4)
Regional returning officer	Section 12(6)
Regional vote	Section 6(2)
Regions and regional member	Section 126(1)
Registered political party	Section 5(9)
Reserved matters	Schedule 5
Retained functions (in relation to the Lord Advocate)	Section 52(6)
Scotland	Section 126(1) and (2)
Scots criminal law	Section 126(5)
Scots private law	Section 126(4)
Scottish Administration	Section 126(6)
Scottish Ministers	Section 44(2)
Scottish public authority	Section 126(1)
Scottish public authority with mixed functions or no reserved functions	Paragraphs 1 and 2 of Part III of Schedule 5
Scottish Seal	Section 2(6)
The Scottish zone	Section 126(1)
Staff of the Parliament	Paragraph 3 of Schedule 2
Standing orders	Section 126(1)
Subordinate legislation	Section 126(1)
Tribunal	Section 126(1)

128 Expenses

(1) There shall be paid out of money provided by Parliament—

(a) any expenditure incurred by a Minister of the Crown by virtue of this Act, and

(b) any increase attributable to this Act in the sums payable out of money so provided under any other enactment.

(2) There shall be paid into the Consolidated Fund any sums received by

a Minister of the Crown by virtue of this Act which are not payable into the National Loans Fund.

129 Transitional provisions etc

(1) Subordinate legislation may make such provision as the person making the legislation considers necessary or expedient for transitory or transitional purposes in connection with the coming into force of any provision of this Act.

(2) If any of the following provisions come into force before the Human Rights Act 1998 has come into force (or come fully into force), the provision shall have effect until the time when that Act is fully in force as it will have effect after that time: sections 29(2)(d), 57(2) and (3), 100 and 126(1) and Schedule 6.

130 Commencement

(1) Sections 19 to 43, Parts II to V, sections 117 to 124 and section 125 (except so far as relating to paragraphs 10, 11, 19 and 23(1) and (6) of Schedule 8) shall come into force on such day as the Secretary of State may by order appoint.

(2) Different days may be appointed under this section for different purposes.

131 Extent

Section 25 extends only to Scotland.

132 Short title

This Act may be cited as the Scotland Act 1998.

SCHEDULE 1

Section 1

Constituencies, Regions and Regional Members

General

1 The constituencies for the purposes of this Act are—
(a) the Orkney Islands,
(b) the Shetland Islands, and
(c) the parliamentary constituencies in Scotland, except a parliamentary constituency including either of those islands.

2 (1) There shall be eight regions for the purposes of this Act.

(2) Those regions shall be the eight European Parliamentary constituencies which were provided for by the European Parliamentary Constituencies (Scotland) Order 1996.

(3) Seven regional members shall be returned for each region.

(4) Sub-paragraphs (2) and (3) are subject to any Order in Council under the Parliamentary Constituencies Act 1986 (referred to in this Schedule as the 1986 Act), as that Act is extended by this Schedule.

Reports of Boundary Commission

3 (1) This paragraph applies where the Boundary Commission for Scotland (referred to in this Schedule as the Commission) submit a report to the Secretary of State under section 3(1) or (3) of the 1986 Act recommending any alteration in any parliamentary constituencies.

(2) In the report the Commission shall recommend any alteration—
(a) in any of the regions, or
(b) in the number of regional members to be returned for any of the regions, which, in their opinion, is required to be made in order to give effect to the rules in paragraph 7.

(3) If in the case of a report under section 3(1) or (3) of that Act the Commission do not make any recommendation within sub-paragraph (2), they shall in the report state that, in their opinion, no such alteration is required.

(4) A report making a recommendation for an alteration in any region shall state—
(a) the name by which the Commission recommend that the region should be known, and
(b) the number of regional members to be returned for the region.

(5) The Commission shall lay any report recommending any alteration in parliamentary constituencies before the Parliament.

4 (1) An Order in Council under section 4 of the 1986 Act which has the effect of making any alteration in any constituency of the Parliament, or makes any alteration within paragraph 3(2), may come into force for the purposes of any election for membership of the Parliament on a different day from the day on which it comes into force for the purposes of any parliamentary election; and paragraph 1(c) shall be read accordingly.

(2) The coming into force of such an Order, so far as it has the effect of making any alteration in any constituency of the Parliament or makes any alteration within paragraph 3(2), shall not affect the return of any member of the Parliament, or its constitution, until the Parliament is dissolved.

Notices

5 (1) Where the Commission have provisionally determined to make recommendations affecting any region, they shall publish in at least one newspaper circulating in the region a notice stating—
(a) the effect of the proposed recommendations and (except in a case where they propose to recommend that no alteration within

paragraph 3(2) be made) that a copy of the recommendations is open to inspection at a specified place or places within the region, and
(b) that representations with respect to the proposed recommendations may be made to the Commission within one month after the publication of the notice;

and the Commission shall take into consideration any representations duly made in accordance with any such notice.

(2) Where the Commission revise any proposed recommendations after publishing notice of them under sub-paragraph (1), the Commission shall comply again with that sub-paragraph in relation to the revised recommendations, as if no earlier notice had been published.

Local inquiries

6 (1) The Commission may, if they think fit, cause a local inquiry to be held in respect of any region.

(2) If, on the publication of a notice under paragraph 5(1) of a recommendation for any alteration within paragraph 3(2), the Commission receive any representation objecting to the proposed recommendation—
(a) from an interested authority, or
(b) from a body of electors numbering 500 or more,

the Commission shall not make the recommendation unless a local inquiry has been held in respect of the region since the publication of the notice.

(3) If a local inquiry was held in respect of the region before the publication of the notice under paragraph 5(1), sub-paragraph (2) shall not apply if the Commission, after considering the matters discussed at the local inquiry, the nature of the representations received on the publication of the notice and any other relevant circumstances, are of the opinion that a further local inquiry would not be justified.

(4) In this paragraph, in relation to any recommendation—
"interested authority" means the council for an area which is wholly or partly included in the region affected by the recommendation, and
"elector" means an elector for the purposes of an election for membership of the Parliament in any constituency included in the region.

(5) Sections 210(4) and (5) of the Local Government (Scotland) Act 1973 (attendance of witnesses at inquiries) shall apply in relation to any local inquiry held under this paragraph.

The rules

7 (1) The rules referred to in paragraph 3 are:

1 A constituency shall fall wholly within a region.

2 The regional electorate of any region shall be as near the regional electorate of each of the other regions as is reasonably practicable having regard, where appropriate, to special geographical considerations.

3 So far as reasonably practicable, the ratio which the number of regional member seats bears to the number of constituency member seats shall be 56 to 73.

4 The number of regional member seats for a region shall be—
(a) one eighth of the total number of regional member seats, or
(b) (if that total number is not exactly divisible by eight) either one eighth of the highest number which is less than that total number and exactly divisible by eight or the number produced by adding one to one eighth of that highest number (as provided by sub-paragraphs (2) to (4)).

(2) If the total number of regional member seats is not exactly divisible by eight, the Commission shall calculate the difference between—
(a) the total number of regional member seats, and
(b) the highest number which is less than that total number and exactly divisible by eight,

and that is the number of residual seats to be allocated by the Commission.

(3) The Commission shall not allocate more than one residual seat for a region.

(4) The Commission shall divide the regional electorate for each region by the aggregate of—
(a) the number of constituencies in the region, and
(b) one eighth of the highest number which is less than the total number of regional member seats and exactly divisible by eight,

and, in allocating the residual seat or seats for a region or regions, shall have regard to the desirability of allocating the residual seat or seats to the region or regions for which that calculation produces the highest number or numbers.

8 (1) For the purposes of any report of the Commission in relation to a region, the regional electorate is the number of persons—
(a) whose names appear on the enumeration date on the registers of local government electors, and
(b) who are registered at addresses within a constituency included in the region.

(2) In sub-paragraph (1), "the enumeration date" means the date on which the notice about the report is published in accordance with section 5(1) of the 1986 Act.

SCHEDULE 2

Section 21

Scottish Parliamentary Corporate Body

Membership

1 A person appointed under section 21(2)(b) shall hold office until another member of the Parliament is appointed in his place unless he previously resigns, ceases to be a member of the Parliament otherwise than by virtue of a dissolution or is removed from office by resolution of the Parliament.

Property

2 (1) The corporation may hold property.

(2) Subordinate legislation may provide—
(a) for the transfer to the corporation of any property belonging to a Minister of the Crown or government department, or
(b) for the corporation to have such rights or interests in relation to any property belonging to a Minister of the Crown or government department as the person making the legislation considers appropriate (whether in connection with a transfer or otherwise).

(3) Subordinate legislation under sub-paragraph (2) in relation to any property may provide for the transfer to the corporation of any liabilities relating to the property to which a Minister of the Crown or government department is subject and which subsist immediately before the subordinate legislation comes into force.

(4) Subordinate legislation under sub-paragraph (2) may only be made if the person making the legislation considers it appropriate to do so to enable the corporation to exercise its functions or to facilitate their exercise or in connection with their exercise or proposed exercise.

Staff

3 (1) The corporation shall appoint Assistant Clerks and may appoint other staff.

(2) The Clerk and other persons appointed by the corporation are referred to in this Act as the staff of the Parliament.

(3) It is for the corporation to determine the terms and conditions of appointment of the staff of the Parliament, including arrangements for the payment of pensions, gratuities or allowances to, or in respect of, any person who has ceased to be a member of the staff of the Parliament.

(4) In particular, the corporation may—
(a) make contributions or payments towards provision for such pensions, gratuities or allowances,
(b) establish and administer one or more pension schemes.

Powers

4 (1) Subject to sub-paragraph (4), the corporation may do anything which appears to it to be necessary or expedient for the purpose of or in connection with the discharge of its functions.

(2) That includes, in particular—
(a) entering into contracts,

(b) charging for goods or services,
(c) investing sums not immediately required in relation to the discharge of its functions, and
(d) accepting gifts.

(3) The corporation may sell goods or provide services, and may make arrangements for the sale of goods or provision of services, to the public.

(4) The corporation may borrow sums in sterling by way of overdraft or otherwise for the purpose of meeting a temporary excess of expenditure over sums otherwise available to meet that expenditure.

(5) The corporation may borrow money only under sub-paragraph (4) and may borrow under that sub-paragraph only in accordance with the special or general approval of the Parliament.

Delegation

5 The corporation may delegate any of its functions to the Presiding Officer or the Clerk.

Proceedings and business

6 (1) The validity of any act of the corporation shall not be affected by any vacancy among the members, or by any defect in the appointment, or qualification for membership, of any member.

(2) The corporation may determine its own procedure.

(3) The Presiding Officer shall preside at meetings of the corporation, but the corporation may appoint another of its members to preside if the office of Presiding Officer is vacant or the Presiding Officer is for any reason unable to act.

Crown status

7 (1) Her Majesty may by Order in Council provide for the corporation to be treated to any extent as a Crown body for the purposes of any enactment.

(2) In particular, the Order may for the purposes of any enactment provide—
(a) for employment under the corporation to be treated as employment under the corporation as a Crown body,
(b) for land held, used or managed by the corporation, or operations carried out by or on behalf of the corporation, to be treated (as the case may be) as land held, used or managed, or operations carried out by or on behalf of, the corporation as a Crown body.

(3) For the purposes of this paragraph, "Crown body" means a body which is the servant or agent of the Crown, and includes a government department

SCHEDULE 3

Section 22

Standing Orders – Further Provision

Preservation of order

1 (1) The standing orders shall include provision for preserving order in the proceedings of the Parliament, including provision for—

(a) preventing conduct which would constitute a criminal offence or contempt of court, and

(b) a sub judice rule.

(2) Such provision may provide for excluding a member of the Parliament from proceedings.

Withdrawal of rights and privileges

2 The standing orders may include provision for withdrawing from a member of the Parliament his rights and privileges as a member.

Proceedings to be in public

3 (1) The standing orders shall include provision requiring the proceedings of the Parliament to be held in public, except in such circumstances as the standing orders may provide.

(2) The standing orders may include provision as to the conditions to be complied with by any member of the public attending the proceedings, including provision for excluding from the proceedings any member of the public who does not comply with those conditions.

Reporting and publishing proceedings

4 The standing orders shall include provision for reporting the proceedings of the Parliament and for publishing the reports.

The Presiding Officer and deputies

5 The standing orders shall include provision for ensuring that the Presiding Officer and deputies do not all represent the same political party.

Committees

6 (1) Standing orders which provide for the appointment of committees may include provision for those committees to have power to appoint sub-committees.

(2) The standing orders shall include provision for ensuring that, in appointing members to committees and sub-committees, regard is had to the balance of political parties in the Parliament.

(3) The standing orders may include provision for excluding from the proceedings of a committee or sub-committee a member of the Parliament who is not a member of the committee or sub-committee.

Crown interests

7 The standing orders shall include provision for ensuring that a Bill containing provisions which would, if the Bill were a Bill for an Act of Parliament, require the consent of Her Majesty, the Prince and Steward of Scotland or the Duke of Cornwall shall not pass unless such consent has been signified to the Parliament.

SCHEDULE 4 Sections 29 and 53(4)

Enactments etc Protected from Modification

PART I
THE PROTECTED PROVISIONS

Particular enactments

1 (1) An Act of the Scottish Parliament cannot modify, or confer power by subordinate legislation to modify, any of the following provisions.

(2) The provisions are—
(a) Articles 4 and 6 of the Union with Scotland Act 1706 and of the Union with England Act 1707 so far as they relate to freedom of trade,
(b) the Private Legislation Procedure (Scotland) Act 1936,
(c) the following provisions of the European Communities Act 1972—
Section 1 and Schedule 1,
Section 2, other than subsection (2), the words following "such Community obligation" in subsection (3) and the words "subject to Schedule 2 to this Act" in subsection (4),
Section 3(1) and (2),
Section 11(2),
(d) paragraphs 5(3)(b) and 15(4)(b) of Schedule 32 to the Local Government, Planning and Land Act 1980 (designation of enterprise zones),
(e) sections 140A to 140G of the Social Security Administration Act 1992 (rent rebate and rent allowance subsidy and council tax benefit),
(f) the Human Rights Act 1998.

The law on reserved matters

2 (1) An Act of the Scottish Parliament cannot modify, or confer power by subordinate legislation to modify, the law on reserved matters.

(2) In this paragraph, "the law on reserved matters" means—
(a) any enactment the subject-matter of which is a reserved matter and which is comprised in an Act of Parliament or subordinate legislation under an Act of Parliament, and
(b) any rule of law which is not contained in an enactment and the subject-matter of which is a reserved matter,

and in this sub-paragraph "Act of Parliament" does not include this Act.

(3) Sub-paragraph (1) applies in relation to a rule of Scots private law or Scots criminal law (whether or not contained in an enactment) only to the extent that the rule in question is special to a reserved matter or the subject-matter of the rule is—
(a) interest on sums due in respect of taxes or excise duties and refunds of such taxes or duties, or
(b) the obligations, in relation to occupational or personal pension schemes, of the trustees or managers.

(4) Sub-paragraph (3)(b) extends to cases where liabilities under orders made in matrimonial proceedings, or agreements made between the parties to a marriage, are to be satisfied out of assets of the scheme.

3 (1) Paragraph 2 does not apply to modifications which—
(a) are incidental to, or consequential on, provision made (whether by virtue of the Act in question or another enactment) which does not relate to reserved matters, and
(b) do not have a greater effect on reserved matters than is necessary to give effect to the purpose of the provision.

(2) In determining for the purposes of sub-paragraph (1)(b) what is necessary to give effect to the purpose of a provision, any power to make laws other than the power of the Parliament is to be disregarded.

This Act

4 (1) An Act of the Scottish Parliament cannot modify, or confer power by subordinate legislation to modify, this Act.

(2) This paragraph does not apply to modifying sections 1(4), 17(5), 19(7), 21(5), 24(2), 28(5), 39(7), 40 to 43, 50, 69(3), 85 and 93 and paragraphs 4(1) to (3) and 6(1) of Schedule 2.

(3) This paragraph does not apply to modifying any provision of this Act (other than sections 64(7), 66(2), 71(7), 77, 78 and 119) which—
(a) charges any sum on the Scottish Consolidated Fund,
(b) requires any sum to be paid out of that Fund without further approval, or
(c) requires or authorises the payment of any sum into that Fund.

(4) This paragraph does not apply to any modifications of Part III which are necessary or expedient for the purpose or in consequence of the establishment of a new fund, in addition to the Scottish Consolidated Fund, out of which loans may be made by the Scottish Ministers.

(5) This paragraph does not apply to—
(a) modifying so much of any enactment as is modified by this Act,
(b) repealing so much of any provision of this Act as amends any enactment, if the provision ceases to have effect in consequence of any enactment comprised in or made under an Act of the Scottish Parliament.

Enactments modified by this Act

5 An Act of the Scottish Parliament cannot modify, or confer power by subordinate legislation to modify—
(a) the effect of section 119(3) in relation to any provision of an Act of Parliament relating to judicial salaries,
(b) so much of any enactment as—
  (i) is amended by paragraph 2, 7 or 32 of Schedule 8, and
  (ii) relates to the Advocate General,
(c) so much of any enactment as is amended by paragraph 9(b) or 29 of Schedule 8.

Shared powers

6 An Act of the Scottish Parliament cannot modify, or confer power by subordinate legislation to modify, any enactment so far as the enactment relates to powers exercisable by a Minister of the Crown by virtue of section 56.

PART II
GENERAL EXCEPTIONS

Restatement, etc

7 (1) Part I of this Schedule does not prevent an Act of the Scottish Parliament—
(a) restating the law (or restating it with such modifications as are not prevented by that Part), or
(b) repealing any spent enactment,

or conferring power by subordinate legislation to do so.

(2) For the purposes of paragraph 2, the law on reserved matters includes any restatement in an Act of the Scottish Parliament, or subordinate legislation under such an Act, of the law on reserved matters if the subject-matter of the restatement is a reserved matter.

Effect of Interpretation Act 1978

8 Part I of this Schedule does not prevent the operation of any provision of the Interpretation Act 1978.

Change of title etc

9 (1) Part I of this Schedule does not prevent an Act of the Scottish Parliament amending, or conferring power by subordinate legislation to amend, any enactment by changing—

(a) any of the titles referred to in sub-paragraph (2), or
(b) any reference to a declarator,

in consequence of any provision made by or under an Act of the Scottish Parliament.

(2) The titles are those of—

(a) any court or tribunal or any judge, chairman or officer of a court or tribunal,
(b) any holder of an office in the Scottish Administration which is not a ministerial office or any member of the staff of the Scottish Administration,
(c) any register.

Accounts and audit and maladministration

10 Part I of this Schedule does not prevent an Act of the Scottish Parliament modifying, or conferring power by subordinate legislation to modify, any enactment for or in connection with the purposes of section 70 or 91.

Subordinate legislation

11 (1) Part I of this Schedule does not prevent an Act of the Scottish Parliament modifying, or conferring power by subordinate legislation to modify, any enactment for or in connection with any of the following purposes.

(2) Those purposes are—

(a) making different provision in respect of the document by which a power to make subordinate legislation within sub-paragraph (3) is to be exercised,
(b) making different provision (or no provision) for the procedure, in relation to the Parliament, to which legislation made in the exercise of such a power (or the instrument or other document in which it is contained) is to be subject,
(c) applying any enactment comprised in or made under an Act of the Scottish Parliament relating to the documents by which such powers may be exercised.

(3) The power to make the subordinate legislation, or a power to confirm or approve the legislation, must be exercisable by—

(a) a member of the Scottish Executive,
(b) any Scottish public authority with mixed functions or no reserved functions,

(c) any other person (not being a Minister of the Crown) within devolved competence.

PART III
CONSEQUENTIAL MODIFICATION OF SECTIONS 53 AND 54

12 (1) This paragraph applies to a function which (apart from this Schedule) would be transferred to the Scottish Ministers by virtue of section 53(2)(c).

(2) If, because of anything in Part I of this Schedule, a provision of an Act of the Scottish Parliament modifying an enactment so as to provide for the function to be exercisable by a different person would be outside the legislative competence of the Parliament, the function is not so transferred.

13 (1) Paragraph 12 does not apply to any function conferred by any provision of—
(a) the European Communities Act 1972,
(b) the Human Rights Act 1998, except sections 1, 5, 14 to 17 and 22 of that Act,
(c) the law on reserved matters (for the purposes of paragraph 2) so far as contained in an enactment.

(2) For the purpose of determining—
(a) whether any function under any of the provisions referred to in sub-paragraph (1) is transferred to the Scottish Ministers by virtue of section 53, and
(b) the extent to which any such function (other than a function of making, confirming or approving subordinate legislation) is exercisable by them,

the references in section 54 to the legislative competence of the Parliament are to be read as if section 29(2)(c) were omitted.

(3) Part I of this Schedule does not prevent an Act of the Scottish Parliament modifying, or conferring power by subordinate legislation to modify, any of the provisions mentioned in sub-paragraph (1) so as to provide for a function transferred to the Scottish Ministers by virtue of section 53 to be exercisable by a different person.

14 If any pre-commencement enactment or prerogative instrument is modified by subordinate legislation under section 105, a function under that enactment or instrument (whether as it has effect before or after the modification) is not transferred by virtue of section 53 if the subordinate legislation provides that it is not to be so transferred.

SCHEDULE 5

Section 30

Reserved Matters

PART I
GENERAL RESERVATIONS

The Constitution

1 The following aspects of the constitution are reserved matters, that is—
(a) the Crown, including succession to the Crown and a regency,
(b) the Union of the Kingdoms of Scotland and England,
(c) the Parliament of the United Kingdom,
(d) the continued existence of the High Court of Justiciary as a criminal court of first instance and of appeal,
(e) the continued existence of the Court of Session as a civil court of first instance and of appeal.

2 (1) Paragraph 1 does not reserve—
(a) Her Majesty's prerogative and other executive functions,
(b) functions exercisable by any person acting on behalf of the Crown, or
(c) any office in the Scottish Administration.

(2) Sub-paragraph (1) does not affect the reservation by paragraph 1 of honours and dignities or the functions of the Lord Lyon King of Arms so far as relating to the granting of arms; but this sub-paragraph does not apply to the Lord Lyon King of Arms in his judicial capacity.

(3) Sub-paragraph (1) does not affect the reservation by paragraph 1 of the management (in accordance with any enactment regulating the use of land) of the Crown Estate.

(4) Sub-paragraph (1) does not affect the reservation by paragraph 1 of the functions of the Security Service, the Secret Intelligence Service and the Government Communications Headquarters.

3 (1) Paragraph 1 does not reserve property belonging to Her Majesty in right of the Crown or belonging to any person acting on behalf of the Crown or held in trust for Her Majesty for the purposes of any person acting on behalf of the Crown.

(2) Paragraph 1 does not reserve the ultimate superiority of the Crown or the superiority of the Prince and Steward of Scotland.

(3) Sub-paragraph (1) does not affect the reservation by paragraph 1 of—
(a) the hereditary revenues of the Crown, other than revenues from bona vacantia, ultimus haeres and treasure trove,
(b) the royal arms and standard,
(c) the compulsory acquisition of property held or used by a Minister of the Crown or government department.

4 (1) Paragraph 1 does not reserve property held by Her Majesty in Her private capacity.

(2) Sub-paragraph (1) does not affect the reservation by paragraph 1 of the subject-matter of the Crown Private Estates Acts 1800 to 1873.

5 Paragraph 1 does not reserve the use of the Scottish Seal.

Political parties

6 The registration and funding of political parties is a reserved matter.

Foreign affairs etc

7 (1) International relations, including relations with territories outside the United Kingdom, the European Communities (and their institutions) and other international organisations, regulation of international trade, and international development assistance and co-operation are reserved matters.

(2) Sub-paragraph (1) does not reserve—
(a) observing and implementing international obligations, obligations under the Human Rights Convention and obligations under Community law,
(b) assisting Ministers of the Crown in relation to any matter to which that sub-paragraph applies.

Public service

8 (1) The Civil Service of the State is a reserved matter.

(2) Sub-paragraph (1) does not reserve the subject-matter of—
(a) Part I of the Sheriff Courts and Legal Officers (Scotland) Act 1927 (appointment of sheriff clerks and procurators fiscal etc),
(b) Part III of the Administration of Justice (Scotland) Act 1933 (officers of the High Court of Justiciary and of the Court of Session).

Defence

9 (1) The following are reserved matters—
(a) the defence of the realm,
(b) the naval, military or air forces of the Crown, including reserve forces,
(c) visiting forces,
(d) international headquarters and defence organisations,
(e) trading with the enemy and enemy property.

(2) Sub-paragraph (1) does not reserve—
(a) the exercise of civil defence functions by any person otherwise than as a member of any force or organisation referred to in sub-paragraph (1)(b) to (d) or any other force or organisation reserved by virtue of sub-paragraph (1)(a),
(b) the conferral of enforcement powers in relation to sea fishing.

Treason

10 Treason (including constructive treason), treason felony and misprision of treason are reserved matters.

PART II

SPECIFIC RESERVATIONS

Preliminary

1 The matters to which any of the Sections in this Part apply are reserved matters for the purposes of this Act.

2 A Section applies to any matter described or referred to in it when read with any illustrations, exceptions or interpretation provisions in that Section.

3 Any illustrations, exceptions or interpretation provisions in a Section relate only to that Section (so that an entry under the heading "exceptions" does not affect any other Section).

Reservations

Head A – Financial and Economic Matters

A1 Fiscal, economic and monetary policy Section A1

Fiscal, economic and monetary policy, including the issue and circulation of money, taxes and excise duties, government borrowing and lending, control over United Kingdom public expenditure, the exchange rate and the Bank of England.

Exception

Local taxes to fund local authority expenditure (for example, council tax and non-domestic rates).

A2 The currency Section A2

Coinage, legal tender and bank notes.

A3 Financial services Section A3

Financial services, including investment business, banking and deposit-taking, collective investment schemes and insurance.

Exception

The subject-matter of section 1 of the Banking and Financial Dealings Act 1971 (bank holidays).

A4 Financial markets Section A4

Financial markets, including listing and public offers of securities and investments, transfer of securities and insider dealing.

A5 Money laundering Section A5

The subject-matter of the Money Laundering Regulations 1993, but in relation to any type of business.

Head B – Home Affairs

B1 Misuse of drugs Section B1

The subject-matter of—
(a) the Misuse of Drugs Act 1971,
(b) sections 12 to 14 of the Criminal Justice (International Co-operation) Act 1990 (substances useful for manufacture of controlled drugs), and
(c) Part V of the Criminal Law (Consolidation) (Scotland) Act 1995 (drug trafficking) and, so far as relating to drug trafficking, the Proceeds of Crime (Scotland) Act 1995.

B2 Data protection Section B2

The subject-matter of—
(a) the Data Protection Act 1998, and
(b) Council Directive 95/46/EC (protection of individuals with regard to the processing of personal data and on the free movement of such data).

Interpretation

If any provision of the Data Protection Act 1998 is not in force on the principal appointed day, it is to be treated for the purposes of this reservation as if it were.

B3 Elections Section B3

Elections for membership of the House of Commons, the European Parliament and the Parliament, including the subject-matter of—
(a) the European Parliamentary Elections Act 1978,
(b) the Representation of the People Act 1983 and the Representation of the People Act 1985, and
(c) the Parliamentary Constituencies Act 1986,

so far as those enactments apply, or may be applied, in respect of such membership.

The franchise at local government elections.

B4 Firearms Section B4

The subject-matter of the Firearms Acts 1968 to 1997.

B5 Entertainment Section B5

The subject-matter of—
(a) the Video Recordings Act 1984, and
(b) sections 1 to 3 and 5 to 16 of the Cinemas Act 1985 (control of exhibitions).

The classification of films for public exhibition by reference to their suitability for viewing by persons generally or above a particular age, with or without any advice as to the desirability of parental guidance.

B6 Immigration and nationality Section B6

Nationality; immigration, including asylum and the status and capacity of persons in the United Kingdom who are not British citizens; free movement of persons within the European Economic Area; issue of travel documents.

B7 Scientific procedures on live animals Section B7

The subject-matter of the Animals (Scientific Procedures) Act 1986.

B8 National security, interception of communications, official secrets and terrorism Section B8

National security.

The interception of communications; but not the subject-matter of Part III of the Police Act 1997 (authorisation to interfere with property etc) or surveillance not involving interference with property.

The subject-matter of—
(a) the Official Secrets Acts 1911 and 1920, and
(b) the Official Secrets Act 1989, except so far as relating to any information, document or other article protected against disclosure by section 4(2) (crime) and not by any other provision of sections 1 to 4.

Special powers, and other special provisions, for dealing with terrorism.

B9 Betting, gaming and lotteries Section B9

Betting, gaming and lotteries.

B10 Emergency powers Section B10

Emergency powers.

B11 Extradition Section B11

Extradition.

B12 Lieutenancies Section B12

The subject-matter of the Lieutenancies Act 1997.

Head C – Trade and Industry

C1 Business associations Section C1

The creation, operation, regulation and dissolution of types of business association.

Exceptions

The creation, operation, regulation and dissolution of—
(a) particular public bodies, or public bodies of a particular type, established by or under any enactment, and
(b) charities.

Interpretation

"Business association" means any person (other than an individual) established for the purpose of carrying on any kind of business, whether or not for profit; and "business" includes the provision of benefits to the members of an association.

C2 Insolvency Section C2

In relation to business associations—
(a) the modes of, the grounds for and the general legal effect of winding up, and the persons who may initiate winding up,
(b) liability to contribute to assets on winding up,
(c) powers of courts in relation to proceedings for winding up, other than the power to resist proceedings,
(d) arrangements with creditors, and
(e) procedures giving protection from creditors.

Preferred or preferential debts for the purposes of the Bankruptcy (Scotland) Act 1985, the Insolvency Act 1986, and any other enactment relating to the sequestration of the estate of any person or to the winding up of business associations, the preference of such debts against other such debts and the extent of their preference over other types of debt.

Regulation of insolvency practitioners.

Co-operation of insolvency courts.

Exceptions

In relation to business associations—
(a) the process of winding up, including the person having responsibility for the conduct of a winding up or any part of it, and his conduct of it or of that part,

(b) the effect of winding up on diligence, and
(c) avoidance and adjustment of prior transactions on winding up.

Floating charges and receivers, except in relation to preferential debts, regulation of insolvency practitioners and co-operation of insolvency courts.

Interpretation

"Business association" has the meaning given in Section C1 of this Part of this Schedule, but does not include any person whose estate may be sequestrated under the Bankruptcy (Scotland) Act 1985 or any public body established by or under an enactment.

"Winding up", in relation to business associations, includes winding up of solvent, as well as insolvent, business associations.

C3 Competition Section C3

Regulation of anti-competitive practices and agreements; abuse of dominant position; monopolies and mergers.

Exception

Regulation of particular practices in the legal profession for the purpose of regulating that profession or the provision of legal services.

Interpretation

"The legal profession" means advocates, solicitors and qualified conveyancers and executry practitioners within the meaning of Part II of the Law Reform (Miscellaneous Provisions) (Scotland) Act 1990.

C4 Intellectual property Section C4

Intellectual property.

Exception

The subject-matter of Parts I and II of the Plant Varieties Act 1997 (plant varieties and the Plant Varieties and Seeds Tribunal).

C5 Import and export control Section C5

The subject-matter of the Import, Export and Customs Powers (Defence) Act 1939.

Prohibition and regulation of the import and export of endangered species of animals and plants.

Exceptions

Prohibition and regulation of movement into and out of Scotland of—
(a) food, animals, animal products, plants and plant products for the purposes of protecting human, animal or plant health, animal welfare or

the environment or observing or implementing obligations under the Common Agricultural Policy, and
(b) animal feeding stuffs, fertilisers and pesticides for the purposes of protecting human, animal or plant health or the environment.

C6 Sea fishing Section C6

Regulation of sea fishing outside the Scottish zone (except in relation to Scottish fishing boats).

Interpretation

"Scottish fishing boat" means a fishing vessel which is registered in the register maintained under section 8 of the Merchant Shipping Act 1995 and whose entry in the register specifies a port in Scotland as the port to which the vessel is to be treated as belonging.

C7 Consumer protection Section C7

Regulation of—
(a) the sale and supply of goods and services to consumers,
(b) guarantees in relation to such goods and services,
(c) hire-purchase, including the subject-matter of Part III of the Hire-Purchase Act 1964,
(d) trade descriptions, except in relation to food,
(e) misleading and comparative advertising, except regulation specifically in relation to food, tobacco and tobacco products,
(f) price indications,
(g) trading stamps,
(h) auctions and mock auctions of goods and services, and
(i) hallmarking and gun barrel proofing.

Safety of, and liability for, services supplied to consumers.

The subject-matter of—
(a) the Hearing Aid Council Act 1968,
(b) the Unsolicited Goods and Services Acts 1971 and 1975,
(c) Parts I to III and XI of the Fair Trading Act 1973,
(d) the Consumer Credit Act 1974,
(e) the Estate Agents Act 1979,
(f) the Timeshare Act 1992,
(g) the Package Travel, Package Holidays and Package Tours Regulations 1992, and
(h) the Commercial Agents (Council Directive) Regulations 1993.

Exception

The subject-matter of section 16 of the Food Safety Act 1990 (food safety and consumer protection).

C8 Product standards, safety and liability Section C8

Technical standards and requirements in relation to products in pursuance of an obligation under Community law.

Product safety and liability.

Product labelling.

Exceptions

Food, agricultural and horticultural produce, fish and fish products, seeds, animal feeding stuffs, fertilisers and pesticides.

In relation to food safety, materials which come into contact with food.

C9 Weights and measures Section C9

Units and standards of weight and measurement.

Regulation of trade so far as involving weighing, measuring and quantities.

C10 Telecommunications and wireless telegraphy Section C10

Telecommunications and wireless telegraphy.

Internet services.

Electronic encryption.

The subject-matter of Part II of the Wireless Telegraphy Act 1949 (electromagnetic disturbance).

Exception

The subject-matter of Part III of the Police Act 1997 (authorisation to interfere with property etc).

C11 Post Office, posts and postal services Section C11

The Post Office, posts (including postage stamps, postal orders and postal packets) and regulation of postal services.

C12 Research Councils Section C12

Research Councils within the meaning of the Science and Technology Act 1965.

The subject-matter of section 5 of that Act (funding of scientific research) so far as relating to Research Councils.

C13 Designation of assisted areas Section C13

The subject-matter of section 1 of the Industrial Development Act 1982.

C14 Industrial Development Advisory Board Section C14

The Industrial Development Advisory Board

C15 Protection of trading and economic interests Section C15

The subject-matter of—
(a) section 2 of the Emergency Laws (Re-enactments and Repeals) Act 1964 (Treasury power in relation to action damaging to economic position of United Kingdom),
(b) Part II of the Industry Act 1975 (powers in relation to transfer of control of important manufacturing undertakings), and
(c) the Protection of Trading Interests Act 1980.

Head D – Energy

D1 Electricity Section D1

Generation, transmission, distribution and supply of electricity.

The subject-matter of Part II of the Electricity Act 1989.

Exception

The subject-matter of Part I of the Environmental Protection Act 1990.

D2 Oil and gas Section D2

Oil and gas, including—
(a) the ownership of, exploration for and exploitation of deposits of oil and natural gas,
(b) the subject-matter of section 1 of the Mineral Exploration and Investment Grants Act 1972 (contributions in connection with mineral exploration) so far as relating to exploration for oil and gas,
(c) offshore installations and pipelines,
(d) the subject-matter of the Pipe-lines Act 1962 (including section 5 (deemed planning permission)) so far as relating to pipelines within the meaning of section 65 of that Act,
(e) the application of Scots law and the jurisdiction of the Scottish courts in relation to offshore activities,
(f) pollution relating to oil and gas exploration and exploitation, but only outside controlled waters (within the meaning of section 30A(1) of the Control of Pollution Act 1974),
(g) the subject-matter of Part II of the Food and Environment Protection Act 1985 so far as relating to oil and gas exploration and exploitation, but only in relation to activities outside such controlled waters,
(h) restrictions on navigation, fishing and other activities in connection with offshore activities,
(i) liquefaction of natural gas, and
(j) the conveyance, shipping and supply of gas through pipes.

Exceptions

The subject-matter of—
(a) sections 10 to 12 of the Industry Act 1972 (credits and grants for construction of ships and offshore installations),
(b) the Offshore Petroleum Development (Scotland) Act 1975, other than sections 3 to 7, and
(c) Part I of the Environmental Protection Act 1990.

The manufacture of gas.

The conveyance, shipping and supply of gas other than through pipes.

D3 Coal Section D3

Coal, including its ownership and exploitation, deep and opencast coal mining and coal mining subsidence.

Exceptions

The subject-matter of—
(a) Part I of the Environmental Protection Act 1990, and
(b) sections 53 (environmental duties in connection with planning) and 54 (obligation to restore land affected by coal-mining operations) of the Coal Industry Act 1994.

D4 Nuclear energy Section D4

Nuclear energy and nuclear installations, including—
(a) nuclear safety, security and safeguards, and
(b) liability for nuclear occurrences.

Exceptions

The subject-matter of—
(a) Part I of the Environmental Protection Act 1990, and
(b) the Radioactive Substances Act 1993.

D5 Energy conservation Section D5

The subject-matter of the Energy Act 1976, other than section 9.

Exception

The encouragement of energy efficiency other than by prohibition or regulation.

Head E – Transport

E1 Road transport Section E1

The subject-matter of—
(a) the Motor Vehicles (International Circulation) Act 1952,

(b) the Public Passenger Vehicles Act 1981 and the Transport Act 1985, so far as relating to public service vehicle operator licensing,
(c) section 17 (traffic regulation on special roads), section 25 (pedestrian crossings), Part V (traffic signs) and Part VI (speed limits) of the Road Traffic Regulation Act 1984,
(d) the Road Traffic Act 1988 and the Road Traffic Offenders Act 1988,
(e) the Vehicle Excise and Registration Act 1994,
(f) the Road Traffic (New Drivers) Act 1995, and
(g) the Goods Vehicles (Licensing of Operators) Act 1995.

Regulation of proper hours or periods of work by persons engaged in the carriage of passengers or goods by road.

The conditions under which international road transport services for passengers or goods may be undertaken.

Regulation of the instruction of drivers of motor vehicles.

Exceptions

The subject-matter of sections 39 and 40 (road safety information and training) and 157 to 159 (payments for treatment of traffic casualties) of the Road Traffic Act 1988.

E2 Rail transport Section E2

Provision and regulation of railway services.

Rail transport security.

The subject-matter of the Channel Tunnel Act 1987.

The subject-matter of the Railway Heritage Act 1996.

Exceptions

Grants so far as relating to railway services; but this exception does not apply in relation to—
(a) the subject-matter of section 63 of the Railways Act 1993 (government financial assistance where railway administration orders made),
(b) "railway services" as defined in section 82(1)(b) of the Railways Act 1993 (carriage of goods by railway), or
(c) the subject-matter of section 136 of the Railways Act 1993 (grants and subsidies).

Interpretation

"Railway services" has the meaning given by section 82 of the Railways Act 1993 (excluding the wider meaning of "railway" given by section 81(2) of that Act).

E3 Marine transport Section E3

The subject-matter of—
(a) the Coastguard Act 1925,
(b) the Hovercraft Act 1968, except so far as relating to the regulation of noise and vibration caused by hovercraft,
(c) the Carriage of Goods by Sea Act 1971,
(d) section 2 of the Protection of Wrecks Act 1973 (prohibition on approaching dangerous wrecks),
(e) the Merchant Shipping (Liner Conferences) Act 1982,
(f) the Dangerous Vessels Act 1985,
(g) the Aviation and Maritime Security Act 1990, other than Part I (aviation security),
(h) the Carriage of Goods by Sea Act 1992,
(i) the Merchant Shipping Act 1995,
(j) the Shipping and Trading Interests (Protection) Act 1995, and
(k) sections 24 (implementation of international agreements relating to protection of wrecks), 26 (piracy) and 27 and 28 (international bodies concerned with maritime matters) of the Merchant Shipping and Maritime Security Act 1997.

Navigational rights and freedoms.

Financial assistance for shipping services which start or finish or both outside Scotland.

Exceptions

Ports, harbours, piers and boatslips, except in relation to the matters reserved by virtue of paragraph (d), (f), (g) or (i).

Regulation of works which may obstruct or endanger navigation.

The subject-matter of the Highlands and Islands Shipping Services Act 1960 in relation to financial assistance for bulk freight services.

E4 Air transport Section E4

Regulation of aviation and air transport, including the subject-matter of—
(a) the Carriage by Air Act 1961,
(b) the Carriage by Air (Supplementary Provisions) Act 1962,
(c) the Carriage by Air and Road Act 1979 so far as relating to carriage by air,
(d) the Civil Aviation Act 1982,
(e) the Aviation Security Act 1982,
(f) the Airports Act 1986, and
(g) sections 1 (endangering safety at aerodromes) and 48 (powers in relation to certain aircraft) of the Aviation and Maritime Security Act 1990,

and arrangements to compensate or repatriate passengers in the event of an air transport operator's insolvency.

Exceptions

The subject-matter of the following sections of the Civil Aviation Act 1982—

(a) section 25 (Secretary of State's power to provide aerodromes),
(b) section 30 (provision of aerodromes and facilities at aerodromes by local authorities),
(c) section 31 (power to carry on ancillary business in connection with local authority aerodromes),
(d) section 34 (financial assistance for certain aerodromes),
(e) section 35 (facilities for consultation at certain aerodromes),
(f) section 36 (health control at Secretary of State's aerodromes and aerodromes of Civil Aviation Authority), and
(g) sections 41 to 43 and 50 (powers in relation to land exercisable in connection with civil aviation) where land is to be or was acquired for the purpose of airport development or expansion.

The subject-matter of Part II (transfer of airport undertakings of local authorities), sections 63 and 64 (airport byelaws) and 66 (functions of operators of designated airports as respects abandoned vehicles) of the Airports Act 1986.

The subject-matter of sections 59 (acquisition of land and rights over land) and 60 (disposal of compulsorily acquired land) of the Airports Act 1986 where land is to be or was acquired for the purpose of airport development or expansion.

E5 Other matters Section E5

Transport of radioactive material.

Technical specifications for public passenger transport for disabled persons, including the subject-matter of—

(a) section 125(7) and (8) of the Transport Act 1985 (Secretary of State's guidance and consultation with the Disabled Persons Transport Advisory Committee), and

(b) Part V of the Disability Discrimination Act 1995 (public transport).

Regulation of the carriage of dangerous goods.

Interpretation

"Radioactive material" has the same meaning as in section 1(1) of the Radioactive Material (Road Transport) Act 1991.

Head F - Social Security

F1 Social security schemes Section F1

Schemes supported from central or local funds which provide assistance for social security purposes to or in respect of individuals by way of benefits.

Requiring persons to—
(a) establish and administer schemes providing assistance for social security purposes to or in respect of individuals, or
(b) make payments to or in respect of such schemes,

and to keep records and supply information in connection with such schemes.

The circumstances in which a person is liable to maintain himself or another for the purposes of the enactments relating to social security and the Child Support Acts 1991 and 1995.

The subject-matter of the Vaccine Damage Payment Scheme.

Illustrations

National Insurance; Social Fund; administration and funding of housing benefit and council tax benefit; recovery of benefits for accident, injury or disease from persons paying damages; deductions from benefits for the purpose of meeting an individual's debts; sharing information between government departments for the purposes of the enactments relating to social security; making decisions for the purposes of schemes mentioned in the reservation and appeals against such decisions.

Exceptions

The subject-matter of Part II of the Social Work (Scotland) Act 1968 (social welfare services), section 2 of the Chronically Sick and Disabled Persons Act 1970 (provision of welfare services), section 50 of the Children Act 1975 (payments towards maintenance of children), section 15 of the Enterprise and New Towns (Scotland) Act 1990 (industrial injuries benefit), and sections 22 (promotion of welfare of children in need), 29 and 30 (advice and assistance for young persons formerly looked after by local authorities) of the Children (Scotland) Act 1995.

Interpretation

"Benefits" includes pensions, allowances, grants, loans and any other form of financial assistance.

Providing assistance for social security purposes to or in respect of individuals includes (among other things) providing assistance to or in respect of individuals—
(a) who qualify by reason of old age, survivorship, disability, sickness, incapacity, injury, unemployment, maternity or the care of children or others needing care,
(b) who qualify by reason of low income, or
(c) in relation to their housing costs or liabilities for local taxes.

F2 Child support Section F2

The subject-matter of the Child Support Acts 1991 and 1995.

Exception

The subject-matter of sections 1 to 7 of the Family Law (Scotland) Act 1985 (aliment).

Interpretation

If section 30(2) of the Child Support Act 1991 (collection of payments other than child support maintenance) is not in force on the principal appointed day, it is to be treated for the purposes of this reservation as if it were.

F3 Occupational and personal pensions Section F3

The regulation of occupational pension schemes and personal pension schemes, including the obligations of the trustees or managers of such schemes.

Provision about pensions payable to, or in respect of, any persons, except—
(a) the persons referred to in section 81(3),
(b) in relation to a Scottish public authority with mixed functions or no reserved functions, persons who are or have been a member of the public body, the holder of the public office, or a member of the staff of the body, holder or office.

The subject-matter of the Pensions (Increase) Act 1971.

Schemes for the payment of pensions which are listed in Schedule 2 to that Act, except those mentioned in paragraphs 38A and 38AB.

Where pension payable to or in respect of any class of persons under a public service pension scheme is covered by this reservation, so is making provision in their case—
(a) for compensation for loss of office or employment, for their office or employment being affected by constitutional changes, or circumstances arising from such changes, in any territory or territories or for loss or diminution of emoluments, or
(b) for benefits in respect of death or incapacity resulting from injury or disease.

Interpretation

"Pension" includes gratuities and allowances.

F4 War pensions Section F4

Schemes for the payment of pensions for or in respect of persons who have a disablement or have died in consequence of service as members of the armed forces of the Crown.

The subject-matter of any scheme under the Personal Injuries (Emergency Provisions) Act 1939, sections 3 to 5 and 7 of the Pensions (Navy, Army,

Air Force and Mercantile Marine) Act 1939 or section 1 of the Polish Resettlement Act 1947.

Illustration

The provision of pensions under the Naval, Military and Air Forces Etc (Disablement and Death) Service Pensions Order 1983.

Interpretation

"Pension" includes grants, allowances, supplements and gratuities.

Head G – Regulation of the Professions

G1 Architects Section G1

Regulation of the profession of architect.

G2 Health professions Section G2

Regulation of the health professions.

Exceptions

The subject-matter of—
(a) section 21 of the National Health Service (Scotland) Act 1978 (requirement of suitable experience for medical practitioners), and
(b) section 25 of that Act (arrangements for the provision of general dental services), so far as it relates to vocational training and disciplinary proceedings.

Interpretation

"The health professions" means the professions regulated by—
(a) the Pharmacy Act 1954,
(b) the Professions Supplementary to Medicine Act 1960,
(c) the Veterinary Surgeons Act 1966,
(d) the Medical Act 1983,
(e) the Dentists Act 1984,
(f) the Opticians Act 1989,
(g) the Osteopaths Act 1993,
(h) the Chiropractors Act 1994, and
(i) the Nurses, Midwives and Health Visitors Act 1997.

G3 Auditors Section G3

Regulation of the profession of auditor.

Head H – Employment

H1 Employment and industrial relations Section H1

Employment rights and duties and industrial relations, including the subject-matter of—
(a) the Employers' Liability (Compulsory Insurance) Act 1969,
(b) the Employment Agencies Act 1973,
(c) the Pneumoconiosis etc (Workers' Compensation) Act 1979,
(d) the Transfer of Undertakings (Protection of Employment) Regulations 1981,
(e) the Trade Union and Labour Relations (Consolidation) Act 1992,
(f) the Industrial Tribunals Act 1996,
(g) the Employment Rights Act 1996, and
(h) the National Minimum Wage Act 1998.

Exception

The subject-matter of the Agricultural Wages (Scotland) Act 1949.

H2 Health and safety Section H2

The subject-matter of the following Parts of the Health and Safety at Work etc Act 1974—
(a) Part I (health, safety and welfare in connection with work, and control of dangerous substances) as extended or applied by section 36 of the Consumer Protection Act 1987, sections 1 and 2 of the Offshore Safety Act 1992 and section 117 of the Railways Act 1993, and
(b) Part II (the Employment Medical Advisory Service).

Exception

Public safety in relation to matters which are not reserved.

H3 Job search and support Section H3

The subject-matter of—
(a) the Disabled Persons (Employment) Act 1944, and
(b) the Employment and Training Act 1973, except so far as relating to training for employment.

Exception

The subject matter of—
(a) sections 8 to 10A of the Employment and Training Act 1973 (careers services), and
(b) the following sections of Part I of the Enterprise and New Towns (Scotland) Act 1990 (Scottish Enterprise and Highlands and Islands Enterprise)—
 (i) section 2(3)(c) (arrangements for the purpose of assisting persons to establish themselves as self-employed persons), and
 (ii) section 12 (disclosure of information).

Head J – Health and Medicines

J1 Abortion Section J1

Abortion.

J2 Xenotransplantation Section J2

Xenotransplantation.

J3 Embryology, surrogacy and genetics Section J3

Surrogacy arrangements, within the meaning of the Surrogacy Arrangements Act 1985, including the subject-matter of that Act.

The subject-matter of the Human Fertilisation and Embryology Act 1990.

Human genetics.

J4 Medicines, medical supplies and poisons Section J4

The subject-matter of—

(a) the Medicines Act 1968, the Marketing Authorisations for Veterinary Medicinal Products Regulations 1994 and the Medicines for Human Use (Marketing Authorisations Etc) Regulations 1994,

(b) the Poisons Act 1972, and

(c) the Biological Standards Act 1975.

Regulation of prices charged for medical supplies or medicinal products which (in either case) are supplied for the purposes of the health service established under section 1 of the National Health Service (Scotland) Act 1978.

Interpretation

"Medical supplies" has the same meaning as in section 49(3) of the National Health Service (Scotland) Act 1978.

"Medicinal products" has the same meaning as in section 130(1) of the Medicines Act 1968.

J5 Welfare foods Section J5

Schemes made by regulations under section 13 of the Social Security Act 1988 (schemes for distribution of welfare foods).

Head K – Media and Culture

K1 Broadcasting Section K1

The subject-matter of the Broadcasting Act 1990 and the Broadcasting Act 1996.

The British Broadcasting Corporation.

K2 Public lending right

Section K2

The subject-matter of the Public Lending Right Act 1979.

K3 Government Indemnity Scheme

Section K3

The subject-matter of sections 16 and 16A of the National Heritage Act 1980 (public indemnities for objects on loan to museums, art galleries, etc).

K4 Property accepted in satisfaction of tax

Section K4

The subject-matter of sections 8 and 9 of the National Heritage Act 1980 (payments to Inland Revenue in respect of property accepted in satisfaction of tax, and disposal of such property).

Head L – Miscellaneous

L1 Judicial remuneration

Section L1

Determination of the remuneration of—
(a) judges of the Court of Session,
(b) sheriffs principal and sheriffs,
(c) members of the Lands Tribunal for Scotland, and
(d) the Chairman of the Scottish Land Court.

L2 Equal opportunities

Section L2

Equal opportunities, including the subject-matter of—
(a) the Equal Pay Act 1970,
(b) the Sex Discrimination Act 1975,
(c) the Race Relations Act 1976, and
(d) the Disability Discrimination Act 1995.

Exceptions

The encouragement (other than by prohibition or regulation) of equal opportunities, and in particular of the observance of the equal opportunity requirements.

Imposing duties on—
(a) any office-holder in the Scottish Administration, or any Scottish public authority with mixed functions or no reserved functions, to make arrangements with a view to securing that the functions of the office-holder or authority are carried out with due regard to the need to meet the equal opportunity requirements, or
(b) any cross-border public authority to make arrangements with a view to securing that its Scottish functions are carried out with due regard to the need to meet the equal opportunity requirements.

Interpretation

"Equal opportunities" means the prevention, elimination or regulation of discrimination between persons on grounds of sex or marital status, on racial grounds, or on grounds of disability, age, sexual orientation, language or social origin, or of other personal attributes, including beliefs or opinions, such as religious beliefs or political opinions.

"Equal opportunity requirements" means the requirements of the law for the time being relating to equal opportunities.

"Scottish functions" means functions which are exercisable in or as regards Scotland and which do not relate to reserved matters.

L3 Control of weapons Section L3

Control of nuclear, biological and chemical weapons and other weapons of mass destruction.

L4 Ordnance survey Section L4

The subject-matter of the Ordnance Survey Act 1841.

L5 Time Section L5

Timescales, time zones and the subject-matter of the Summer Time Act 1972.

The calendar; units of time; the date of Easter.

Exceptions

The computation of periods of time.

The subject-matter of—

(a) section 1 of the Banking and Financial Dealings Act 1971 (bank holidays), and

(b) the Term and Quarter Days (Scotland) Act 1990.

L6 Outer space Section L6

Regulation of activities in outer space.

PART III

GENERAL PROVISIONS

Scottish public authorities

1 (1) This Schedule does not reserve any Scottish public authority if some of its functions relate to reserved matters and some do not, unless it is a cross-border public authority.

(2) Sub-paragraph (1) has effect as regards—

(a) the constitution of the authority, including its establishment and dissolution, its assets and liabilities and its funding and receipts,

(b) conferring or removing any functions specifically exercisable in relation to the authority.

(3) Sub-paragraph (2)(b) does not apply to any function which is specifically exercisable in relation to a particular function of the authority if the particular function relates to reserved matters.

(4) An authority to which this paragraph applies is referred to in this Act as a Scottish public authority with mixed functions.

2 Paragraph 1 of Part I of this Schedule does not reserve any Scottish public authority with functions none of which relate to reserved matters (referred to in this Act as a Scottish public authority with no reserved functions).

Reserved bodies

3 (1) The reservation of any body to which this paragraph applies has effect to reserve—
(a) its constitution, including its establishment and dissolution, its assets and liabilities and its funding and receipts,
(b) conferring functions on it or removing functions from it,
(c) conferring or removing any functions specifically exercisable in relation to it.

(2) This paragraph applies to—
(a) a body reserved by name by Part II of this Schedule,
(b) each of the councils reserved by Section C12 of that Part,
(c) the Commission for Racial Equality, the Equal Opportunities Commission and the National Disability Council.

Financial assistance to industry

4 (1) This Schedule does not reserve giving financial assistance to commercial activities for the purpose of promoting or sustaining economic development or employment.

(2) Sub-paragraph (1)—
(a) does not apply to giving financial assistance to any activities in pursuance of a power exercisable only in relation to activities which are reserved,
(b) does not apply to Part I of this Schedule, except paragraph 9, or to a body to which paragraph 3 of this Part of this Schedule applies,
(c) is without prejudice to the exceptions from the reservations in Sections E2 and E3 of Part II of this Schedule.

(3) Sub-paragraph (1) does not affect the question whether any matter other than financial assistance to which that sub-paragraph applies is reserved.

Interpretation

5 (1) References in this Schedule to the subject-matter of any enactment are to be read as references to the subject-matter of that enactment as it has effect on the principal appointed day or, if it ceased to have effect at any time within the period ending with that day and beginning with the day on which this Act is passed, as it had effect immediately before that time.

(2) Subordinate legislation under section 129(1) may, in relation to the operation of this Schedule at any time before the principal appointed day, modify the references to that day in sub-paragraph (1).

SCHEDULE 6

Section 98

Devolution Issues

PART I
PRELIMINARY

1 In this Schedule "devolution issue" means—

(a) a question whether an Act of the Scottish Parliament or any provision of an Act of the Scottish Parliament is within the legislative competence of the Parliament,

(b) a question whether any function (being a function which any person has purported, or is proposing, to exercise) is a function of the Scottish Ministers, the First Minister or the Lord Advocate,

(c) a question whether the purported or proposed exercise of a function by a member of the Scottish Executive is, or would be, within devolved competence,

(d) a question whether a purported or proposed exercise of a function by a member of the Scottish Executive is, or would be, incompatible with any of the Convention rights or with Community law,

(e) a question whether a failure to act by a member of the Scottish Executive is incompatible with any of the Convention rights or with Community law,

(f) any other question about whether a function is exercisable within devolved competence or in or as regards Scotland and any other question arising by virtue of this Act about reserved matters.

2 A devolution issue shall not be taken to arise in any proceedings merely because of any contention of a party to the proceedings which appears to the court or tribunal before which the proceedings take place to be frivolous or vexatious.

PART II
PROCEEDINGS IN SCOTLAND

Application of Part II

3 This Part of this Schedule applies in relation to devolution issues in proceedings in Scotland.

Institution of proceedings

4 (1) Proceedings for the determination of a devolution issue may be instituted by the Advocate General or the Lord Advocate.

(2) The Lord Advocate may defend any such proceedings instituted by the Advocate General.

(3) This paragraph is without prejudice to any power to institute or defend proceedings exercisable apart from this paragraph by any person.

Intimation of devolution issue

5 Intimation of any devolution issue which arises in any proceedings before a court or tribunal shall be given to the Advocate General and the Lord Advocate (unless the person to whom the intimation would be given is a party to the proceedings).

6 A person to whom intimation is given in pursuance of paragraph 5 may take part as a party in the proceedings, so far as they relate to a devolution issue.

Reference of devolution issue to higher court

7 A court, other than the House of Lords or any court consisting of three or more judges of the Court of Session, may refer any devolution issue which arises in proceedings (other than criminal proceedings) before it to the Inner House of the Court of Session.

8 A tribunal from which there is no appeal shall refer any devolution issue which arises in proceedings before it to the Inner House of the Court of Session; and any other tribunal may make such a reference.

9 A court, other than any court consisting of two or more judges of the High Court of Justiciary, may refer any devolution issue which arises in criminal proceedings before it to the High Court of Justiciary.

References from superior courts to Judicial Committee

10 Any court consisting of three or more judges of the Court of Session may refer any devolution issue which arises in proceedings before it (otherwise than on a reference under paragraph 7 or 8) to the Judicial Committee.

11 Any court consisting of two or more judges of the High Court of Justiciary may refer any devolution issue which arises in proceedings before it (otherwise than on a reference under paragraph 9) to the Judicial Committee.

Appeals from superior courts to Judicial Committee

12 An appeal against a determination of a devolution issue by the Inner House of the Court of Session on a reference under paragraph 7 or 8 shall lie to the Judicial Committee.

13 An appeal against a determination of a devolution issue by—

(a) a court of two or more judges of the High Court of Justiciary (whether in the ordinary course of proceedings or on a reference under paragraph 9), or

(b) a court of three or more judges of the Court of Session from which there is no appeal to the House of Lords,

shall lie to the Judicial Committee, but only with leave of the court concerned or, failing such leave, with special leave of the Judicial Committee.

PART III

PROCEEDINGS IN ENGLAND AND WALES

Application of Part III

14 This Part of this Schedule applies in relation to devolution issues in proceedings in England and Wales.

Institution of proceedings

15 (1) Proceedings for the determination of a devolution issue may be instituted by the Attorney General.

(2) The Lord Advocate may defend any such proceedings.

(3) This paragraph is without prejudice to any power to institute or defend proceedings exercisable apart from this paragraph by any person.

Notice of devolution issue

16 A court or tribunal shall order notice of any devolution issue which arises in any proceedings before it to be given to the Attorney General and the Lord Advocate (unless the person to whom the notice would be given is a party to the proceedings).

17 A person to whom notice is given in pursuance of paragraph 16 may take part as a party in the proceedings, so far as they relate to a devolution issue.

Reference of devolution issue to High Court or Court of Appeal

18 A magistrates' court may refer any devolution issue which arises in proceedings (other than criminal proceedings) before it to the High Court.

19 (1) A court may refer any devolution issue which arises in proceedings (other than criminal proceedings) before it to the Court of Appeal.

(2) Sub-paragraph (1) does not apply to—

(a) a magistrates' court, the Court of Appeal or the House of Lords, or

(b) the High Court if the devolution issue arises in proceedings on a reference under paragraph 18.

20 A tribunal from which there is no appeal shall refer any devolution issue which arises in proceedings before it to the Court of Appeal; and any other tribunal may make such a reference.

21 A court, other than the House of Lords or the Court of Appeal, may refer any devolution issue which arises in criminal proceedings before it to—

(a) the High Court (if the proceedings are summary proceedings), or
(b) the Court of Appeal (if the proceedings are proceedings on indictment).

References from Court of Appeal to Judicial Committee

22 The Court of Appeal may refer any devolution issue which arises in proceedings before it (otherwise than on a reference under paragraph 19, 20 or 21) to the Judicial Committee.

Appeals from superior courts to Judicial Committee

23 An appeal against a determination of a devolution issue by the High Court or the Court of Appeal on a reference under paragraph 18, 19, 20 or 21 shall lie to the Judicial Committee, but only with leave of the High Court or (as the case may be) the Court of Appeal or, failing such leave, with special leave of the Judicial Committee.

PART IV

PROCEEDINGS IN NORTHERN IRELAND

Application of Part IV

24 This Part of this Schedule applies in relation to devolution issues in proceedings in Northern Ireland.

Institution of proceedings

25 (1) Proceedings for the determination of a devolution issue may be instituted by the Attorney General for Northern Ireland.

(2) The Lord Advocate may defend any such proceedings.

(3) This paragraph is without prejudice to any power to institute or defend proceedings exercisable apart from this paragraph by any person.

Notice of devolution issue

26 A court or tribunal shall order notice of any devolution issue which arises in any proceedings before it to be given to the Attorney General for Northern Ireland and the Lord Advocate (unless the person to whom the notice would be given is a party to the proceedings).

27 A person to whom notice is given in pursuance of paragraph 26 may take part as a party in the proceedings, so far as they relate to a devolution issue.

Reference of devolution issue to Court of Appeal

28 A court, other than the House of Lords or the Court of Appeal in Northern Ireland, may refer any devolution issue which arises in any proceedings before it to the Court of Appeal in Northern Ireland.

29 A tribunal from which there is no appeal shall refer any devolution issue which arises in any proceedings before it to the Court of Appeal in Northern Ireland; and any other tribunal may make such a reference.

References from Court of Appeal to Judicial Committee

30 The Court of Appeal in Northern Ireland may refer any devolution issue which arises in proceedings before it (otherwise than on a reference under paragraph 28 or 29) to the Judicial Committee.

Appeals from Court of Appeal to Judicial Committee

31 An appeal against a determination of a devolution issue by the Court of Appeal in Northern Ireland on a reference under paragraph 28 or 29 shall lie to the Judicial Committee, but only with leave of the Court of Appeal in Northern Ireland or, failing such leave, with special leave of the Judicial Committee.

PART V
GENERAL

Proceedings in the House of Lords

32 Any devolution issue which arises in judicial proceedings in the House of Lords shall be referred to the Judicial Committee unless the House considers it more appropriate, having regard to all the circumstances, that it should determine the issue.

Direct references to Judicial Committee

33 The Lord Advocate, the Advocate General, the Attorney General or the Attorney General for Northern Ireland may require any court or tribunal to refer to the Judicial Committee any devolution issue which has arisen in proceedings before it to which he is a party.

34 The Lord Advocate, the Attorney General, the Advocate General or the Attorney General for Northern Ireland may refer to the Judicial Committee any devolution issue which is not the subject of proceedings.

35 (1) This paragraph applies where a reference is made under paragraph 34 in relation to a devolution issue which relates to the proposed exercise of a function by a member of the Scottish Executive.

(2) The person making the reference shall notify a member of the Scottish Executive of that fact.

(3) No member of the Scottish Executive shall exercise the function in the manner proposed during the period beginning with the receipt of the

notification under sub-paragraph (2) and ending with the reference being decided or otherwise disposed of.

(4) Proceedings relating to any possible failure by a member of the Scottish Executive to comply with sub-paragraph (3) may be instituted by the Advocate General.

(5) Sub-paragraph (4) is without prejudice to any power to institute proceedings exercisable apart from that sub-paragraph by any person.

Expenses

36 (1) A court or tribunal before which any proceedings take place may take account of any additional expense of the kind mentioned in sub-paragraph (3) in deciding any question as to costs or expenses.

(2) In deciding any such question, the court or tribunal may award the whole or part of the additional expense as costs or (as the case may be) expenses to the party who incurred it (whatever the decision on the devolution issue).

(3) The additional expense is any additional expense which the court or tribunal considers that any party to the proceedings has incurred as a result of the participation of any person in pursuance of paragraph 6, 17 or 27.

Procedure of courts and tribunals

37 Any power to make provision for regulating the procedure before any court or tribunal shall include power to make provision for the purposes of this Schedule including, in particular, provision—
(a) for prescribing the stage in the proceedings at which a devolution issue is to be raised or referred,
(b) for the sisting or staying of proceedings for the purpose of any proceedings under this Schedule, and
(c) for determining the manner in which and the time within which any intimation or notice is to be given.

Interpretation

38 Any duty or power conferred by this Schedule to refer a devolution issue to a court shall be construed as a duty or (as the case may be) power to refer the issue to the court for decision.

SCHEDULE 7

Section 115

Procedure for Subordinate Legislation

General provision

1 (1) Subordinate legislation (or a statutory instrument containing it) under a provision listed in the left-hand column is subject to the type of procedure in the right-hand column.

(2) This paragraph is subject to paragraphs 3 and 4.

Provision of the Act	*Type of procedure*
Section 2(1)	Type C
Section 12(1)	Type C
Section 15	Type D
Section 18(5)	Type J
Section 30	Type A
Section 35	Type I
Section 38	Type J
Section 56(2)	Type G
Section 58	Type I
Section 60	Type G
Section 62	Type G
Section 63	Type A
Section 64(5)	Type K
Section 67(3)	Type E
Section 71(6)	Type K
Section 79	Type E
Section 88	Type I
Section 89	Type F
Section 90	Type F
Section 93	Type H
Section 97	Type A
Section 103(3)(a) and (b)	Type I
Section 104	Type G
Section 105	Type G
Section 106	Type G
Section 107	Type G
Section 108	Type A
Section 109	Type H
Section 110(1)	Type C
Section 110(2)	Type I
Section 111	Type A
Section 116(9)	Type G
Section 124(1)	Type G
Section 126(2)	Type B
Section 126(8)	Type H
Section 129(1)	Type G
Schedule 2, paragraph 2	Type G
Schedule 2, paragraph 7	Type H

Notes

The entry for section 58 does not apply to an instrument containing an order merely revoking an order under subsection (1) of that section.

The entry for section 79, in relation to an instrument containing an order which makes only such provision as is mentioned in section 79(3), is to be read as referring to type K instead of type E.

Types of procedure

2 The types of procedure referred to in this Schedule are—

Type A: No recommendation to make the legislation is to be made to Her Majesty in Council unless a draft of the instrument—
(a) has been laid before, and approved by resolution of, each House of Parliament, and
(b) has been laid before, and approved by resolution of, the Parliament.

Type B: No recommendation to make the legislation is to be made to Her Majesty in Council unless a draft of the instrument has been laid before, and approved by resolution of, each House of Parliament.

Type C: No Minister of the Crown is to make the legislation unless a draft of the instrument has been laid before, and approved by resolution of, each House of Parliament.

Type D: No recommendation to make the legislation is to be made to Her Majesty in Council unless a draft of the instrument has been laid before, and approved by resolution of, the Parliament.

Type E: No Minister of the Crown is to make the legislation unless a draft of the instrument has been laid before, and approved by resolution of, the House of Commons.

Type F: The instrument containing the legislation, if made without a draft having been approved by resolution of each House of Parliament and of the Parliament, shall be subject to annulment in pursuance of—
(a) a resolution of either House, or
(b) a resolution of the Parliament.

Type G: The instrument containing the legislation, if made without a draft having been approved by resolution of each House of Parliament, shall be subject to annulment in pursuance of a resolution of either House.

Type H: The instrument containing the legislation shall be subject to annulment in pursuance of—
(a) a resolution of either House of Parliament, or
(b) a resolution of the Parliament.

Type I: The instrument containing the legislation shall be subject to annulment in pursuance of a resolution of either House of Parliament.

Type J: The instrument containing the legislation shall be subject to annulment in pursuance of a resolution of the Parliament.

Type K: The instrument containing the legislation shall be subject to annulment in pursuance of a resolution of the House of Commons.

Special cases

3 (1) This paragraph applies if—
(a) the instrument containing the legislation would, apart from this paragraph, be subject to the type F, G, H, I or K procedure, and

(b) the legislation contains provisions which add to, replace or omit any part of the text of an Act.

(2) Where this paragraph applies—
(a) instead of the type F procedure, the type A procedure shall apply,
(b) instead of the type G procedure, the type B or (as the case may be) C procedure shall apply,
(c) instead of the type H procedure, the type A procedure shall apply,
(d) instead of the type I procedure, the type B or (as the case may be) C procedure shall apply,
(e) instead of the type K procedure, the type E procedure shall apply.

4 If legislation under section 129(1) makes provision as mentioned in section 112(2) then, instead of the type G procedure, the type D procedure shall apply.

5 (1) An instrument containing an Order in Council or order under an open power which revokes, amends or re-enacts subordinate legislation under an open power may (in spite of section 14 of the Interpretation Act 1978) be subject to a different procedure under this Schedule from the procedure to which the instrument containing the original legislation was subject.

(2) An instrument containing an Order in Council under section 89 or 90 which revokes, amends or re-enacts an Order under either section may (in spite of section 14 of the Interpretation Act 1978) be subject to a different procedure under this Schedule from the procedure to which the instrument containing the original Order was subject.

SCHEDULE 8

Section 125

Modifications of Enactments

Public Revenue (Scotland) Act 1833 (c 13)

1 In section 2 of the Public Revenue (Scotland) Act 1833 (regulation of Queen's and Lord Treasurer's Remembrancer), for "Treasury" in both places there is substituted "Scottish Ministers".

Crown Suits (Scotland) Act 1857 (c 44)

2 (1) The Crown Suits (Scotland) Act 1857 is amended as follows.

(2) In section 1 (Crown suits may be brought by or against Lord Advocate)—
(a) after "Crown" there is inserted "(including the Scottish Administration)", and
(b) for "Her Majesty's Advocate for the time being" there is substituted "the appropriate Law Officer".

(3) In section 2 (authority of Crown required)—
(a) for "Her Majesty's Advocate" there is substituted "the appropriate Law Officer", and

(b) after "Majesty" there is inserted "of the part of the Scottish Administration".

(4) In section 3 (absence of authority cannot be founded upon), for "Her Majesty's Advocate" there is substituted "the appropriate Law Officer".

(5) After section 4 there is inserted—

"4A Meaning of "the appropriate Law Officer"

In this Act "the appropriate Law Officer" means—
(a) the Lord Advocate, where the action, suit or proceeding is on behalf of or against any part of the Scottish Administration, and
(b) the Advocate General for Scotland, in any other case."

(6) In section 5 (change of Lord Advocate not to affect proceedings)—
(a) for "Her Majesty's Advocate" there is substituted "the Lord Advocate or the Advocate General for Scotland", and
(b) for "the office of Her Majesty's Advocate" there is substituted "that office".

Sheriff Courts and Legal Officers (Scotland) Act 1927 (c 35)

3 (1) The Sheriff Courts and Legal Officers (Scotland) Act 1927 is amended as follows.

(2) In section 1(2) (appointment etc of procurator fiscal), "with the consent of the Treasury" is omitted.

(3) In section 2 (appointment of sheriff clerk and procurator fiscal deputes), "with the consent of the Treasury as to numbers and salaries" is omitted.

(4) In section 3 (whole-time sheriff clerks and procurators fiscal and deputes), "and in either case with the consent of the Treasury" is omitted.

(5) In section 5 (whole-time clerks), "with the consent of the Treasury as to numbers and salaries" is omitted.

(6) In section 12 (prosecutions at instance of procurator fiscal), "after consultation with the Treasury" is omitted.

Administration of Justice (Scotland) Act 1933 (c 41)

4 In the Administration of Justice (Scotland) Act 1933, in sections 24(7) and 25 (officers of Court of Session etc), "and shall be exercised on nomination by the Lord Advocate" is omitted.

Private Legislation Procedure (Scotland) Act 1936 (c 52)

5 In section 1 of the Private Legislation Procedure (Scotland) Act 1936 (application for provisional order: notices), after subsection (4) there is added—

"(5) This section shall not apply where any public authority or any persons desire to obtain parliamentary powers the conferring of which is wholly within the legislative competence of the Scottish Parliament."

United Nations Act 1946 (c 45)

6 In section 1 of the United Nations Act 1946 (measures to give effect to decisions of Security Council), in subsection (4), for the words following "shall" there is substituted

"forthwith after it is made be laid—
(a) before Parliament; and
(b) if any provision made by the Order would, if it were included in an Act of the Scottish Parliament, be within the legislative competence of that Parliament, before that Parliament."

Crown Proceedings Act 1947 (c 44)

7 (1) The Crown Proceedings Act 1947 is amended as follows.

(2) In section 38(2) (interpretation)—
(a) in the definition of "His Majesty's aircraft", after "Kingdom" there is inserted "or the Scottish Administration",
(b) in the definition of "His Majesty's ships", after "Kingdom" there is inserted "or the Scottish Administration" and after "said Government" there is inserted "or Administration", and
(c) in the definition of "officer", after "Minister of the Crown" there is inserted "and a member of the Scottish Executive".

(3) In section 40 (savings)—
(a) in subsection (2), after "in the United Kingdom", in each place where those words appear, there is inserted "or the Scottish Administration", and
(b) after subsection (3) there is inserted—

"(3A) A certificate of the Scottish Ministers to the effect that—
(a) any alleged liability of the Crown arises otherwise than in respect of the Scottish Administration,
(b) any proceedings by the Crown are proceedings otherwise than in right of the Scottish Administration,

shall, for the purposes of this Act, be conclusive as to that matter."

(4) In the proviso to section 44 (remit from sheriff court to Court of Session on Lord Advocate's certificate)—
(a) for "Lord Advocate" there is substituted "appropriate Law Officer", and
(b) at the end there is inserted—

"In this proviso, "the appropriate Law Officer" means—
(a) the Lord Advocate, where the proceedings are against any part of the Scottish Administration, and
(b) the Advocate General for Scotland, in any other case."

(5) In section 50 (application to Scotland of section 35), subsection (2) of section 35 as substituted for Scotland is amended as follows—

(a) in paragraph (d)—

(i) after "Crown" there is inserted "in right of Her Majesty's Government in the United Kingdom",

(ii) for "Lord Advocate" there is substituted "Advocate General for Scotland", and

(iii) after "department", in the second place where it appears, there is inserted—

"(i) shall not be entitled to avail itself of any set-off or counterclaim if the subject matter thereof relates to the Scottish Administration, and

(ii)", and

(b) after that paragraph there is inserted—

"(e) a part of the Scottish Administration, in any proceedings against that part or against the Lord Advocate on its behalf, shall not be entitled to avail itself of any set-off or counterclaim if the subject matter thereof relates to another part of the Scottish Administration or to the Crown in right of Her Majesty's Government in the United Kingdom."

(6) In section 51(2) (application to Scotland of section 38), in paragraph (ii), after "Lord Advocate" there is inserted "or the Advocate General for Scotland".

Public Registers and Records (Scotland) Act 1948 (c 57)

8 In section 1(1) of the Public Registers and Records (Scotland) Act 1948 (appointment etc of Keeper of the Registers and Keeper of the Records), for "Secretary of State" there is substituted "Scottish Ministers".

Lands Tribunal Act 1949 (c 42)

9 In section 2 of the Lands Tribunal Act 1949 (members etc of Lands Tribunal for Scotland)—

(a) in subsection (9)—

(i) after "effect" there is inserted "with the omission of subsection (8) and", and

(ii) in paragraph (a), for "(8)" there is substituted "(7)", and

(b) after that subsection there is inserted—

"(10) The remuneration of members of the Lands Tribunal for Scotland shall be charged on the Scottish Consolidated Fund."

Defamation Act 1952 (c 66)

10 In section 10 of the Defamation Act 1952 (limitation on privilege at elections), after "local government authority" there is inserted "to the Scottish Parliament".

Defamation Act (Northern Ireland) 1955 (c 11 (NI))

11 In section 10(2) of the Defamation Act (Northern Ireland) 1955 (limitation on privilege at elections), after "Parliament of the United Kingdom" there is inserted "or to the Scottish Parliament".

Registration of Births, Deaths and Marriages (Scotland) Act 1965 (c 49)

12 In section 1(1) of the Registration of Births, Deaths and Marriages (Scotland) Act 1965 (power of Secretary of State to appoint Registrar General), for "Secretary of State" there is substituted "Scottish Ministers".

Pensions (Increase) Act 1971 (c 56)

13 In Part II of Schedule 2 to the Pensions (Increase) Act 1971 (official pensions out of local funds), before paragraph 39 there is inserted—

"Scottish Parliament and Scottish Executive

38AB A pension payable under a scheme established by virtue of section 81(4)(b) of, or paragraph 3(4)(b) of Schedule 2 to, the Scotland Act 1998."

Superannuation Act 1972 (c 11)

14 In section 1(6) of the Superannuation Act 1972 (superannuation as respects civil servants etc), for "or the Consolidated Fund" there is substituted "the Consolidated Fund or the Scottish Consolidated Fund".

European Communities Act 1972 (c 68)

15 (1) The European Communities Act 1972 is amended as follows.

(2) In section 2 (general implementation of Treaties)—
(a) references to a statutory power or duty include a power or duty conferred by an Act of the Scottish Parliament or an instrument made under such an Act, and
(b) references to an enactment include an enactment within the meaning of this Act.

(3) In relation to regulations made by the Scottish Ministers, or an Order in Council made on the recommendation of the First Minister, under section 2—
(a) in subsection (2), "designated" in the first sentence, and the second sentence, shall be disregarded,
(b) references to an Act of Parliament shall be read as references to an Act of the Scottish Parliament, and
(c) paragraph 2(2) of Schedule 2 shall have effect as if the references to each, or either, House of Parliament were to the Scottish Parliament.

(4) In section 3(4) (evidence), references to a government department include any part of the Scottish Administration.

Interpretation Act 1978 (c 30)

16 (1) The Interpretation Act 1978 is amended as follows.

(2) After section 23 there is inserted—

"23A Acts of the Scottish Parliament etc

(1) This Act applies in relation to an Act of the Scottish Parliament and an instrument made under such an Act only to the extent provided in this section.

(2) Except as provided in subsection (3) below, sections 15 to 18 apply to—
(a) an Act of the Scottish Parliament as they apply to an Act,
(b) an instrument made under an Act of the Scottish Parliament as they apply to subordinate legislation.

(3) In the application of those sections to an Act and to subordinate legislation—
(a) references to an enactment include an enactment comprised in, or in an instrument made under, an Act of the Scottish Parliament, and
(b) the reference in section 17(2)(b) to subordinate legislation includes an instrument made under an Act of the Scottish Parliament.

(4) In the application of section 20 to an Act and to subordinate legislation, references to an enactment include an enactment comprised in, or in an instrument made under, an Act of the Scottish Parliament."

(3) In Schedule 1 (words and expressions defined), the following definitions are inserted in the appropriate places—
""Act" means an Act of Parliament."
""Enactment" does not include an enactment comprised in, or in an instrument made under, an Act of the Scottish Parliament."

Education (Scotland) Act 1980 (c 44)

17 In section 135(1) of the Education (Scotland) Act 1980 (interpretation), in the definition of "Her Majesty's inspectors", "on the recommendation of the Secretary of State" is omitted.

Civil Jurisdiction and Judgments Act 1982 (c 27)

18 (1) Section 46 of the Civil Jurisdiction and Judgments Act 1982 (domicile and seat of the Crown) is amended as follows.

(2) In subsection (3), after paragraph (a) there is inserted—

"(aa) the Crown in right of the Scottish Administration has its seat in, and in every place in, Scotland,".

(3) In subsection (7), after "Kingdom" there is inserted ", the Scottish Administration".

Mental Health Act 1983 (c 20)

19 In section 141 of the Mental Health Act 1983 (members of the House of Commons suffering from mental illness), after subsection (7), there is added—

"(8) This section also has effect in relation to members of the Scottish Parliament but as if—
(a) any references to the House of Commons or the Speaker were references to the Scottish Parliament or (as the case may be) the Presiding Officer, and
(b) subsection (7) were omitted."

National Audit Act 1983 (c 44)

20 Sections 6 and 7 of the National Audit Act 1983 (value for money studies) shall not apply in relation to—
(a) the Scottish Administration or any part of it, or
(b) any Scottish public authority with mixed functions or no reserved functions.

Tourism (Overseas Promotion) (Scotland) Act 1984 (c 4)

21 In section 1 of the Tourism (Overseas Promotion) (Scotland) Act 1984 (power of Scottish Tourist Board to promote tourism in Scotland outside UK), subsection (2) is omitted.

Bankruptcy (Scotland) Act 1985 (c 66)

22 For section 1 of the Bankruptcy (Scotland) Act 1985 there is substituted—

"1 Accountant in Bankruptcy

(1) The Accountant in Bankruptcy shall be appointed by the Scottish Ministers.

(2) The Scottish Ministers may appoint a member of the staff of the Accountant in Bankruptcy to be Depute Accountant in Bankruptcy to exercise all of the functions of the Accountant in Bankruptcy at any time when the Accountant in Bankruptcy is unable to do so."

Insolvency Act 1986 (c 45)

23 (1) The Insolvency Act 1986 is amended as follows.

(2) Anything directed to be done, or which may be done, to or by—
(a) the registrar of companies in Scotland by virtue of any of the provisions mentioned in sub-paragraph (3), or
(b) the assistant registrar of friendly societies for Scotland by virtue of any of those provisions as applied (with or without modification) in relation to friendly societies, industrial and provident societies or building societies,

shall, or (as the case may be) may, also be done to or by the Accountant in Bankruptcy.

(3) Those provisions are: sections 53(1), 54(3), 61(6), 62(5) (so far as relating to the giving of notice), 67(1), 69(2), 84(3), 94(3), 106(3) and (5), 112(3), 130(1), 147(3), 170(2) and 172(8).

(4) Anything directed to be done to or by—
(a) the registrar of companies in Scotland by virtue of any of the provisions mentioned in sub-paragraph (5), or
(b) the assistant registrar of friendly societies for Scotland by virtue of any of those provisions as applied (with or without modification) in relation to friendly societies, industrial and provident societies or building societies,

shall instead be done to or by the Accountant in Bankruptcy.

(5) Those provisions are: sections 89(3), 109(1), 171(5) and (6), 173(2)(a) and 192(1).

(6) In section 427 (members of the House of Commons whose estates are sequestrated etc), after subsection (6) there is inserted—

"(6A) Subsections (4) to (6) have effect in relation to a member of the Scottish Parliament but as if—
(a) references to the House of Commons were to the Parliament and references to the Speaker were to the Presiding Officer, and
(b) in subsection (4), for "under this section" there were substituted "under section 15(1)(b) of the Scotland Act 1998 by virtue of this section"."

Public Order Act 1986 (c 64)

24 In section 26(1) of the Public Order Act 1986 (savings for reports of parliamentary proceedings), after "Parliament" there is inserted "or in the Scottish Parliament".

Copyright, Designs and Patents Act 1988 (c 48)

25 (1) The Copyright, Designs and Patents Act 1988 is amended as follows.

(2) In section 12(9) (duration of copyright in literary, dramatic, musical or artistic works), for "166" there is substituted "166A".

(3) In section 153(2) (qualification for copyright protection), for "166" there is substituted "166A".

(4) In section 163(6) (Crown copyright), for "and 166" there is substituted "to 166A".

(5) In section 164(1) (Crown copyright in Acts of Parliament etc), after "Parliament" there is inserted "Act of the Scottish Parliament".

(6) After section 166 there is inserted—

"166A Copyright in Bills of the Scottish Parliament

(1) Copyright in every Bill introduced into the Scottish Parliament belongs to the Scottish Parliamentary Corporate Body.

(2) Copyright under this section subsists from the time when the text of the Bill is handed in to the Parliament for introduction—
(a) until the Bill receives Royal Assent, or
(b) if the Bill does not receive Royal Assent, until it is withdrawn or rejected or no further parliamentary proceedings may be taken in respect of it.

(3) References in this Part to Parliamentary copyright (except in section 165) include copyright under this section; and, except as mentioned above, the provisions of this Part apply in relation to copyright under this section as to other Parliamentary copyright.

(4) No other copyright, or right in the nature of copyright, subsists in a Bill after copyright has once subsisted under this section; but without prejudice to the subsequent operation of this section in relation to a Bill which, not having received Royal Assent, is later reintroduced into the Parliament."

(7) In section 178 (minor definitions)—
(a) in the definition of "the Crown", after "of" there is inserted "the Scottish Administration or of", and
(b) in the definition of "parliamentary proceedings", after "Assembly" there is inserted "of the Scottish Parliament".

(8) In section 179 (index of defined expressions), in column 2 of the entry for "Parliamentary copyright", for "and 166(6)" there is substituted "166(6) and 166A(3)".

Official Secrets Act 1989 (c 6)

26 (1) Section 12 of the Official Secrets Act 1989 (meaning of "Crown servant" and "government contractor" for the purposes of that Act) is amended as follows.

(2) In subsection (1), after paragraph (a) there is inserted—

"(aa) a member of the Scottish Executive or a junior Scottish Minister;".

(3) In subsection (2)(a), after "above," there is inserted "of any office-holder in the Scottish Administration,".

(4) After subsection (3) there is inserted—

"(4) In this section "office-holder in the Scottish Administration" has the same meaning as in section 126(7)(a) of the Scotland Act 1998.".

Prisons (Scotland) Act 1989 (c 45)

27 (1) The Prisons (Scotland) Act 1989 is amended as follows.

(2) Section 2 of that Act (appointment of officers etc) is omitted.

(3) In section 3(1) (prison officers), for the words following "Secretary of State" there is substituted—

"(1A) Every prison shall have a governor and such other officers as may be necessary."

(4) In section 3A (medical services)—
(a) in subsection (2), for "appointing" there is substituted "providing" and for "appointment" there is substituted "provision", and
(b) in subsection (4), for "appointed" there is substituted "provided".

European Communities (Amendment) Act 1993 (c 32)

28 In section 6 of the European Communities (Amendment) Act 1993 (persons who may be proposed for membership of the Committee of the Regions), after "he is" there is inserted "a member of the Scottish Parliament".

Scottish Land Court Act 1993 (c 45)

29 In section 1 of the Scottish Land Court Act 1993 (the Scottish Land Court)—
(a) in subsection (2), for "Secretary of State" there is substituted "First Minister", and
(b) after subsection (2) there is inserted—

"(2A) Before recommending the appointment of a person as Chairman, the First Minister shall consult the Lord President of the Court of Session."

Value Added Tax Act 1994 (c 23)

30 In section 41 of the Value Added Tax Act 1994 (application to the Crown), in subsection (6), after "includes" there is inserted "the Scottish Administration".

Requirements of Writing (Scotland) Act 1995 (c 7)

31 In section 12(1) of the Requirements of Writing (Scotland) Act 1995 (interpretation)—
(a) in the definition of "Minister", after "1975" there is inserted "and also includes a member of the Scottish Executive", and
(b) in paragraph (a) of the definition of "officer", after "Department" there is inserted "or, as the case may be, as a member of the staff of the Scottish Ministers or the Lord Advocate".

Criminal Procedure (Scotland) Act 1995 (c 46)

32 (1) The Criminal Procedure (Scotland) Act 1995 is amended as follows.

(2) After section 288 there is inserted—

"Devolution issues

288A Rights of appeal for Advocate General: devolution issues

(1) This section applies where—
(a) a person is acquitted or convicted of a charge (whether on indictment or in summary proceedings), and
(b) the Advocate General for Scotland was a party to the proceedings in pursuance of paragraph 6 of Schedule 6 to the Scotland Act 1998 (devolution issues).

(2) The Advocate General for Scotland may refer any devolution issue which has arisen in the proceedings to the High Court for their opinion; and the Clerk of Justiciary shall send to the person acquitted or convicted and to any solicitor who acted for that person at the trial, a copy of the reference and intimation of the date fixed by the Court for a hearing.

(3) The person may, not later than seven days before the date so fixed, intimate in writing to the Clerk of Justiciary and to the Advocate General for Scotland either—
(a) that he elects to appear personally at the hearing, or
(b) that he elects to be represented by counsel at the hearing,

but, except by leave of the Court on cause shown, and without prejudice to his right to attend, he shall not appear or be represented at the hearing other than by and in conformity with an election under this subsection.

(4) Where there is no intimation under subsection (3)(b), the High Court shall appoint counsel to act at the hearing as amicus curiae.

(5) The costs of representation elected under subsection (3)(b) or of an appointment under subsection (4) shall, after being taxed by the Auditor of the Court of Session, be paid by the Advocate General for Scotland out of money provided by Parliament.

(6) The opinion on the point referred under subsection (2) shall not affect the acquittal or (as the case may be) conviction in the trial.

288B Appeals to Judicial Committee of the Privy Council

(1) This section applies where the Judicial Committee of the Privy Council determines an appeal under paragraph 13(a) of Schedule 6 to the Scotland Act 1998 against a determination of a devolution issue by the High Court in the ordinary course of proceedings.

(2) The determination of the appeal shall not affect any earlier acquittal or earlier quashing of any conviction in the proceedings.

(3) Subject to subsection (2) above, the High Court shall have the same powers in relation to the proceedings when remitted to it by the Judicial Committee as it would have if it were considering the proceedings otherwise than as a trial court."

(3) In section 307(1) (interpretation), after the definition of "crime" there is inserted—

> ""devolution issue" has the same meaning as in Schedule 6 to the Scotland Act 1998;".

Defamation Act 1996 (c 31)

33 (1) The Defamation Act 1996 is amended as follows.

(2) In section 17(1) (interpretation), in the definition of "statutory provision", after "1978" there is inserted—

> "(aa) a provision contained in an Act of the Scottish Parliament or in an instrument made under such an Act,".

(3) In paragraph 11(1)(c) of Schedule 1 (qualified privilege), after "Minister of the Crown" there is inserted "a member of the Scottish Executive".

Damages Act 1996 (c 48)

34 In section 6 of the Damages Act 1996 (guarantees for public sector settlements), after subsection (8) there is inserted—

> "(8A) In the application of subsection (3) above to Scotland, for the words from "guidelines" to the end there shall be substituted "the Minister"."

SCHEDULE 9 Section 125

Repeals

Chapter	Short title	Extent of repeal
1927 c 35	The Sheriff Courts and Legal Officers (Scotland) Act 1927.	In section 1(2), "with the consent of the Treasury".
		In section 2, "with the consent of the Treasury as to numbers and salaries".
		In section 3, "and in either case with the consent of the Treasury".
		In section 5, "with the consent of the Treasury as to numbers and salaries".

Chapter	Short title	Extent of repeal
		In section 12, "after consultation with the Treasury".
1933 c 41	The Administration of Justice (Scotland) Act 1933.	In sections 24(7) and 25, "and shall be exercised on nomination by the Lord Advocate".
1975 c 24	The House of Commons Disqualification Act 1975.	In Schedule 2, the entries for the Lord Advocate and the Solicitor General for Scotland.
1975 c 27	The Ministerial and other Salaries Act 1975.	In Part III of Schedule 1, the entries for the Lord Advocate and the Solicitor General for Scotland.
1980 c 44	The Education (Scotland) Act 1980.	In section 135(1), in the definition of "Her Majesty's inspectors", "on the recommendation of the Secretary of State".
1984 c 4	The Tourism (Overseas Promotion) (Scotland) Act 1984.	Section 1(2).
1986 c 56	The Parliamentary Constituencies Act 1986.	In Schedule 2, rule 1(2).
1989 c 45	The Prisons (Scotland) Act 1989.	Section 2.

Index